ROCKEFELLER CENTER

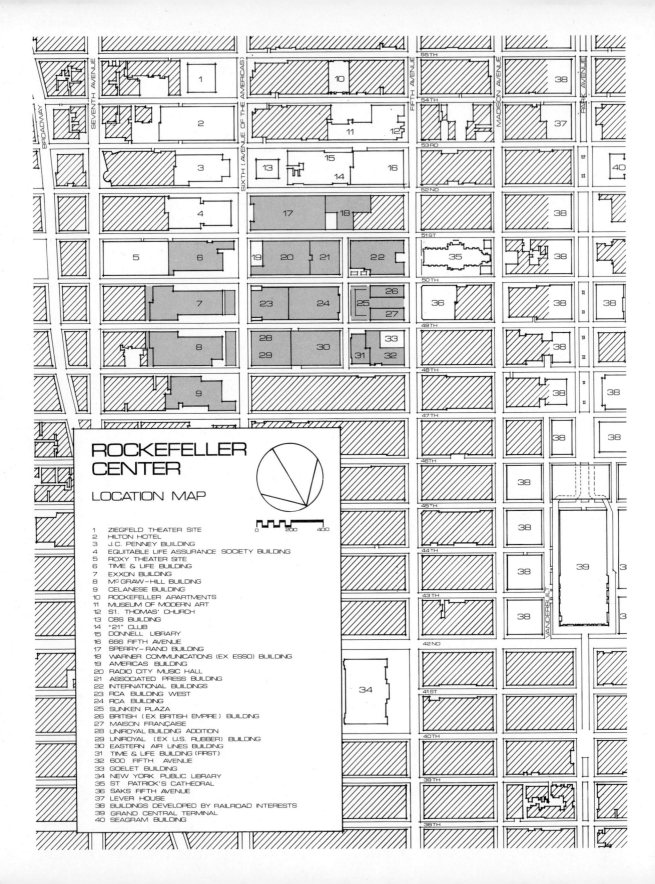

ROCKEFELLER CENTER

LOCATION MAP

1   ZIEGFELD THEATER SITE
2   HILTON HOTEL
3   J.C. PENNEY BUILDING
4   EQUITABLE LIFE ASSURANCE SOCIETY BUILDING
5   ROXY THEATER SITE
6   TIME & LIFE BUILDING
7   EXXON BUILDING
8   McGRAW-HILL BUILDING
9   CELANESE BUILDING
10 ROCKEFELLER APARTMENTS
11 MUSEUM OF MODERN ART
12 ST. THOMAS' CHURCH
13 CBS BUILDING
14 "21" CLUB
15 DONNELL LIBRARY
16 666 FIFTH AVENUE
17 SPERRY-RAND BUILDING
18 WARNER COMMUNICATIONS (EX ESSO) BUILDING
19 AMERICAS BUILDING
20 RADIO CITY MUSIC HALL
21 ASSOCIATED PRESS BUILDING
22 INTERNATIONAL BUILDINGS
23 RCA BUILDING WEST
24 RCA BUILDING
25 SUNKEN PLAZA
26 BRITISH (EX BRITISH EMPIRE) BUILDING
27 MAISON FRANÇAISE
28 UNIROYAL BUILDING ADDITION
29 UNIROYAL (EX U.S. RUBBER) BUILDING
30 EASTERN AIR LINES BUILDING
31 TIME & LIFE BUILDING (FIRST)
32 600 FIFTH AVENUE
33 GOELET BUILDING
34 NEW YORK PUBLIC LIBRARY
35 ST. PATRICK'S CATHEDRAL
36 SAKS FIFTH AVENUE
37 LEVER HOUSE
38 BUILDINGS DEVELOPED BY RAILROAD INTERESTS
39 GRAND CENTRAL TERMINAL
40 SEAGRAM BUILDING

ROCKEFELLER CENTER

Carol Herselle Krinsky

OXFORD UNIVERSITY PRESS
Oxford   London   New York
1978

OXFORD UNIVERSITY PRESS

Oxford   London   Glasgow   New York   Toronto   Melbourne
Wellington   Ibadan   Nairobi   Dar es Salaam   Lasaka   Cape Town
Kuala Lumpur   Singapore   Jakarta   Hong Kong   Tokyo   Delhi
Bombay   Calcutta   Madras   Karachi

Library of Congress Cataloging in Publication Data
Krinsky, Carol Herselle.
     Rockefeller Center.

     Bibliography: p.
     Includes index.
     1. Rockefeller Center, inc., New York. I. Title.
NA6233.N5R64   725′.09747′1   77-23735
ISBN 0-19-502317-X
ISBN 0-19-502404-4 pbk

Printed in the United States of America

To Robert, Alice, and John

Acknowledgments

I am glad to have the opportunity to acknowledge my debt to many people who have helped me during the preparation of this book.

The owners and officers of Rockefeller Center, Inc., have been most generous in allowing a completely independent analysis to be made of Rockefeller Center's development. Nelson A. Rockefeller answered my questions about it and about the Empire State Plaza in Albany. Alton G. Marshall, President of Rockefeller Center, Inc., granted an interview and had the Corporation's records placed at my disposal. Caroline Hood, former Vice-President for Public Relations, gave me the benefit of her four decades of experience at the Center, and also supplied otherwise unobtainable information about Raymond Hood which I hope to use in an extended study. Rita Gallagher, present Vice-President for Public Relations, extended innumerable courtesies and encouraged her gracious staff to do the same. It is also a pleasure to thank Patricia H. Robert, Director of Publicity at the Radio City Music Hall. During a period of several months, Dr. Joseph Ernst, Director of the Rockefeller Family Archives, and his assistant, Linda Edgerly, offered hospitality, patience, and generous assistance. G. S. Eyssell, retired President of Rockefeller Center, Inc., Louis G. Schoeller, retired Executive Vice-President, and Remsen Walker and Bertram Hegeman, Vice-Presidents, kindly granted helpful interviews.

Past and present architects at Rockefeller Center answered many questions and located such drawings as still exist. Wallace K. Harrison deserves my special thanks; I hope that he will make his own permanent record of his career. Michael Harris, partner in the architectural firm of Harrison & Abramovitz, offered an illuminating account of the architectural development of the Center's latest buildings. Walter H. Kilham, Jr., biographer of Raymond Hood, was more than generous with his time, his unpublished material, and his photographs. His partner, Robert B. O'Connor, now retired from practice, allowed me to ask him many questions about the Center's early stages with which he was associated. Edward Durell Stone and William Delehanty described the development of the Radio City Music Hall. James Norton, Morris Weiss, and Nicholas Haritonoff also assisted me in many ways.

Amongst those associated with Rockefeller Center in its early stages, Ruth Reinhard, widow of architect L. Andrew Reinhard, placed her personal papers and her memory at my disposal. Webster Todd granted a particularly helpful interview near the start of my research, and made available the privately printed autobiography of his father. Donald Deskey allowed me to review his files and photographs and to draw upon his knowledge. Harold Rambusch, whose firm of decorators worked at the Radio City Music Hall, Center Theater, Lincoln Center, and the Roxy Theater also gave me the benefit of his memories which go back to the mid-1920s. Francis T. Christy, Esq., kindly clarified several matters for me.

Wide-ranging interviews with Peter Grimm, Chairman of the Board of William A. White & Sons, Inc., with Douglas Haskell, former editor of *Architectural Forum,* and with Lauren Otis, Deputy Director of the Mayor's Office of Midtown Planning and Development, proved to be more than useful and more than pleasant.

At Columbia University, Alice Bonnell made the Columbiana Collection available, and at the Avery Library, Dr. Adolf K. Placzek, Neville Thompson, and Joanne Simonds extended themselves, as always, to assist research.

Space will not permit a precise explanation of my debt to those who have supplied additional assistance, but I can at least record the names of Mary-Anne Berman, Robert Benish, Fran Black, Jeanne Bliss, David Chelimer, Ernest M. Conrad, Elaine Evans Dee, Wilson Duprey, Shirley diEduardo, Helen diMaio, John J. Fleming, Ellen Hemminger, William Holabird, Charlotte LaRue, Alfred F. Loritsch, Grace Mayer, Barbara L. Michaels, Nancy Jane Ruddy, Eloise Pressey, Catha Grace Rambusch, Michael Rubinstein, Irving Sandler, Leon Shimkin, Otto J. Teegen, Gretl Urban, and Thomas C. Young. I regret that the late Earl Lundin, Eleanor Pearson, Ralph T. Walker, and Robert C. Weinberg cannot read this expression of my gratitude to them.

For helpful and stimulating suggestions about the text, I am most grateful to Reyner Banham and John Fleming and to James Raimes, the editor of this book.

For special photographic work and help in obtaining illustrations, I am happy to thank Sarah Bradford Landau, Jerry Robinson, and Vaughn Vekony, and for their typing skill and speed, Frances Petrow and Sonya Brockstein deserve special mention.

Without the assistance of Edward Kresky, Earl Palay, and H. W. Janson, I could never have written this book.

New York   C. H. K.
June 1977

Contents

List of Illustrations   **xiii**

Introduction   **xxiii**

I   The Mid-Century Cathedral   **2**

II   Background: The Limits to Power   **14**

III   The Opera House Project, 1927–1929:
Maximum Profit with Maximum Beauty   **22**

IV   Expert Advice   **30**

V   The Commercial Project, 1929–1933:
Disaster Averted   **44**

VI   Publicity and Management   **70**

VII   Grand Plans, 1934–1935   **82**

VIII   The Commercial Project, 1935–1940:
Filling the Gaps   88

  IX   First Postwar Expansion, 1941–1960   102

   X   Recent Expansion, 1960–1974   116

  XI   The RCA Building   130

 XII   Five Office Buildings   150

XIII   Theaters   164

 XIV   A Future Half a Century Old   196

           Notes   200

           Bibliography   214

           Index   218

List of Illustrations

1. Rockefeller Center, air view looking northwest. Photographed 1974.   xxiv

2. Simplified map of midtown Manhattan, 1977.   xxv

3. Rockefeller Center, grade level plan, 1974.   4

4. Underground pedestrian concourse plan, West 47th-West 54th Streets, 1974.   6

5. Rockefeller Center, air view looking northeast. Photographed May 1940.   7

6. Rockefeller Center, air view looking southwest. Photographed 1947.   8

7. Rockefeller Center, air view looking southwest. Photographed January 1956.   9

8. Montreal, Place Ville Marie. I. M. Pei and Partners, architects.   10

9. Atlanta, Peachtree Center. John Portman & Associates, architects.   10

10. Lincoln Center for the Performing Arts.   11

11. Albany, Empire State Plaza, model. Harrison & Abramovitz *et al.,* architects.   12

12. Albany, Empire State Plaza, air view photographed June 1974.   13

13. Grand Central Terminal and related buildings. Photographed *c.* 1938–39.   18

14. Grand Central Terminal, 1903–13, section. Reed & Stem, Warren & Wetmore, architects.   19

15. "Terminal Park" project, 1929. Ralph T. Walker, architect.   20

16. Sixth Avenue (Avenue of the Americas), toward north. Photographed April 1932.   26

17. Metropolitan Club Dinner scheme, Metropolitan Opera House, April 1928. Benjamin Wistar Morris, architect. Rendering by Chester B. Price.   27

18. Metropolitan Club Dinner scheme, model. April 1928.   28

19. Plan of September 1928. Reinhard & Hofmeister, architects.   34

20. Triple-deck street system, designed *c.* 1925–30. Harvey Wiley Corbett, architect.   37

21. New York about 1975, designed *c.* 1925–30. Harvey Wiley Corbett, architect.   38

22. Symposium project, Spring 1929. Corbett, Harrison & MacMurray, architects. Published 1931 as "Arts Center."   41

23. Daily News Building, 1930. Hood & Howells, archi-

tects. Right background: Tudor City Apartments, 1923–28. Photographed 1935.   45

24. McGraw-Hill Building, 1931. Hood, Godley & Fouilhoux, architects.   46

25. Plan G-3, January 8, 1930.   51

26. Plan H-1 revised, May 20, 1930. Reinhard & Hofmeister; Corbett, Harrison & MacMurray; Hood, Godley & Fouilhoux, architects.   54

27. "Fling" model, Summer 1930. Raymond Hood, architect.   56

28. "Oilcan" model, exhibited March 6, 1931.   58

29. Project in effect between mid-March and Autumn 1931, close to Plan F-19. Rendering by John Wenrich.   59

30. Roof garden proposed for Radio City Music Hall, 1932. Rendering by John Wenrich.   60

31. Project in effect between Spring 1932 and January 1934. Rendering by John Wenrich.   62

32. Promenade ("Channel Gardens") between La Maison Française (left) and British Building (right), looking west toward RCA Building. Photographed August 1972.   63

33. Left to right: La Maison Française, Promenade, RCA Building, British Empire Building, International Building, looking west. Photographed c. 1936.   64

34. Paul Manship, *Prometheus*. Photographed c. 1933–36.   65

35. Sunken plaza with City Garden Club Exhibition

and *Prometheus* fountain, looking southwest. Photographed May 1934.   67

36. Plan in effect between Spring 1932 and January 1934.   68

37. Rockefeller Center model flanked by models of the Pantheon and Column of Marcus Aurelius in same scale.   69

38. Sunken plaza with summer restaurant, toward RCA Building. Photographed Summer *c.* 1936.   72

39. Underground levels, rendering.   75

40. RCA Building, observation roof, looking west.   79

41. Rainbow Room lounge. Photographed September 1934.   80

42. Rainbow Room. Mrs. M. B. Schmidt, decorator.   81

43. Municipal Art Center project. Harrison & Fouilhoux, Morris & O'Connor, architects. Rendering by Hugh Ferriss.   86

44. Music Center project, 1938. Aymar Embury II, architect.   87

45. Project in effect between January 1934 and Spring 1937. Rendering by John Wenrich.   89

46. RCA Building, Museum of Science and Industry. Edward Durell Stone, architect.   90

47. RCA Building, eleventh floor roof. Gardens of the Nations. Dutch Garden.   91

48. Sunken plaza with Christmas tree. Photographed December 1972.   92

49. First Time & Life Building (One Rockefeller Plaza), looking south from Rockefeller Plaza (private street). Photographed April 1937.   94

50. Associated Press Building. Left background: RKO (Amax) Building. Left foreground: RCA Building. Right foreground: International Building with relief by Lawrie over entrance to East River Savings Bank. Photographed *c.* 1940.   95

51. Isamu Noguchi, *News*. Associated Press Building.   96

52. Eastern Air Lines Building, looking southwest. Photographed *c.* 1939–40.   97

53. Sixth Avenue (Avenue of the Americas), looking north, immediately after demolition of the elevated railway. Photographed April 1939.   98

54. U.S. Rubber Company (Uniroyal) Building. Photographed *c.* 1940.   99

55. "Plaza of the Americas" proposal, 1941. Edward Durell Stone *et al.,* architects.   100

56. Rockefeller Plaza (private street), looking north from 48th Street. Left: Eastern Air Lines Building. Photographed July 1945.   104

57. Rockefeller Plaza (private street), looking north from 48th Street. Left: Eastern Air Lines Building. At north end: Esso (Warner Communications) Building. Photographed July 1948.   105

58. Rockefeller Plaza (private street), looking south from 51st Street. Photographed December 1961.   106

59. Left to right: Eastern Air Lines Building, RCA Showroom, 1947; Garage entrance; U.S. Rubber Company (Uniroyal) Building Addition. Photographed December 1955.   109

60. Rockefeller Center, air view looking northwest. Photographed June 1964.   110

61. Sixth Avenue (Avenue of the Americas), looking northwest.   113

62. Left to right: RKO (Amax) Building, Radio City Music Hall, RCA Building West, U.S. Rubber Company (Uniroyal) Buildings. Photographed October 1961.   118

63. Sixth Avenue (Avenue of the Americas), looking southwest from 51st Street. Photographed 1974.   119

64. View from a terrace restaurant into the Ville Contemporaine, project of 1921–22. Le Corbusier, architect.   120

65. City Planning Commission, Urban Design Group, theoretical study for mid-block *galleria, c.* 1968.   123

66. Section through Sixth Avenue and McGraw-Hill Building and Plaza, as planned *c.* 1969–71.   124

67. Celanese Building *galleria* with Ibram Lassaw sculpture, *Pantheon*. Photographed July 1974.   125

68. "Minipark" west of Exxon Building. Photographed July 1974.   126

69. "Minipark" west of McGraw-Hill Building. Photographed 1974.   127

70. Fifth Avenue, looking south from 51st Street. Photographed September 1955.   131

71. View looking west from 7th floor roof garden of Palazzo d'Italia. Photographed July 1974.   132

72. RCA Building, street level plan.   133

73. RCA Building, plan of 19th–31st floors.   134

74. RCA Building, three sketch models, 1930–31.   135

75. RCA Building, alternative exterior designs, 1931.   136

76. Three-story high NBC Broadcasting studio, rendering *c.* 1931–32.   139

77. Margaret Bourke-White, photomurals showing radio transmission equipment. RCA Building, NBC visitors' reception lobby.   140

78. Margaret Bourke-White, photomurals showing radio transmission equipment. RCA Building, NBC visitors' reception lobby.   141

79. RCA Building. Municipal Art Exhibit, May 1934.   142

80. RCA Building lobby. Photographed July 1974.   143

81. Lee Lawrie, *Genius.* RCA Building, east façade.   144

82. Gaston Lachaise, *Gifts of Earth to Mankind* and *The Spirit of Progress.* RCA Building West, façade.   145

83. Leo Friedlander, *Transmission and Reception.* RCA Building, 49th Street entrance.   145

84. Diego Rivera, *Man at the Crossroads,* formerly RCA Building lobby.   146

85. José María Sert, *Triumph of Man's Accomplishments,* RCA Building lobby.   147

86. RCA Management Conference Center, proposed 1974. Ford and Earl Associates, architects.   148

87. Underground pedestrian concourse showing original lighting. Photographed July 1952.   149

88. Palazzo d'Italia, International Building entrance, and International Building North. Photographed *c.* 1950.   151

89. International Building lobby, rendering *c.* 1935.   152

90. International Building lobby, looking out toward St. Patrick's Cathedral. Photographed 1935–36.   153

91. Carl Milles, *Man and Nature,* first Time & Life Building (One Rockefeller Plaza) lobby. Photographed 1941.   155

92. Eastern Air Lines Building. View from underground pedestrian concourse level to street-level lobby. Photographed July 1974.   156

93. Second Time & Life Building, showing Americas Plaza.   159

94. Josef Albers, *Portals,* second Time & Life Building lobby. Photographed 1961.   160

95. Exxon Building lobby. Photographed July 1974.   161

96. Ann Arbor, University of Michigan. Hill Auditorium, interior, 1914. Albert Kahn and Ernest Wilby, architects.   166

97. Music Center auditorium project, sections, *c.* 1927–29. Joseph Urban, architect.   167

98. Radio City Music Hall, Roxy's studio, reception room. Donald Deskey, designer.   168

99. Radio City Music Hall, plans and section.   169

100. Radio City Music Hall, grand lobby looking north.   170

101. Radio City Music Hall, grand lobby looking south.   171

102. Ezra Winter, *Fountain of Youth*, Radio City Music Hall, grand lobby.   172

103. Radio City Music Hall, basement lounge. Photographed 1932–33.   173

104. Radio City Music Hall sculptures in art studio before installation in theater. Photographed 1932.   174

105. Radio City Music Hall, auditorium toward stage.   175

106. Radio City Music Hall, auditorium showing sides and rear mezzanines.   176

107. Berlin, Grosses Schauspielhaus. Hans Poelzig, architect.   177

108. Hartford, Bushnell Memorial Auditorium, interior. Corbett, Harrison & MacMurray, architects.   177

109. Radio City Music Hall, preliminary auditorium model. Photographed May 1931.   178

110. Metropolitan Opera House project, 1927. Joseph Urban, architect.   179

111. Radio City Music Hall, preliminary auditorium model. Photographed August 1931.   181

112. Stuart Davis, mural, and furniture by Donald Deskey. Radio City Music Hall, men's smoking room. Photographed May 1974.   184

113. Yasuo Kuniyoshi, floral murals, and furniture by Donald Deskey. Radio City Music Hall, women's powder room. Photographed May 1974.   185

114. Radio City Music Hall, women's powder room, Donald Deskey, designer. Photographed May 1974.   186

115. Center Theater, preliminary model. Photographed May 1931.   188

116. Center Theater, preliminary model. Photographed January 1932.   188

117a,b,c. Center Theater, façade and marquee studies. Photographed June 1931.   189

118. Center Theater, grand foyer.   190

119. Center Theater, auditorium. Photographed 1932.   191

120. Center Theater, women's lounge. Eugene Schoen, designer.   192

121. Maurice Heaton, *Amelia Earhart Crossing the Atlantic* and furniture by Eugene Schoen. Center Theater, women's lounge.   193

122. Edward Steichen, *Story of Aviation*. Center Theater, men's lounge.   194

123. Edward Steichen, *Story of Aviation*. Center Theater, men's lounge.   194

124. Center Theater, roof. Simon & Schuster offices, 1940. Photographed 1940 or 1941.   195

125. McGraw-Hill sunken plaza during concert performance. Photographed 1974.   197

126. Rockefeller Center, Christmas, 1940.   199

Introduction

"The Heavens themselves, the Planets and this Center
Observe degree, priority and place."
Shakespeare, *Troilus and Cressida* I. iii. 85

Rockefeller Center is a group of twenty-one office buildings, theaters, underground streets, and open public spaces in midtown Manhattan, a coordinated group of commercial buildings under unified control [1–4]. Here, for the first time, the concept of a skyscraper city was realized in practice. During the 1930s, its original fourteen buildings were confined to the three blocks between 48th and 51st Streets, Fifth to Sixth Avenues, occupying all the property there which belonged to Columbia University, as well as a few parcels of land bordering Sixth Avenue which were contiguous to the Columbia site [5]. After the Second World War, the Center grew outside the original site when its owners constructed an office building extending from 51st to 52nd Streets [6], acquired another at the northwest corner of Fifth Avenue and 48th Street, and built a third replacing one of its unprofitable theaters [7]. In 1957 the Center expanded to the northwest across Sixth Avenue by building the second Time & Life Building; it then helped to finance the Sperry-Rand Building and the Hilton Hotel on Sixth Avenue [1]. At the end of 1973 the last of its three newest buildings planned in 1963 was finished.

A list of buildings alone cannot describe Rockefeller Center. It is not simply a group of interrelated rectilinear prisms, and it is not just another financial corporation. It is a complex of structures which has created a new core for the city of New York. It is the prototype of countless urban renewal projects around the world. It was originally intended to provide the maximum beauty consistent with profitability, a fundamental interrelationship between architecture as an art and building as business wills. It was the only executed model for the cities

1. Rockefeller Center, air view looking northwest. Photographed 1974.

of towers that a past generation expected. It anticipated the city of the future.

It has more than thirty restaurants, an outdoor ice-skating rink, shops at street level and underground. It has murals and statues and flags of the United Nations. It contains public exhibition rooms and broadcasting studios. The Center's Christmas tree is probably the most famous on earth [126], and its horticultural displays are changed with the seasons. About 240,000 people use the Center on every working day, and its largest theater, the Radio City Music Hall, counted about 240,000,000 paid admissions since it opened at the end of December 1932.

Because it offers the city far more than office space and theater seats, it has been a focal point of Manhattan for almost a half-century, and shows no signs of abandoning its position. Because it still offers lessons to major builders, it is time to understand what lies behind its ability to do so.

ROCKEFELLER CENTER

I.

The Mid-Century Cathedral

"The newcomer to New York City, American or foreigner, doesn't spend a glance on St. John's of Morningside Heights, or on St. Patrick's on Fifth Avenue, or on the Russian basilica on Fourth Avenue, or thereabouts; but makes for Rockefeller Center where he can get an eyeful worth seeing."

Sean O'Casey, *Rose and Crown*

Office buildings are built to house businesses and make money. When the profit motive looms as large as the buildings, artistic standards may decline. Even innovative planning can present an unwelcome risk to conservative investors and rental managers. Such mundane circumstances do not ordinarily engage our sympathy or flatter our view of what men do at their best. And so, although general accounts of office building design may be written, entire books are seldom devoted to individual commercial towers.

Cathedrals and castles, mansions and museums, designed to be beautiful or grand, with practicalities and financial considerations sometimes sacrificed to a brilliant effect—these typically attract more attention from architectural historians. These buildings were commissioned by an aesthetically sensitive elite which separated its buildings from the surrounding cities by walls and by customs, and the buildings are often discussed in isolation from the towns around them. But office buildings are created and properly perceived only as part of the totality of our modern cities. Their effect on the urban environment demands to be assessed.

When they are outstanding in planning and design, as they sometimes are, and when they are wide-ranging in their effects, they hold a place in a capitalist democracy comparable to the monuments of traditional institutions of other times.[1] To a remarkable degree, Rockefeller Center exemplifies such building. It may even be appropriate to think of it as a cathedral of the mid-twentieth century. Multi-building complexes used to be universities, religious establishments, and, in the nineteenth century, factories; in our century, the major ones are the premises of government and corporate employees. And this one, a success for so long, has been an example to many others.

The idea of comparing twenty-one office buildings with a monument to faith, art, and ethics is not quite as outrageous as it may seem at first.[2] We still accept the ideals of revering God, nature, and country, although much of America spends hours faithfully traveling to work in offices but not to church on Sundays. The minister of a church adjacent to Rockefeller Center said that his church saw itself as part of the life of the Center, in which he believed there was room for the altar.[3] In past centuries, men of commerce saw themselves as part of the life of the church and hoped that there was room for them.

If we look at other aspects of cathedrals and major office buildings, we come closer to the significance of Rockefeller Center to mid-twentieth-century America. Both types of buildings are monuments conceived by institutions which, along with government, were the determining institu-tions of the day—in earlier centuries the church, in the twentieth century petro-chemical and banking industries, for example. The strength of these institutions is proclaimed by means of size and height (which altered their cities' fabric significantly), their messages further explained with the help of painting and sculpture. Advanced technology available at the period was used in both cases without necessarily employing the most daring techniques or most advanced forms theoretically possible. While neither cathedrals nor office buildings are spontaneous popular creations, both were intended to attract masses of people and to satisfy the demands—not always profound or sophisticated, sometimes pressing and sometimes soothing—of those who come to them. They are meeting points, city landmarks, centers of memorable public life. It is one ironic sign of twentieth-century reality that Rockefeller Center dwarfs St. Patrick's Cathedral across Fifth Avenue [1, 5-7].

The essence of New York is not its native artistic heritage, if by that we mean a centuries' old cultivation of local painting and sculpture, or a series of self-conscious architectural masterpieces. The essence of New York is not to be found in traditional spirituality or philosophical refinement, nor in respect for the established order of political or social life. Rather, the essence of the city is its drive toward the future, its constant experimentation, its attempts to make the best of its physical limitations and its financial problems, its position in international trade, and its international social composition. Visitors regard it as the embodiment of material progress, of

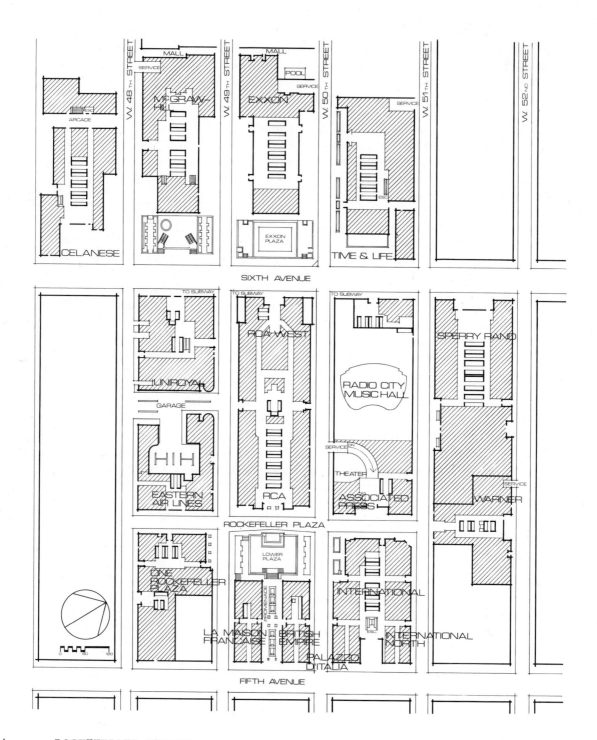

W. 48th STREET W. 49th STREET W. 50th STREET W. 51st STREET W. 52nd STREET

MALL
SERVICE
McGRAW-HILL
ARCADE
ESC

MALL
POOL
SERVICE
EXXON

SERVICE
ESC

CELANESE
EXXON PLAZA
TIME & LIFE

SIXTH AVENUE

TO SUBWAY
TO SUBWAY
TO SUBWAY

RCA WEST
SPERRY RAND

UNIROYAL
RADIO CITY MUSIC HALL

GARAGE

H H
SERVICE
THEATER

EASTERN AIR LINES
RCA
ASSOCIATED PRESS
WARNER
SERVICE

ROCKEFELLER PLAZA

ONE ROCKEFELLER PLAZA
LOWER PLAZA
INTERNATIONAL

PROMENADE
ESC

LA MAISON FRANÇAISE
BRITISH EMPIRE
INTERNATIONAL NORTH

PALAZZO D'ITALIA

FIFTH AVENUE

twentieth-century forces of physical size, of speed, of compromise, of ambition.

There is no better representative of these forces than Rockefeller Center which established its neighborhood as the heart of New York City. Its owners built office and theater space of unprecedented extent, and provided a coordinated plan blending commerce and art, plants and limestone, in a way perhaps dreamed of but never realized before. It was intended to last far longer than the twenty-five years' span on which speculative builders now reckon, and incorporated more popular technology—rotating theater stages, high-speed elevators, narrow-tread moving stairs—than any earlier project and many later ones. The planners left a legacy of concern for channeling vehicular and pedestrian traffic in segregated areas, for providing landscaped open space, and for the use of an area for leisure activity as well as for business premises. The open space and the provision of covered pedestrian passages supplementing the usual city sidewalks suggested New York City's recent zoning amendments which offer incentives to builders who provide such facilities as these.

Ambition, flexibility, the idealism possible within enlightened self-interest, astute management—all are important signs of successful commercial culture, which Rockefeller Center exemplifies.

Today we tend to assume that a conscientious private developer will think of the coordinated planning of all the buildings on a large site, arranging and graduating their sizes to give each the maximum open space and view, and providing for adequate pedestrian as well as vehicular passageways. Zoning refinements may, in fact, oblige him to offer these features of design, or to provide landscaping or links to mass transportation or a covered parking garage. But few of these aspects of planning were common in commercial building in late 1927 when John D. Rockefeller Jr.'s associates first became interested in acquiring a lease on the three blocks of midtown Manhattan where Rockefeller Center rose a few years later. It was primarily because the economic predictions for the project they had in mind were radically altered during its planning stages that the directors were forced to find new and more agreeable ways of designing a large commercial development. Their research forecast later projects in North America and abroad.

Rockefeller Center showed how well-conceived new construction could increase retail sales and restaurant patronage in an area. It proved that the value of its own buildings, and those of its satellite neighborhood, could rise to heights gratifying to the municipal tax collector. Its population made civic improvements urgent, such as the completion of the Sixth Avenue subway and a 49th-50th Street bus line. City planners used the Center as the starting point of grand urban schemes; one was a boulevard extending from the RCA Building westward to the Hudson River, and another was Mayor LaGuardia's dream of a Municipal Art Center adjacent to Rockefeller Center [43].[4] Public opinion welcomed the smooth, clean towers which replaced older buildings, and the public has always enjoyed the

3. Rockefeller Center, grade level plan, 1974.
(*Redrawn by Nancy Jane Ruddy*)

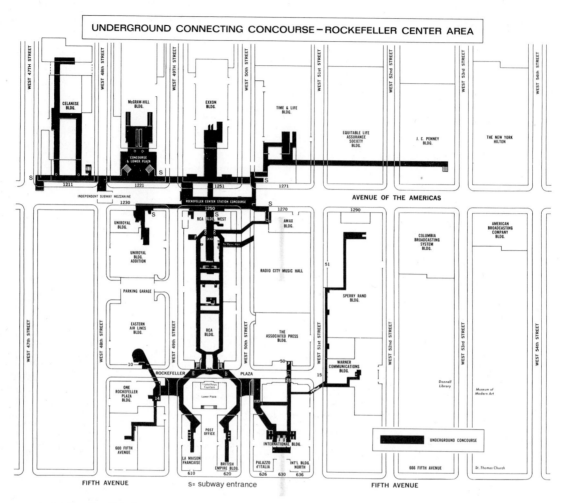

UNDERGROUND CONNECTING CONCOURSE – ROCKEFELLER CENTER AREA

4. Underground pedestrian concourse plan, West 47th-West 54th Streets, 1974.
(*Courtesy Rockefeller Center, Inc.*)

open spaces, plants, and works of art. Tourists find that Rockefeller Center gives them vantage points, whereas the Empire State and Chrysler Buildings are crowded against the sidewalks so that their towers are only visible from afar.

After the Second World War, the Center inspired dozens of urban renewal ventures which were meant to make equally profitable city centers rise over equally unprepossessing neighborhoods. The fact that a business center could be used to shift both commerce and prestige from one area of a city to another is part of the background of La Défense zone in Paris, and the Peachtree Center in Atlanta [9]. Los Angeles, Denver and Detroit, Montreal [8] and Johannesburg,

Pittsburgh and Kansas City are only a few cities in which developers built co-ordinated commercial complexes with multi-level shopping centers, sculpture and foliage, flags, public entertainment, and hard-working public relations staffs. Rockefeller Center's way of having business present a smiling face to attract shoppers and diners to its facilities was not lost on developers from Philadelphia to Brooklyn, Minnesota, and from Houston to Berlin, who installed ice-skating rinks in commercial centers.

The flowers, café umbrellas, and sculpture which soften the effect of dense office construction have been an obvious source of inspiration to architect-developer John Portman, who has designed center-city building groups in Georgia [9], Michigan, and California which have given importance and focus to downtown areas. It has been Portman more than any other designer or builder who has understood the prescription combining adequate financing, adequate—and sometimes superior—architectural quality, and well-publicized urban amenity as a remedy for urban blight.[5] Other architects such as I. M. Pei at Place Ville Marie in Montreal [8] [6] or Mies van der Rohe and his successors at Illinois Center in Chicago [7] have added the public pleasures of Rockefeller Center to buildings over railroad station tracks, an idea inspired by the Grand Central Terminal neighborhood in New York.

The influence of Rockefeller Center extends even to Walt Disney World, also de-signed under single-minded control. Like the Center, it has underground facilities, plants, an almost obsessive interest in cleanliness, and an up-to-date if not avant-garde standard of modern architecture.[8]

The value of new buildings and open space as regenerators of a moribund neighborhood was fully apparent to Rockefeller's sons. John D. Rockefeller 3rd was the principal private sponsor of Lincoln Center for the Performing Arts [10] [9], a classicistic complex of buildings replacing blocks of tenements. It was designed under the supervision of Wallace Harrison, one of the designers of Rockefeller Center, and his partner, Max Abramovitz, and it incorporates most of the features

5. Rockefeller Center, air view looking northeast. Photographed May 1940.
(*Courtesy Rockefeller Center, Inc.*)

once proposed for the abandoned Municipal Art Center. David Rockefeller understood the same lessons, when he promoted the development of the Chase Manhattan Bank's art-filled headquarters building in the Wall Street area where no large building had been built for an entire generation, but where many have been built since then.[10] Nelson Rockefeller's monument to what he learned is the most extraordinary of all—the Empire State Plaza in Albany, New York, where he served as state governor for over a decade [11, 12]. This multi-level complex of office buildings for state bureaus, auditoria, cafeterias, scientific laboratories, educational and cultural facilities was intended to bring new life and work to an old city center and to clear away a slum at the same time. It has overtones of Washington, D.C., with its marble covered buildings flanking a central reflecting pool; memories of Versailles with its clipped trees in formal rows; echoes of Brasilia with its sleek buildings rising ostentatiously high on a windy platform. Nelson Rockefeller said, too, that he had always very much admired the Palace of the Dalai Lama which inspired the Albany towers rising over a wall, with access at the base of a mural cliff. But the reasonable possibility of having Harrison & Abramovitz come up with a practical design for this more-than-a-billion-dollar project was based upon Nelson Rockefeller's intimate familiarity with Rockefeller Center, which he has served as director, renting agent, corporation president, and part owner. The Empire State Plaza has been the subject of almost endless criticism, which Nelson Rockefeller dismisses as his father ignored criticisms of Rockefeller Center. Perhaps he noticed that some Albany residents began to feel happier about it during the cold winter of 1976-77 when part of its surface was flooded and used as an ice-skating rink, the very hallmark of his father's Center in New York.[11]

6. Rockefeller Center, air view looking southwest. Photographed 1947.
(*Courtesy Rockefeller Center, Inc.*)

Unquestionably, Rockefeller Center has reminded developers both good and bad that the architecture of individual buildings need not be exquisite to be functional and an improvement to the city; that the open spaces do not have to be very large if they are well designed; that people seldom complain about uninteresting side streets if there are compensating amenities close by. The creation of an area which is active day and night is another legacy of Rockefeller Center to its own city and to other building projects designed to become essential parts of downtown areas.

Some people do not learn the right lessons. Developers fare badly if they try to build large projects without making sure that transit facilities exist to provide a steady flow of shop and restaurant customers. Developers who build shoddy shopping centers and fail to supervise the quality of tenants have generally not done well in the long run. People who build sunken plazas beside office buildings usually find that they are unprofitable unless the public can be forced downward into the plaza level shops; Rockefeller Center did not solve this problem fully. Rockefeller Center should have taught developers that neither a miser nor a prodigal is likely to produce a project that enjoys half a century of success.

All this is not to say that Rockefeller Center is architecturally or conceptually perfect. When the building plans were first revealed, they were criticized for being too extensive and dense. People said that they altered the building scale of the neighborhood and would introduce thou-

7. Rockefeller Center, air view looking southwest showing Esso (now Warner Communications) Building in center foreground, Sinclair Oil Building (now 600 Fifth Avenue) in left center. Photographed January 1956.
(*Courtesy Rockefeller Center, Inc.*)

sands of people to an area with insufficient transit facilities to accommodate them. Later, the management drew criticism from several quarters for its policies regarding painted and sculptural decoration —decoration which exemplifies certain "Art Deco" modes. Some critics wanted more art by Americans, or at least different procedures for selecting artists, and other critics objected to the themes, to the ideology, or simply to the quality of the art. Later still, people found the last of the original group of buildings erected before the Second World War to be less sensitive in design and planning, a criticism leveled at the later buildings as well. The Center was occasionally chastised for including insufficient space to produce a new park around the midtown office towers, but the architects never intended to bring the country to the city or to mix the informality of nature with the strict demands of the site; the Center's architects were all urban-based and were generally inclined to do their landscaping in brick and limestone. The postwar growth of the Center made some real estate people wonder when the expansion would end.

9. Atlanta, Peachtree Center. John Portman & Associates, architects.
(*Courtesy John Portman & Associates*)

8. Montreal, Place Ville Marie. I. M. Pei and Partners, architects.
(*Joseph Molitor*)

Nevertheless, Rockefeller Center is a place where people go not only because their offices are there or because they want to see a show at a theater within the complex, but also because the Center has become a focal point of our urban experience. It is one of the country's greatest tourist attractions. It gives people the sense of the best that money could buy for a city, which is not the same as seeing expensive buildings. It is a place for meeting friends and for sitting beside some of the few ornamental plants in the neighborhood [32]. People come to watch the ice-skaters in the original sunken plaza [48] or free concerts in the later McGraw-Hill Plaza to the west [125]. They browse in shops which sell products more exotic or more costly than those offered in the average New York neighborhood. Rockefeller Center offers accessible open public space, accommodates restaurants and theaters, a skating rink and dance floors. It maintains carefully cleaned lobbies and public restrooms, and provides sheltered underground streets [4, 87] which many people use to avoid crowds and inclement weather. In other words, by careful planning and constant attention to its public image, it has made itself into a busy center of many kinds of activity, not simply of office work and entertainment. As such, it draws visitors and local people and provides them with an orientation point, a stopping place within a city designed on a monotonous grid plan.

For a city to be coherent to its inhabitants and visitors, it needs certain reference points which shape the neighborhoods and mark one's progress around the town. A single tower may suffice, but a clearly definable group of buildings, distinct from their neighbors but not totally different from them, will provide orientation for a far larger area.

Cathedrals and their precincts used to provide the main reference points of this kind. In the modern world it is our office buildings that attract and inspire through their dramatic height, unusual size, or public amenities. Rockefeller Center coordinated and related a group of high and low office buildings, gathering them into a group and making the already familiar skyscraper form intelligible.

Rockefeller Center was the only large private permanent construction project planned and executed between the start of the Depression and the end of the Second World War. There were other important building enterprises during these

10. Lincoln Center for the Performing Arts. Left to right around plaza: New York State Theater, 1964, Philip Johnson and Richard Foster, architects; Metropolitan Opera House, 1966, Wallace K. Harrison, architect; Avery Fisher Hall, 1962, Max Abramovitz, architect. Center background: Vivian Beaumont Theater, 1965, Eero Saarinen & Associates, architects; right background: Juilliard School of Music, 1968, Pietro Belluschi with Eduardo Catalano and Westermann & Miller, architects.
(*Serating Photograph, Courtesy Harrison & Abramovitz*)

11. Albany, Empire State Plaza, model. Harrison & Abramovitz *et al.,* architects.
(*Courtesy Office of General Services*)

years, of course, but almost all of them were sponsored by government to stimulate employment, to provide housing for the third of the nation in desperate need of it, or to give benefits of enormous importance to the country. Because these enterprises were not private, they involved risks and problems different from those of private developments. The World's Fairs of the 1930s were privately sponsored, it is true, but there was abundant public investment in transit facilities, city park improvements, and in government pavilions to help the fairs to succeed financially. Besides, those expositions offered a hopeful but transitory vision of a future made simple through modern design and technology. They were events intended for immediate impact and not for permanent life as integral parts of cities.

Rockefeller Center was unique in its purpose, in its sponsorship, and necessarily, then, in its results. Nothing comparable could be built at the time, so that nothing else looks like it. Apart from its virtues, its very uniqueness makes it a monument.

12. Albany, Empire State Plaza, air view photographed June 1974.
(*Courtesy Office of General Services*)

II.

Background:

The Limits
to Power

"Assuming that the Regional Plan Association, the Rockefeller Family, and LeCorbusier have been the principal forces in shaping the city since 1930, we may ask ourselves if they will continue to be so."

Henry Hope Reed, "The Vision Spurned: Classical New York. The Story of City Planning in New York, Part II," *Classical America* I, 1973.

The story of Rockefeller Center tells us many things, one of which is that a successful building project like this one is built upon a solid foundation of money. The money must be as reliable and as available as the bedrock of Manhattan Island, whose existence is the essential precondition of the city's skyscrapers. Another part of the story is less obvious— that money alone will not produce a superior product and that there were obstacles which even the Rockefeller millions could not dislodge.

Rockefeller Center was, of course, built by one of the richest men in America, John D. Rockefeller Jr. (1874-1960). It remains the property of his sons who hold the stock of Rockefeller Center, Inc.,[12] which built and operates the development. In order of their birth, Rockefeller's children were a daughter, Abby (Mrs. Jean Mauzé, 1903-77); and five sons, John D. Rockefeller 3rd (1906-), a philanthropist; Nelson Aldrich (1908-), his outgoing brother who was Governor of

New York for fifteen years and who was the Vice-President of the United States; Laurance Spelman (1910-), who supports environmental conservation and develops resort hotels; Winthrop (1912-73), former Governor of his adopted state of Arkansas; and David (1915-), Chairman and Chief Executive Officer of the Chase Manhattan Bank.

John D. Rockefeller Jr. controlled the building development by selecting the Board of Directors of Rockefeller Center, Inc. (originally called Metropolitan Square Corporation), and of the various corporations associated with it as holding companies and operating subsidiaries. Rockefeller had final authority over expenditure, work schedules, and the appointment of architects and artists, although he did not participate in the daily work process or in preliminary planning sessions. He had years of experience of being the interested but detached executive who knew how to pick his associates and delegate authority to boards of directors and to building managers.

For John D. Rockefeller Jr., though a personally retiring man, had already proved to be a prodigious builder of bold projects.[13] A considerable number of his many charitable activities took architectural form—Riverside Church in New York (1927-30); the restoration of Versailles, starting in 1924; Colonial Williamsburg restoration in Virginia (1926-); the Paul Laurence Dunbar Apartments in Harlem (1926-28). He provided land and buildings for The Cloisters, for Rockefeller University, and International House student residences from New York to Tokyo. Later, in 1946, he bought and gave to the United Nations the land on which its buildings stand.

John D. Rockefeller Jr. kept himself informed about the finances of his buildings, but was just as eager to know about the plans. A young architect who brought drawings for him to examine would quickly learn about the folding ruler which his patron kept in his pocket, and Rockefeller was as interested in examining the width of an elevator as in seeing a handsome but inevitably glamorized presentation drawing. He was not attracted to modern styles, except insofar as costs might be kept down by omitting superfluous decoration. He was attracted to the Egyptian style for its suggestion of permanence and solidity, to the Gothic style for its religious connotations, and to the classical modes probably for their familiar intimations of substantial earthly status. He liked realistic sculpture and generally had aesthetic tastes not unlike those of the other barons of business whose steel-framed, stone-faced office buildings culminated in rooftop water towers disguised as miniature temples.

His wife, née Abby Greene Aldrich (1874-1948), was far more interested in art than he was, and her taste was wider in range. She actively supported the recording and institutional collecting of folk art and modern art, especially that of France, Mexico, and the United States. She was a co-founder of the Museum of Modern Art and introduced contemporary materials and display techniques into her private print gallery. A woman of strong tastes and widely admired character, she was the first artistic mentor of her children, several of whom have become important patrons of the arts.

There were, however, aspects of the Rockefeller Center project over which the owner and his wife had little or no control. He did not own the land on which the original group of buildings was constructed. Columbia University did, and does.[14] The University's treasurer and lawyers and president and trustees all had a say in approving the original agreement to build and any amendments or alterations to it. They also had to agree to extend or renew the leases, and stood to benefit under the terms of renewed leases if the development proved to be profitable.

The Rockefeller Center project was originally conceived with the thought of providing a new home for the Metropolitan Opera within the Columbia property. But Rockefeller could not influence the stockholders of the Metropolitan Opera and Real Estate Company which owned the Metropolitan Opera House. When these American aristocrats decided that the Opera would not enter his project after all, Rockefeller's entire plan had to be changed.

Nor did Rockefeller have any control over the effects of the stock market crash of 1929, or the subsequent Depression, other factors which affected the development. Because of the Depression, for instance, there was available a large pool of construction men eager for work and less inclined to strike than they might have been in a period of high employment. Costs of materials were considerably lower, too, and contracts could be negotiated on terms favorable to developers because suppliers were eager for any profitable business. But most American companies were not expanding, or moving into new premises without being offered special inducements. The Center's character and finances were affected by this factor, and we see reflections of this situation in a decision to attract international tenants, in the early provision of air conditioning in several buildings, provision of an on-site bonded warehouse, and a hundred other things large and small, from rental agreements to cleaning the Center's sidewalks.

When Metropolitan Life Insurance Company agreed to provide a mortgage to help finance the project, it gained certain rights of approval or disapproval of changes in the plans. The insurance company also brought in its own architect, Daniel Everett Waid, to inspect and report on the plans; and if Waid had wanted to, he could probably have exercised a considerable influence upon the development. The insurance company was particularly alert to materials or layouts that were potentially hazardous, and its advice probably saved the Center some lawsuits.

More important than the involvement of the insurance company was the effect of municipal legislation. New York City has a building code that regulates such matters as safety, construction materials, and avoidance of hazards to passers-by. The building code for theaters in effect at the time prohibited office building above theaters, so there had to be limits on the total height of any part of the development where there were theaters. To compensate for necessary office space lost on this account, other parts of the Center might have to include taller buildings. The silhouette of the project and the amount of pedestrian traffic would vary from area to area. The Code prevented New York architects from using concrete framing for tall buildings, or structural steel without fireproof cladding, or broad expanses of glass. Since the tall buildings at the Center could not be designed fully to exploit modern materials either structurally or visually, they could be open to criticism for their lack of structurally expressive modernity. On the other hand, the Code forbade copies of a bold Renaissance cornice or anything else with ornamental forms projecting more than eighteen inches. Then the total building bulk was affected by a Code revision of 1931, which permitted the installation of high-speed elevators. If elevators move people quickly, they can make more trips and thus serve as many passengers as a larger number of slower elevators. Fewer elevators mean that fewer total square feet of building need be constructed and financed.

New York City's Zoning Resolution of 1916 and its amendments had an even more fundamental influence upon the Center. This measure regulated land use, permitting only low-rise residences in one area of the city, factories and industrial installations in another, department stores, offices, and similar agreeable premises in another, unrestricted development in other areas.

The Zoning Resolution had been introduced originally for reasons having more to do with economics than aesthetics. The increasing centralization of commerce in the late nineteenth century—symbolized by the growth of cartels, trusts, and giant corporations—had led to increasing centralization of business offices in a single location. The location might have spread over several adjacent blocks, or might have been found in vacant land in the country or suburbs. But in the early twentieth century, there was every incentive to stay in the heart of town, because personal and even telephone contact were easier there, because staff was available in the center but could not easily reach—or was not willing to travel to—out-of-town locations before rapid mass transit facilities were developed, and because for the same reason there were not many commuter suburbs where staff could be recruited. Reliable water supplies, electric power, and other necessities were also available primarily in town. But as the population rose, the available land in cities became more valuable, and landholders built upward rather than horizontally, a solution made possible by the introduction of structural steel and by the elevator.[15] There was so much construction upward that the buildings crowded each other, deprived their neighbors of light and air, and therefore threatened eventually to reduce even their own land values. In addition, every sort of business was crowding every other. There was, at the time, no way to prevent tanneries or sweatshop clothing factories from standing beside the elegant department stores which sold their products. This situation, which influential citizens of the gentler class found disagreeable, also threatened to reduce land values, and there was even reason to fear that factories might intrude upon the traditional dwelling areas of these articulate members of the community. Zoning for size restriction, zoning for the provisions of even minimal light and air, and zoning for limited uses were adopted in New York in 1916 and later by every major American city except Houston, Texas.[16]

Zoning for use limited the ability of the development to expand to the north of the Columbia University property, where 52nd-55th Streets were zoned for residential, not commercial purposes [2]. John D. Rockefeller Jr. and other members of his family lived on one of those blocks, and he may have become interested in undertaking a high-quality building project partly in order to preserve the quality of his neighborhood.

The Resolution also regulated the size of buildings by providing that a new structure could rise only to a certain multiple of the width of the street which it faced before being stepped back. The Resolution established dimensions for side lots and back areas, and it required setbacks after certain limits on these sides as well. When a building had contracted tc cover only a quarter of its site, the floors could be built up to any height the owners desired. This accounts for the stepped silhouette of New York's tall buildings for which plans were filed between 1916 and 1961, when a comprehensively amended Resolution went into effect.

13. Grand Central Terminal and related buildings, to the west (left) and north (rear). Photographed c. 1938–39.
(*Courtesy Penn Central Railroad*)

The setback requirement also stimulated a change in the style of office buildings, which had generally been designed with Gothic details or with Italian Renaissance design principles (massive lower floors, lighter intermediate floors, elaborate "cornice" floors). It is impossible to design a convincing *palazzo* with setbacks, or a stepped pseudo-cathedral. The setback rule, according to journalists and architects and critics of the time, required, and had inspired, a new style in architecture which would be simpler, independent of the past, more direct in expression, "a study in form whereas the sky-scraper of yesterday was a study of surface and academic proportion." [17] The planners of new buildings would henceforth call more often on the professional model-maker, since architects had to design in the round rather than put façades on the simple rectangular buildings of the years before 1916.

The Zoning Resolution affected much more than the single building. It gave impetus to the idea of assembling huge plots of land, including the creation of super-blocks by closing off streets running between several blocks. This would be done for the sake of the immense tower which could be erected on one-quarter of the land, or for the sake of a coordinated, varied group built up according to the demands of the total area and of potential tenants. Comprehensive design on large tracts could also make the city more beautiful. If a super-block could not be formed, builders could emulate the Grand Central Terminal neighborhood, where from about 1910 onward the New York Central Railroad had leased the land above the tracks to builders who erected a dense row of large buildings [13], creating the Midtown business district where building far outpaced development in the old business district, the Wall Street area.

In the Grand Central neighborhood,

14. Grand Central Terminal, 1903–13, section. Reed & Stem, Warren & Wetmore, architects. (*Courtesy Penn Central Railroad*)

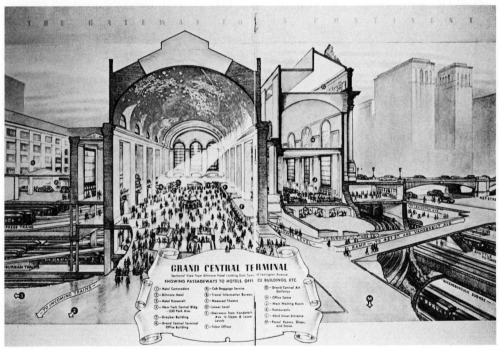

tall, profitable cliffs of offices and shops, hotels, clubs and apartment houses—one pushed right beside the other and rising from the sidewalk building line—spread in three directions from the multi-level Terminal [13, 14]. The idea of such a development obviously grew out of the earlier practice of putting a hotel and a railroad office building beside major stations, but the New York Central Railroad's immense magnification of those earlier schemes enabled it to alter the character of an entire city district. To facilitate motor vehicle traffic and de-

liveries in the neighborhood, the railroad owners created Vanderbilt Avenue, a new street beside the Terminal, on which many of their buildings fronted. (Rockefeller Center would have a new street, too.)

Successful as it was, the Grand Central development stimulated nearby office buildings under other ownership, such as the Chanin and Chrysler Buildings nearby. For those who disliked commuting, the Fred F. French real estate and building company erected the Tudor City apartment houses and hotel a few blocks to the east [23]. A few years later, Raymond Hood and Kenneth Murchison designed the two large Beaux-Arts apartment buildings just north of Tudor City to serve childless Midtown employees.

The Grand Central development also inspired other commercial building groups, including several connected with railroad terminals. Such projects, and others which demonstrate the contemporary American interest in tightly knit, massive building groups include the Cleveland, Ohio, Union Station area and the Federal Triangle government office buildings in Washington, D.C. Among the others were an unexecuted project for a hotel and apartment houses at Abingdon Square in New York and the Terminal Park project of 1929 for Chicago, a dense group of office buildings and apartments framing a central parklike mall built over railroad tracks at the meeting point of the

15. "Terminal Park" project, 1929. Ralph T. Walker, architect.
(*Courtesy Haines, Lundberg & Waehler, Architects*)

Chicago River and Lake Michigan [15], where the Illinois Center development is now going up.[18]

Terminal Park (by Raymond Hood; Ralph Walker; Holabird & Root, 1929) and the Cleveland project (by Graham, Anderson, Probst & White, 1926-30) were, like Grand Central, proposed for sites adjacent to and elevated over commuter railroad tracks. They were immediately adjacent to already existing business districts, however, whereas Grand Central and Rockefeller Center stimulated new development. Terminal Park also introduced its own permanent residential accommodation as Grand Central "City" has not done (but as Rockefeller Center may do in the future). But the midwestern projects did share with the New York railroad development a generally rectilinear arrangement related to established street patterns. They also subordinated aesthetic distinction to considerations of profit and of such efficiency as concentration might produce. The owners and managers and architects of all these American projects evidently believed in the virtue of concentration, using high-rise buildings on a vast scale. Tall buildings seemed to be efficient, reducing street traffic and travel time between offices. They used precious city land economically. They substituted single boiler plants and water towers for many smaller ones. Skyscrapers sometimes made good corporate advertisements, and most people found them thrilling, whether the buildings were isolated or massed as at the lower tip of Manhattan. Hardly anyone at the time worried about the limits to growth, or about pro-

viding appropriately human scale and historic continuity in a city. Buildings just increased in size, like the fortunes from stocks bought on margin.

Enlightened planners were quick to see the threat of large-scale development done only for profit, and architects such as Ernest Flagg, or younger critics such as Lewis Mumford and Douglas Haskell called for open space, generous light, and measures to curb congestion. It soon became customary for developers interested in respectable rents to advertise projects that included green spaces, even tiny ones produced by complying with the Zoning Resolution. Among high-rise projects, two well-known New York housing developments included patches of green— Tudor City (1925-28) with apartment houses and hotels relieved by two small private parks [23], and London Terrace (1929-30), where a long block entirely surrounded by twenty-story contiguous apartment houses has an elevated grassy inner courtyard. So did Terminal Park.

Not only laws, then, but also the attitudes they fostered, helped to determine the building development that John D. Rockefeller Jr. undertook at the end of the prosperous 1920s. Law and public opinion, conservative and symmetrical design habits characteristic of the years since the mid-1890s, economic expectations, the interests of landowners and moneylenders, current technological advances in elevators and air-conditioning, the changing business outlook of the 1930s—all these factors contributed to the shaping of a project that one might have thought was the result of a single man's interests.

III.

The Opera House Project, 1927–1929:

Maximum Profit with Maximum Beauty

"The Rockefeller Center project started in 1928 . . . The Metropolitan Opera organization had been negotiating for the purchase of a large plot in the center of the area owned by Columbia University, and planned to build a new opera house on it. I was asked to join with others in acquiring an adjacent plot to be given to the city for a street and public square, in order to provide an adequate setting for the opera house. The plan commended itself to me as a highly important civic improvement and I agreed to participate in it. Materially changed and greatly enlarged in scope, the project finally took the form of my personally acquiring from Columbia on a twenty-four year lease, later extended to thirty-four years, with renewal options, the substantially three blocks which it owned . . . I had the option to purchase a part of the property for a site for the Opera House and to transfer it at the same price to the Opera House group, also to purchase the public square site and donate it to the City . . . The opera people were unable to finance their building project. They asked me to make a very large contribution to it in addition to making the necessary land available for a public square and street. Feeling that I had done my full share, I asked to be excused. Shortly thereafter because of financial and legal difficulties, the opera people withdrew entirely from the undertaking—an undertaking which they themselves had initiated and which I had become interested in solely at their instance."

John D. Rockefeller Jr., address to employees of Rockefeller Center, Inc., September 30, 1939. Rockefeller Family Archives, Box 69, General Envelope no 3, 1951-62.

On December 27, 1927, Thomas M. Debevoise, Esq., counsel to John D. Rockefeller Jr., and his charitable organizations, wrote a short and cryptic memorandum to Charles O. Heydt who supervised the Rockefeller real estate interests. The memorandum said: 'It has occurred to me that it may save you a great deal of trouble and get Mr. Cutting down to business—if he is not there already—if you arrange to have Mr. Hall or whoever is handling the matter for William A. White & Sons, deal directly with him [Mr. Cutting] T.M.D.' [19]

Since R. Fulton Cutting was the President of the Metropolitan Opera and Real Estate Company which owned the Opera House and the land on which it was built, since the Opera had been hoping to find a site for a new Opera House since 1926, and since the White firm was a real estate company, the matter to which Debevoise referred must have been that of co-ordinating Rockefeller interests with those of the other parties. They were trying to arrange for a gift of land on one of Columbia University's Midtown blocks, which Rockefeller would donate to the Opera in order to provide a new Opera House with a plaza. They were actually initiating the activities that led to the creation of Rockefeller Center.

Almost two years earlier, in January of 1926, Otto Kahn, a financier and owner of most of the stock of the Metropolitan Opera Company (which produced the performances) had written to Cutting, explaining why the Opera had to move from its house at Broadway and 39th Street. The reasons included an inelegant location, insufficient backstage space, traffic congestion outside, some poor sightlines, and some inadequate sanitary standards.[20] Moreover, the lease on the old Opera House would expire in a few years, providing extra impetus for a move. The Metropolitan Opera and Real Estate Company directors voted on January 21, 1926, to proceed with a new Opera House.

Within the next few months, the search for a site began. As early as April 26, 1926, Cutting had learned from the William A. White real estate firm that many leases on sites which Columbia University owned in three adjacent blocks between Fifth and Sixth Avenue, 48th and 51st Street, would expire between 1928 and the end of 1931.[21]

Other sites were considered first. The architect Benjamin Wistar Morris (1870-1944) was engaged to study the project in detail and prepare estimates of the cost. Morris was a man of patrician background who had executed grand offices, clubs, and residences using classical forms. Joseph Urban (1872-1933), an Austrian architect and scene designer for the Opera was appointed Morris's associate until October 1927 (when they quarreled because Urban had repeatedly made public his own remarkable suggestions [97, 110] instead of deferring to Morris as he ought to have done). Before the end of 1927, Morris proposed an Opera House only a few stories high on property owned by Otto Kahn on 57th Street, with a twelve-story studio-office building behind it. The taller building was included to produce income which would offset the cost of constructing and running the Opera. This project was abandoned in February 1928 with the explanation that costs would be too high. By that time, the Metropolitan Opera and Real Estate Company's board of directors had also considered and rejected several sites farther to the north, on 59th, 63rd, 96th, and 110th Streets. For an Opera House and office towers on the Century Theater site at 63rd Street just west of Central Park, Morris proposed a landscaped plaza, an idea retained in subsequent proposals for a new Opera House.[22] Unfortunately, the plaza would cost a great deal of money but would not produce any income. Morris, who was well aware of this fact, informed the Opera directors in February 1928 that their only hope for the realization of the Opera and the plaza lay in acquiring a large endowment fund. A new patron who had not hitherto concerned himself with the Opera's factions and personalities might therefore suit the Opera's needs particularly well.

John D. Rockefeller was considered an excellent person to approach. He was not a boxholder or even a noteworthy opera lover, nor did he move in the same social circles as many of the prominent opera supporters. He had already received public attention for other new building. His family might be especially interested in a project in Midtown where three family members owned houses and where John D. Rockefeller Jr. and Sr. had been buying parcels of land north of Columbia University's property for twenty-five years. The William A. White firm would have been particularly aware of this, as Mr. White himself had known the elder Rockefeller in Cleveland when both

were young men, and had handled some real estate transactions for the Rockefellers in New York.

John D. Rockefeller Jr., his father, and his sister occupied large houses on 53rd and 54th Street between Fifth and Sixth Avenues, just three blocks away from the north end of the Columbia University property. By the end of 1928, the Rockefeller family owned or controlled the following properties:

666, 668, 670, 672, 680, 684, and 690 Fifth Avenue in the blocks between 52nd and 55th Streets

2, 4, 16, 22, 24, 28, and 5, 7, 11, 13, 17, 19, and 27 West 53rd Street

2, 4, 6, 8, 10, 12, 14, 16, 20, 22, 24 and 13, 17, 23, and 29 West 54th Street

By the end of 1929, they added 18 and 27 West 53rd Street and 26, 28, 30, 32, 34, and 36 West 55th Street.[23]

They had acquired these properties for several reasons. The more widely publicized reason was that they wished to protect the tranquility and domestic amenity of the streets on which they lived. Other property owners shared this desire. In 1928, thirty-eight of the forty-eight property owners in 53rd and 54th Streets petitioned the Board of Estimate to rezone 53rd Street between Fifth and Sixth Avenues as a commercial rather than residential street, claiming that rising taxes occasioned by the construction of the Queens branch of the subway under 53rd Street could not be offset from purely residential rents. They said they could not afford to keep their properties if current zoning restrictions were upheld. Both John D. Rockefellers and the elder's son-in-law, E. P. Prentice of 5-7 West 53rd Street, joined seven other prosperous parties and spokesmen for St. Thomas Episcopal Church at the Fifth Avenue end of the street and for the University Club one block north; they successfully opposed the rezoning.[24] Having kept 52nd through 55th Streets, from Fifth to Sixth Avenue from being zoned for commercial use when the first city zoning map was drawn in 1916, they intended to continue living in their accustomed surroundings.

Wealthy, personally retiring gentlemen may go to great lengths to preserve the charm of their neighborhoods, but Rockefeller and his advisors also knew about the potential value of real estate in this area. Rockefeller had already bought buildings on Fifth Avenue for investment and was collecting rents from high quality retail tenants. Within a few blocks, new luxury hotels and office buildings had recently been completed. Although the area was still inadequately served by mass transit and was not convenient to the commuter railroad terminals, people might take the trouble to reach it if its character was sufficiently prestigious. It is true that these improvements occurred primarily on Fifth Avenue, or to the east of it, rather than toward Sixth Avenue to the west where the Rockefellers owned property. It is also true that the Rockefellers sought—successfully—to keep their immediate neighborhood residential. But one could imagine a time in the near future when these residential blocks would be considered so

well located that rents charged for houses and flats there would rise impressively. The subway line under 53rd Street might raise the tax assessments on 53rd Street properties but it also increased the accessibility of shops, offices, and housing in this part of Midtown. Loud noise from the subway construction was keeping land prices down temporarily. The relatively low prices of land would not remain low forever.[25] One could imagine demolishing some row houses and rebuilding them as modern flats—as was done, in fact, at the Rockefeller Apartments of 1935-36. Such properties would become available for purchase if the thirty-eight small landowners were really serious about being unable to support the financial burdens of their houses and became willing to sell to enterprising bidders—which also happened, although the Rockefellers were not the only buyers when the sales were made during the 1930s. And it was certainly possible to envisage the reopening of the matter of rezoning at some time in the future. If Rockefeller moved—as he did, to a Park Avenue apartment in 1937 —he would no longer seek so earnestly to preserve the residential calm of the side streets. The streets could then be rezoned for commercial development, or large plots could be assembled which could automatically be used for business premises if they had Sixth Avenue frontage— and this, too, happened.

It was no less easy to speculate about the eventual improvement of Sixth Avenue, although that street remained seedy [16] until 1957 when Rockefeller Center itself boldly expanded to the

16. Sixth Avenue (Avenue of the Americas), toward north. Photographed April 1932.
(Photograph by Byron. The Byron Collection. Museum of the City of New York)

northwest by building the Time & Life Building in partnership with Time Inc. across Sixth Avenue from the older Center. Nevertheless, the prospects for the street were not at all dim before the stock market crash altered the business and rental situation. The avenue was darkened by the elevated railway, but ever since 1920 there had been plans to tear it down and replace it with an underground line. The subway would bring more passengers to the neighborhood than the under-utilized "El" had done, and they could come from points farther away in the city. And in 1923 parts of the raised track were actually removed, freeing the

blocks from 53rd Street to Central Park from gloom, noise and dirt, and opening up the prospect of a grand artery from Greenwich Village to Central Park. The Sixth Avenue Association, founded in 1921, prepared literature and illustrations about such a project for publication in the first issue of its magazine, optimistically entitled *The Boulevard,* in 1931, and from time to time between 1920 and 1957, grand plans were formulated for the development of buildings flanking the wide roadway [55]. Rockefeller prudently confined his land purchases almost exclusively to the Fifth Avenue half of each crosstown block, wisely refusing to invest in mere dreams for the future of Sixth Avenue, but he was certainly buying more land than he really needed to safeguard the tranquility of his house.

If, then, we examine the situation at the end of 1927, we find the Opera directors and Benjamin Wistar Morris searching for an accessible and agreeable location, and for a suitable type of building. These problems had recently been made more complicated because the planners found it hard to give up Morris's idea of a plaza in front of the Opera House. We find Columbia University in possession of a suitably large plot of land in central Midtown, an area familiar to all the Opera boxholders, near the main entertainment areas, and accessible to the railroad stations without being so close that Opera and station traffic would conflict. We find that the William A. White firm, among other real estate brokers, know that most of the leaseholds on the Columbia property will expire at about the same time. And we find that they and Cutting of the

Opera have been in contact with Heydt and Debevoise of the office of John D. Rockefeller Jr., who might become interested in the Opera's problems and in Columbia's property.

The perfect opportunity presented itself for offering benefits to a large number of people. They took the opportunity seriously. Columbia entertained proposals for developing its holdings on which stood about two hundred row buildings paying only $300,000 in combined rent each year;

17. Metropolitan Club Dinner scheme, Metropolitan Opera House, April 1928. Benjamin Wistar Morris, architect. Rendering by Chester B. Price. (*Courtesy Metropolitan Opera Association*)

the buildings housed shops, speakeasies, bistros, and residential tenants, not all of whom were of good reputation. William A. White & Sons would find it profitable to be the brokers for Columbia's property transactions.

In January 1928 John Tonnelé of the White firm contacted Cutting, as Debevoise had recommended. He proposed that a controlling company be formed to coordinate these plans, the lease to the Opera of the plaza site, and the development of the corner sites.

18. Metropolitan Club Dinner scheme, model. April 1928.
(*Courtesy Metropolitan Opera Association*)

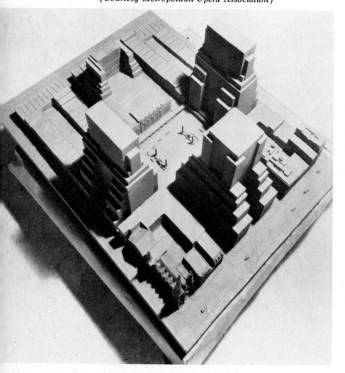

On March 2, Harry Hall of the White company sent Heydt a blueprint of the Columbia University buildings, marking the Opera site over them. The Opera project was shown as designed for the south block, but Hall wrote that difficulties about the new street had led to studies of a new idea which affected the entire later project—that of locating the Opera on the central block.[26]

Morris and Tonnelé corresponded about this idea, and by April 13, 1928, Morris had produced his fourth suggestion for the central site.[27] The Opera could face a plaza which would provide a new breathing space for the city and a handsome setting for the Opera. In exchange for that—especially if a donor were to purchase the plaza site and give it to the city—the University and lessees who built on its land could expect concessions from the city government, allowing the builders to erect more profitable structures than they might be allowed to do under the zoning provisions which limited the size of buildings.

Morris's April 13 proposal and his development of it through May 21 [17, 18] envisioned the Opera House façade on the west side of the plaza, and three thirty-five-story income-producing buildings on the south, east, and north sides. Each building would have a setback above the ground floor, and on the terrace thus provided would be a pedestrian walk giving access to a second floor of shops, adding to the shops foreseen for the street level. This design would increase the revenue to be derived from the buildings, because retailers' rentals were higher per square foot than those paid by office tenants; besides, it would add to the attractive and lively appearance of the square. Shoppers could reach all three buildings at this upper level by means of four bridges, two over 49th and two over 50th Street. In order further to increase the shop window area, Morris proposed cutting a very large arcade into the building opposite the center of the Opera House, from Fifth Avenue to the plaza, and he recommended pedestrian arcades through each of the north and south buildings. These would also connect the square on its axial line with 48th and 51st Streets. Finally, Morris proposed a triple deck garage to be constructed under the plaza, with a capacity of 400 cars; when not in use by Opera patrons, it could be operated profitably for use by the general public.

Morris assumed with quite a remarkable gift of prophecy, that the Opera House would be "symmetrical and monumental and that due reference will be made to what is termed Classical Architectural tradition . . . , its sense of proportion, scale, simplicity and restraint, but it is quite unnecessary that classic details and elements shall prevail where they are meaningless or useless and therefore objectionable." The office buildings around the plaza were to be far too high for classical precedent, so Morris pointed out that "we can use only the principles of design and composition which would ap-

peal to the Classic mind and the Classic taste." [28]

The proposal was ambitious, but not beyond realization: 1927 and 1928 were vigorous years in the New York construction and real estate industries. A great model for a comprehensive development was nearing completion—the Grand Central neighborhood on 42nd Street. [13, 14]

His proposal, however, had drawbacks. One was that he neglected the plots abutting his tall buildings and Opera House. Another was Columbia's lack of enthusiasm for selling any of its land, even for an Opera plaza. A third was that cars driving in and out of the garage would proceed on ramps which started in the central open space, and that would be unsightly [17]. Then, too, the square itself would cost about $2,500,000, a sum which few donors were prepared to give. Besides, the building heights and density depended on the city's willingness to grant height and bulk variances in exchange for a plaza. The city officials might not do that, especially if the plaza remained in private hands.

But John D. Rockefeller Jr. might be induced to do another fine thing for the city and for culture by donating the Opera plaza. He would also have a voice in the development of the area near his home. The problem was simply that of getting him to do it.

IV.

Expert
Advice

"While the prime consideration in this enterprise must be its financial success, the importance of a unified and beautiful architectural whole must be constantly kept in mind, and attained, to the fullest extent possible compatible with an adequate return on the investment."

> John D. Rockefeller Jr. memorandum, August 28, 1929. Rockefeller Family Archives, Box 79, Todd & Brown file.

"There is probably no other firm just like Todd, Robertson & Todd anywhere. Its services run the gamut of building, from promotion to management, including architecture, engineering, and construction. Though they frequently work with architects or with general contractors, there is never any doubt about who is running the job. It is always the two Todds and Robertson."

> "A Phenomenon of Exploitation," *Architectural Forum* LXI, October, 1934.

Robert Fulton Cutting made arrangements for a dinner party to be held on May 21, 1928, at the Metropolitan Club in New York. His guest list included most of the multi-millionaires in the city, although not all of them came. The after-dinner speaker was Benjamin Wistar Morris, presenting his proposals for the development of the Columbia property [17, 18]. About forty guests attended, among them Ivy Lee, who handled Rockefeller public relations, sitting in for his employer. He heard about the plaza and about plans for office buildings to be built by unnamed "lessees from Columbia, as and when demand occurs for the construction and occupancy of permanent units facing 49th and 50th Street." Morris urged his listeners to consider the proposals quickly because other parties were thinking of building on the Columbia land.[29]

Ivy Lee was interested and on May 25 wrote to Rockefeller outlining the proposal which he said would "make the square and the immediate surroundings the most valuable shopping district in the world." He told Rockefeller about the $2,500,000 necessary to purchase the ground (Rockefeller wrote in the margin "What ground?" either asking for the exact location or showing that he had heard little or nothing about these plans earlier)[30] and that Kahn would suggest that Rockefeller himself provide the entire sum or join a small group to do so.[31]

Rockefeller was not interested in contributing the total cost of the square, but felt that the cost should be divided between the Opera and the surrounding properties. He considered taking a part interest in a syndicate which would buy all the property and donate part of it as a square for public use. Or he "might even be interested in a syndicate which might take over a 99-year lease with one or two renewals" from Columbia, "on condition that Columbia would allow the public square to be dedicated."[32] He still had no idea of taking a lease on the property all by himself, let alone constructing all the buildings.

Later in June, however, Charles O. Heydt estimated the annual rent to Col-

umbia at about $3,000,000[33] and asked for authority to negotiate on Rockefeller's behalf. Potential competitors withdrew their project in July. On August 9, Harry Hall and Frederick A. Goetze, treasurer of Columbia University, established the terms on which Rockefeller might take over the Columbia property with a lease beginning on October 1, 1928. A New York real estate executive once declared that Columbia owed a gigantic monument to the late Mr. Goetze!

John D. Rockefeller Jr. was not in the habit of signing contracts in haste. He and his staff had a great deal of work to do before the October 1 contract date arrived. He had to learn everything he could about potential profits and he had to find the men to help him get those profits. This was another situation in which money alone could not solve problems. Money could pay for experts, but Rockefeller had to be able to evaluate their expertise.

On August 23, Rockefeller asked real estate firms for advice on the return that would be necessary to justify his investment, and for advice on the best means of developing the land. He solicited the opinions of Harry Hall and Peter Grimm at the White company, and asked for advice from Albert B. Ashforth, John A. Osborne, the C. G. Edwards Company and Todd, Robertson & Todd Engineering Corporation, who replied in early September. These firms received maps of the site showing Morris's plans for the center block. All based their advice upon the idea of Rockefeller leasing the property and subleasing it to groups who would erect their own buildings. They made many suggestions which were eventually adopted, and all shared Morris's taste for symmetrical plans which would clearly define the irregularly shaped enclave inserted into the city's regular gridiron plan.[34]

Ashforth recommended that Rockefeller develop an outstanding shopping district with offices, a department store, a hotel, apartments, a garage, and a bus terminal. Existing streets could be widened and a new north–south street added. He was not at all certain that the Opera would help it, since "past experience would indicate a slowing down of business improvements surrounding opera houses as the opera is generally closed in the day time." If the Opera were included, it ought to have shops on its 49th and 50th Street flanks (although architects could have told him that this might conflict with the city's fire code). John Osborne thought that the Opera square should not be given to the city; while it would save Rockefeller the taxes on it, the city might turn it to some undesirable use in the future. He thought it might be unnecessary to build more than a couple of tall buildings. The real estate men shared Morris's view that all building surfaces should be uniform, preferably stone. They also pointed out the necessity of controlling all leases and choosing tenants with care. Their estimates of the rent which Rockefeller would have to pay ranged from about $5,500,000 down to about $3,100,000. The lowest estimates were the most accurate.

The consultants were members of firms well known then and even today. But the name John R. Todd (1867-1945) is unfamiliar to most people, although he was responsible for much of the original character of Rockefeller Center.[35]

The son of a midwestern Presbyterian minister, Todd worked his way through Princeton University, took his M.A. and a law degree in New York, and was admitted to the bar in 1894. Soon thereafter his law partner found himself involved as a principal in the financial affairs of a client, a builder who could not pay his debts. Todd brought money to the aid of his partner, and they found themselves in the construction and rental business, which Todd never left. Their firm, Todd & Irons, built and then quickly sold at considerable profit a large number of apartment houses, and they erected hotels, the Architects' Building, the Brooks Brothers store, and other commercial structures. They astutely attracted related tenants to their buildings, such as shipping companies or architects. The firm's last project was the Cunard Building at 25 Broadway, an office building with a great domed and vaulted lobby designed by Benjamin Wistar Morris and decorated in a Roman Renaissance mode by Ezra Winter. (Todd supposedly suggested the lavish lobby although he did not normally approve of such "architectural" display if it reduced profit.) This building was unquestionably well known to Rockefeller since it stood across the street from the Standard Oil Building at 26 Broadway. When Henry Irons retired in 1919, Todd formed another firm, Todd, Robertson & Todd with his brother, Dr. James M. Todd (c. 1870-1939) and yet another minister's son, Hugh S. Robertson (1880-1951), who had been Dr. Todd's partner in the Center Realty Company, builders of apartment houses and apartment hotels. Dr. Todd was a physician by training, a quiet, painstaking man who spent much of his working life taking care of defects in buildings rather than men. Robertson was a highly intelligent and diplomatic person, expert at real estate and financial management. These men worked on renting and internal layout on several well-known buildings including those in the Grand Central zone such as 379 and 385 Madison Avenue, the Barclay Hotel, and the Graybar Building, which John R. Todd suggested should be linked to the Terminal by corridors. Shortly after moving to Summit, New Jersey, in 1901, he met Thomas M. Debevoise, a member of a law firm which did much of Todd's company's legal work. Todd, who believed that "business is not only what you do, but how you do it and whom you get to know in the process," [36] felt that it was his friendship with Debevoise that brought about his association with Rockefeller Center. When in 1928 the Rockefeller interests needed engineering assistance with the Colonial Williamsburg restoration in Virginia, Debevoise asked Todd if the firm headed by Todd's son, Webster, and John R. Todd's chief engineer, Joseph O. Brown, would be interested in doing this work. From this experience in land developing, Todd and Brown, as well as the older men who assisted with some of the Williamsburg work, became acquainted with other Rockefeller advisers including Charles O. Heydt.

Todd himself, now over sixty and aware that the building boom of the 1920s could not last, was still available as a consultant. He submitted proposals for the Rockefeller project, stressing that if it were well done with a beautiful Opera House and with traffic through the site conducted underground, it might be-

come the center of the city's retail district. This would make it even more profitable than the original isolated development would be. His report implied that beauty should serve profit, an attitude with which the Rockefeller advisers agreed.

Todd suggested building two twenty-five-story buildings at the eastern end of the central block [19], linked by an arcade leading to the Opera plaza. South of the plaza would be a thirty-seven-story hotel, with a thirty-five story apartment hotel to the north. One private north–south street would separate these buildings from lofts or apartment houses to the west. Another private street would separate the central buildings from a department store at the eastern end of the north block, and from St. Nicholas Church and the property of Robert Goelet who was planning an office building (built in 1931) at the eastern end of the south block. Todd's intensive development provided for the greatest number of building types and it asked the city only for permission to open new streets. Since the streets would serve the public as well as private interests (for example, in an increase in high-rent shop frontage), the city could be counted on to agree to having them. The mix of residential, cultural, and commercial buildings is exactly what municipal planning officials have been promoting during the 1970s.

To give John R. Todd exclusive credit for these early September plans (generally known as the Labor Day Plans) is misleading, for the men who actually worked out the distribution of buildings and their shapes were two obscure architects in their late thirties, the efficient,

SIXTH AVENUE

EXISTING BUILDINGS

49TH STREET

EXISTING BUILDINGS

50TH STREET

EXISTING BUILDINGS

LOFT or APT. BUILDINGS

ENTER TO LEVEL B

OPERA HOUSE

LOFT or APT. BUILDINGS

FROM LEVEL B EXIT

PRIVATE

STREET

EXIT FROM LOWER LEVEL A OR B

HOTEL

ARCADE

SIDEWALK

TO LOWER ENTER LEVEL A OR B

ARCADE

SIDEWALK

APT. HOTEL

OPERA PLAZA

PRIVATE

STREET

EXISTING BUILDINGS

0   60   120

20 FT CONCOURSE

SHOP

40 FT. PROMENADE

MART

DEPARTMENT STORES

FIFTH AVENUE

34   *ROCKEFELLER CENTER*

19. Plan of September 1928. Reinhard & Hofmeister, architects.
(*Redrawn by Nancy Jane Ruddy*)

personally retiring Henry Hofmeister and
his more dynamic and ambitious partner,
L. Andrew Reinhard. Todd summoned
them just as they were preparing to begin
their Labor Day holidays. He gave them
a map of the Columbia property, showed
them Morris's scheme for the center block,
and asked them to prepare a plot plan for
the entire site by the time the weekend
was over. The two architects got little
sleep for several days.

Colleagues remember Henry Hofmeister (1891-1962) for his methodical and
responsible work habits and they admired
his knowledge of practical matters such as
plumbing and ventilation. He was exceptionally good at interior layouts that saved
space and money, and quietly relished
such difficult tasks as planning the RKO
office building partly over the Music Hall
entrance. He organized the Rockefeller
Center architectural office and saw to it
that drawings were produced on time and
accurately. In about 1928 he had become
the partner of L. Andrew Reinhard (1891-
1964), another alumnus of the Todd
building enterprise.[37]

Reinhard was the son of a carpenter-
cabinetmaker and a mother who determined that her son would not follow his
father's career. She shepherded her four-
teen-year-old son to architects' offices on
14th Street, where Reinhard became an
office boy for Morris, then studied at the
Mechanics' Institute, and later won a
medal from the Beaux-Arts Society of Design where he received his most advanced
schooling. He obtained practical experi-

ence by working as a junior designer and
designer for prominent New York firms,
including Morris's, and worked on competition drawings with other architects,
including Raymond Hood. Reinhard resigned from Morris's firm, and worked
with Todd for eight years. During this
period, he and Hofmeister did interior
layouts as well as renting work for the
Graybar Building. They worked on the
renting committee and layout program of
the Chrysler Building. John R. Todd
would certainly entrust these men with
the task of producing a plan that could be
executed under the zoning and building
codes, and that used space profitably.

Todd must have been told of Rockefeller's interest in his ideas, for he had his
two architects produce an improved plan,
dated September 18 [19]. Rockefeller
found the prospects reassuring and entered into a definitive agreement and a
separate lease with the Trustees of Columbia University, dated October 1, 1928;
the lease was not actually signed until
December 31, 1928. Rockefeller leased the
entire Columbia property in the three
blocks from October 1, 1928 to September 30, 1952, with options for three renewals of twenty-one years each. The
annual rent paid between 1928 and 1973
ranged from approximately $3.6 million to
$3.8 million. The lease included an option
allowing Rockefeller until April 1, 1930,
to purchase the Opera House site if an
Opera House were built; if it were not
built, the site would revert to the University, and Rockefeller could rent it.

Rockefeller could, and on January 22,
1929, did, "assign the right to take the
lease to" a holding company, organized on
December 6, 1928, which he called Metro-

politan Square Corporation after the name of the Opera plaza. The corporation president was his trusted associate Col. Arthur Woods, who had been a police commissioner at one time and was related by marriage to J. P. Morgan. But Rockefeller "would remain liable as a principal and not as a surety on all of the covenants and promises contained in the Agreement of October 1, 1928." This clearly fixed financial responsibility on "Mr. Jr." himself.[38]

In October, Rockefeller asked two eminent conservative architects, John Russell Pope and William T. Aldrich, for names of architects who could do suitable work on this project. Aldrich praised Morris, Cass Gilbert and Delano & Aldrich (not his own firm), and said that Cross & Cross and Raymond Hood were "the two most brilliant performers whom I know personally." Just before the end of the year, Rockefeller and Todd asked Pope to solicit ideas from other architects as to the appropriate development of the site. By February 20, Pope had enlisted the aid of nine other architects. Two would help him to judge the proposals of the other seven. The judges were Cass Gilbert, who designed grand business and civic edifices adorned with ornament imitating everything from gargoyles to the dome of St. Peter's, and Milton B. Medary Jr. (1874-1929), whose most modern work is a carillon tower in Florida.

The architects from whom ideas were solicited included William Aldrich, who was related to Rockefeller, and well-established firms that are best known for spacious banks in almost every historic style (York & Sawyer), and for office towers and expensive apartment houses

(Charles Adams Platt; Cross & Cross). Morris's ideas were solicited, too, as were those of two other architects, E. H. Bennett and Harvey Wiley Corbett (1873-1954). Bennett's activities ranged from work with Daniel Burnham on the comprehensive plan for Chicago (1909) to designs made with other architects for the first American building erected on the principle of suspended construction, the Travel and Transport Building at the 1933-34 Chicago Century of Progress Exposition (designed 1929-32). Corbett, of the firm of Corbett, Harrison & MacMurray, was among the more up-to-date architects in New York during the 1920s when most were thoroughly conservative. His contemporaneity had little to do with that of the modern architects who were between ten years and half a generation younger than he was—Gropius, Wright, Mies van der Rohe, and Le Corbusier. Rather than wanting a near revolution in style and technique and planning, Corbett contented himself with designing within the general limitations of budget, taste, and construction methods, while remaining alert to factors of cityscape and urban design. He was a consultant to the enlightened Regional Plan Association, suggesting elevated walkways between Fifth and Sixth Avenue to alleviate traffic congestion [20] [39] and advocating a tunnel from midtown Manhattan to New Jersey, like the one that was eventually built. But he had neither the patronage nor the inclination for the younger geniuses' experiments with office floors cantilevered from

20. Triple-deck street system, designed *c.* 1925–30. Harvey Wiley Corbett, architect.
(*Courtesy Avery Library, Columbia University*)

a service core, for a glass-walled business building or a white stuccoed skyscraper. He knew the problems such experimental structures would cause in the North American climate and the soot of American cities. He was a practical architect, not without dreams about how New York might change [21], but one whose practice was devoted to satisfying clients within the limits generally accepted in established society. Corbett was capable of adjusting to a modernistic vocabulary, as in the Master Apartments and Roerich Museum Building on Riverside Drive (1929). He was not averse to architectural experiments and praised the aluminum "Magic House" designed by Kocher and Frey, saying that this and other "machine houses" would prove economical to build and would be popular once people got to know and use them. From 1929 onward, he directed the planning at the Chicago Century of Progress Exposition (1933-34), superintending the first American exhibition grounds which were disposed on an irregular plan rather than according to

the formal and symmetrical schemes admired at the Ecole des Beaux-Arts. The buildings frankly proclaimed their amusing and ephemeral nature and their impermanent structure and materials by their eccentric shapes, areas of bright color, and dramatic lighting effects. He was personally attractive as well—a tall, gray-haired gentleman with a lively but dignified expression, an agreeable after-dinner speaker at civic gatherings and ladies' societies. Corbett wore gloves and carried his walking stock into the drafting room. He was exactly the sort of architect who should have been invited to the Rockefeller "symposium."

At the time that he was invited to enter the "symposium," Corbett had two relatively new partners—William Mac-Murray (1868-1941), who was good at handling the partnership's business affairs and had little to do with the Rockefeller project, and Wallace K. Harrison, a young man who had come to Corbett's attention.[40] After leaving school at fourteen, Harrison worked first for a Worcester, Massachusetts, building contractor and then as a junior draftsman for a local architectural firm. He studied some construction engineering at Worcester Polytechnic Institute, and departed for New York where he became a draftsman for McKim, Mead & White. To refine his training, he entered Corbett's atelier, where the educational methods of the Paris Ecole des Beaux-Arts were employed. Not long afterward, he joined the

21. New York about 1975, designed c. 1925–30. Harvey Wiley Corbett, architect.
(*Courtesy Avery Library, Columbia University*)

Naval Coastal Defense Reserve, and it may have been there, during the First World War, that he became friendly with young men of means who welcomed him into prominent social circles. Later, he traveled on a scholarship, studied at the Ecole des Beaux-Arts itself, returned briefly to McKim, Mead & White, and studied mathematics. By 1922 he was prepared to be a designer for the classical department of another important American firm, that of Bertram G. Goodhue, who was at work on the skyscraper state capitol for Lincoln, Nebraska. Harrison assisted on this project, among others, until the classical department was disbanded after Goodhue's death in 1924. Intermittently, from his early professional days to the start of his partnership with Corbett, Harrison worked on projects for his future associates at Rockefeller Center, such as drawings for the newly famous Raymond Hood who had won the international competition for the Chicago Tribune Tower in 1922. Although Harrison became familiar with modern tendencies in architecture, he was not intimately associated with the avant-garde. In 1926 he married Ellen Milton, whose brother was then married to Abby Rockefeller, the oldest child and only daughter of John D. Rockefeller Jr. When Corbett needed a new and promising partner, this engaging and hard-working young man appeared to be a logical candidate.

The architects invited to the "symposium" received plot plans of the Columbia property showing Morris's Opera House, open square, and underground garage, and plan of the Opera House at basement level. For a fee of $5000 each, they were to present specified drawings and written reports describing the "economic elements of the problem and the manner of their recognition and incorporation in the aesthetic results proposed." The architects were to consider the "possibility of open areas, additional streets, traffic circulation, access, automobile parking or storage; appropriate classes of buildings, and use of arcades, bridges, porticoes, terraces, and similar elements affecting the whole problem." By May 13 when the results were due, the architects proposed a variety of projects ranging from an expensive octagonal tower on Fifth Avenue, which could have blocked the view of the Opera, to more sensible proposals.

Morris designed two forty-four story office towers on Fifth Avenue, shifting them to the north and south so that they would bridge 49th and 50th Street, and thereby opened a wide path between them to the Opera plaza. The other major idea he introduced was that of including in the plans the plots between the Columbia property line and Sixth Avenue; these plots would have to be purchased, but the three blocks could be developed more rationally, more completely, more spaciously, and thus perhaps more profitably. Other noteworthy features of his plan were terraced gardens on the setbacks of the low buildings on the side blocks, and a more hesitant suggestion that the approach to the Opera from Fifth Avenue might slope gently upward.

Although Corbett did not propose enlarging the whole plot as Morris did, he shared Morris's understanding of the urgent need to widen the access to the interior of the site so that the 1500 feet of property all around the Opera's plaza would have a value equal to or better than the Fifth Avenue frontage. Corbett suggested leaving the central block front on Fifth Avenue open, sacrificing 120 feet of valuable frontage for the sake of higher prestige and rental in the entire three-block project [22]. A broad ramp would start at Fifth Avenue and reach to a second-story level where it met the Opera House. The ramp would provide the principal pedestrian access to the Opera House, and would be linked to an arcaded promenade serving the second (i.e. principal) stories of the buildings surrounding the square. This was an idea already familiar from the proposals of the Regional Plan Association which may have inspired Tonnelé's and Morris's similar ideas. Cars would deliver patrons to the Opera at an automobile entrance at grade level, using new north–south streets to the east and west of the Opera building; cars could also drive up a ramp to second-story level at the west (rear) of the Opera House. The Opera House itself was to be located farther to the east than Morris had planned, so that two new streets could flank it and—more importantly—so that there would be room at the west end of the Columbia property for one tall commercial building on each block. This arrangement offered a grand approach to the Opera and a monumental backdrop for it; provided for two levels for pedestrian and vehicular traffic segregation, in which Corbett had long been interested, as well as for doubling the retail shop frontage; made the entire square enticingly visible and grand and therefore valuable; provided for several kinds of commercial space—low buildings on the north and south blocks, three tall towers

at the west—each of which Corbett imagined devoted to tenants of a single type; and included the further significant idea of planning the western towers to connect to the proposed Sixth Avenue subway station which would someday replace the elevated line.[41]

Corbett's plan forecast several of the actual Center's important features—tall buildings at the western end of each block, the open approach from Fifth Avenue which draws people into the central space, related groups of tenants. Like all the plans made for the Center, it was a response to demands for profit-making in real-estate; architects had not even been consulted until the general economic prospects for the development were understood, and Corbett himself had the Ashforth real estate company compute the profit that could be obtained if the plan were accepted. It is significant that Corbett's plan, which was not profitable enough, was published later as a model cultural center,[42] the sort of thing not expected to be built for commercial profit.

Before Morris had worked out his two "symposium" proposals which were intended to benefit both the Opera and the Rockefeller interests, he made public an idea for a new north–south avenue named "Metropolitan Boulevarde" which was to run from Pennsylvania Station to the new Metropolitan Opera square. Morris proposed moving the Opera and its square to the north block so that the Opera property would face St. Patrick's Cathedral. He proposed acquiring the plots at the west end of the block so that the square could extend from Fifth Avenue to the "Boulevarde" and the Opera could reach to Sixth Avenue.[43] Of course, this proposal meant cutting the square off from the Opera House with a large traffic artery. It meant additional land acquisition costs, and the Sixth Avenue property owners would surely hold out for high land prices. It denied the value of fronting on the open area to the plots on the south block, while offering that frontage to property that the Rockefellers did not control between 51st and 52nd Streets. Naturally enough, Heydt wrote to Morris rejecting the proposal.[44] Morris's overall idea was unwise, but palatable parts of it reappeared in plans of the 1930s for Rockefeller Center, especially the long north–south avenue (because avenue frontage could be rented for more money than side-street frontage), and the links between the Center, Grand Central and Pennsylvania Stations.

While Gilbert, Medary, and Pope analyzed the "symposium" proposals, the board of directors of the Metropolitan Square Corporation discussed the possibility of planning comparatively low buildings for high quality shops, with only three or four tall buildings for hotels, apartments, or offices.[45] The three architects' analysis, dated one week later, suggested that the project be built as high as the projected absorption rate of new building indicated would be profitable, not higher. They noted, however, that the "symposium" participants had all recommended construction of from four to five million square feet of rentable area—a dense development with several tall build-

ings in each plan. They emphasized the general agreement on segregation of pedestrian traffic at one or more levels above the street, and the use of underground parking, although problems of proper ventilation underground would require careful study. Overall, the three architects were in favor of Corbett's proposal, but recommended that an architectural organization be hired to do a detailed preliminary study of the development.[46] The Rockefeller advisers followed this last suggestion and received Morris's ideas based in part on the "symposium" projects and in part on consultation with the William A. White firm. He thought of flanking a central access path with low buildings (as was eventually done) and of keeping the plaza at grade level. He also moved the Opera building eastward, as Corbett had recommended. He designed

22. Symposium project, Spring 1929. Corbett, Harrison & MacMurray, architects. Published 1931 as "Arts Center."
(*Brown Brothers*)

two circulation levels and used the idea of private streets. In August he revised many of his July proposals, partly to include freight and delivery rooms in the building basements, an idea adopted in the actual Center. But Heydt was afraid that Morris would be away on account of a recent illness. Perhaps he also thought that the "Metropolitan Boulevarde" scheme showed that Morris had the Opera's prestige more firmly in mind than the needs of John D. Rockefeller Jr. Heydt also complained that the Opera's lawyers had taken from June of 1928 to January of 1929 to prepare a lease.

Morris and the Opera were not helping to develop the site efficiently in Heydt's opinion, and on August 15, he wrote to Rockefeller, who had left about a month earlier for his summer home in Seal Harbor, Maine, saying that a strong personality should take charge of this project which had been plagued by the delays and outlays. He found Todd a suitable person, experienced in building "large structures, taking full charge of all details and turning over the completed project in each case fully manned and rented and in successful operation. Mr. Todd . . . has never made a failure of any of his undertakings." Four days later Heydt wrote again, praising Todd's understanding of finance and leases over railroad lines and he reminded Rockefeller that Thomas Debevoise knew Todd thoroughly.[47]

Heydt received permission to invite Todd to Seal Harbor for three days. Todd and Rockefeller got along so well, discussing horses and sizing each other up, that Rockefeller delegated the work to Todd's own firm and Todd & Brown. "We had about the same powers we would have had if he had owned the land," Todd wrote later. "We were to build the thing, put it on a profitable basis, and sell it to the world." [48] Todd proposed having Reinhard & Hofmeister do the architectural work, although Rockefeller felt that some well-known architect, perhaps Morris, should be employed as coadjutant in order to direct the "artistic architectural appearance" of the building rather than the "practical working aspect." [49] The Todd organizations would agree to take on no new work and to complete outstanding work expeditiously or turn it over to others. In return, Rockefeller would provide secondary financing of a building on Lexington Avenue which the Todds had under way. The Todd companies would be paid $250,000 a year for the term of their contract, as well as other minor compensation. Todd persuaded his colleagues to undertake this "important and different" project which clearly fascinated him, and soon made a presentation which convinced them and the Rockefeller circle as well.[50] Todd was apparently quite willing to adhere to "Mr. Jr.'s" wish that "while the prime consideration in this enterprise must be its financial success, the importance of a unified and beautiful architectural whole must constantly be kept in mind, and attained, to the fullest extent possible with adequate return on the investment." [51] To increase the potential return, Rockefeller had a holding company organized to buy the property fronting on Sixth Avenue. With a rare bit of whimsy it was called the Underel Holding Corporation because the land was under the elevated railway.

On September 30, Heydt wrote a memorandum suggesting that land near the Columbia property be acquired in case the rail terminal idea was revived in the future.[52]

Heydt's estimate of the goals of the entire development are summarized in a memorandum that he wrote probably at about this time.

Essentials, First! Success. A. Artistic—harmonized development. B. Commercial—Full return to Mr. R. not less than 33⅓ % C. Lasting—continuous over entire period. Second. Prompt, energetic, skillful handling of negotiations with Architects—for plans and specifications to be approved by Board. Columbia—for approval of plans. Lessees—for leases. Real Estate Brokers—for leases. Contractors—for buildings constructed either by ourselves or lessees. City Authorities—for permits for building, overhead and underground construction, in and across streets. Van Sweringens—possible railroad terminal. Labor—all trades. For publicity.[53]

The memorandum is interesting on several accounts. Most startling is the optimistic financial return for which he hoped. The memorandum and the signing of the managers' contract also make it obvious that commercial architecture is not simply an aesthetic exercise but the outcome of negotiation—which often means compromise—among designers, engineers, contractors, tenants, business partners, the real estate industry, public representatives, legal experts, and construction workers. Any one of these factions could overturn fundamental plans of the others; and great skill, good fortune, or perfect community of interests would be required to achieve success in a huge project unlike anything else in the world.

Good fortune was not the lot of the planners, for soon after Todd and Rockefeller had agreed to collaborate, the stock market began its disastrous decline.

V.

The Commercial Project, 1929–1933:

Disaster Averted

"The Opera House would be a dead spot and greatly reduce shopping values in all property facing it. I am saying this because I am hoping so keenly that the matter will not be re-opened."

John R. Todd to Winthrop Aldrich. December 4, 1929 Rockefeller Family Archives, Box 82, Metropolitan Square Corporation Sale to Opera Company file.

The precarious situation on Wall Street in early October had no immediate effect on the Center's plan and the project went on as if prosperity could continue forever.

On October 1, John R. Todd signed the contract making his company the managers of the project and employing Todd & Brown. Although John D. Rockefeller Jr. retained final control over the plans and design and details, the essential work would be done by the two managerial companies controlled by the firm—or rather, the iron—hand of John R. Todd.

On October 22, Todd presented Reinhard & Hofmeister as the general architects. They were to be paid for drafting costs and overhead plus $50,000 each year, with a new arrangement to be made if they did satisfactory work and if there was an additional need for their services. This arrangement could terminate on two months' notice by either party. At the same time, Todd suggested that Raymond Hood (1881-1934) and Harvey Wiley Corbett be engaged as consultants on architectural style and grouping, with Morris to be a third consultant (although he declined to serve after December 1929). The consultants would be paid each month for work that they did, but would not be on anyone's regular payroll or receive a fixed fee in advance.[54]

Todd wanted architects "who would be primarily interested in good planning, utility, cost, income, low operating expenses and progress . . . We work . . . from the inside out, first to get good plans for what we had to have and then to clothe those plans, as simply and attractively as possible, with clean-looking exteriors. We didn't want men who were too much committed to the architectural past or who were too much interested in wild modernism." The architects were to be entirely subordinate to the managers throughout Todd's term of office. (This arrangement was—and is—common in firms like Todd's which were primarily developers.) Todd said that Reinhard & Hofmeister "had worked with us before on our theory that in business property income production supersedes pure aesthetics."[55] He thought Corbett had a "mind open toward the modern trend" and that he was admired especially by young architects. He considered Harrison an able designer and an agreeable colleague, and praised Hood for his original ideas.

Hood was useful in ways that Todd did not record—primarily in his publicity value. After living hand-to-mouth by working for a number of firms including Cram, Goodhue & Ferguson, he won the Chicago Tribune competition, and although the avant-garde was horrified at the Gothic tower he designed, Hood became well known. He designed a con-

23. Daily News Building, 1930. Hood & Howells, architects. Right background: Tudor City Apartments, 1923–28. Photographed 1935. *(Photograph by Berenice Abbott for Federal Art Project "Changing New York." Museum of the City of New York)*

spicuous black and gold skyscraper over-looking Bryant Park in New York for the American Radiator Company (1924) [56] and was watching his gleaming white-and-russet-striped Daily News Building [23] rise near the east end of 42nd Street when Todd hired him. At the same time, he was submitting his ideas for Terminal Park [15] in Chicago, and was working with Corbett on plans for the Chicago Century of Progress Exposition of 1933-34. He may already have proposed to the McGraw-Hill company his pre-liminary designs for its famous blue-green headquarters (1931) near the west end of 42nd Street [24]. Todd is said to have told Hood that he was being em-ployed despite the modern style of the News skyscraper, so there was a limit to Todd's admiration for him. But Hood had an engagingly informal way with clients, and Todd surely knew that Hood pro-duced far better buildings than the clients expected and that those buildings gen-erated a great deal of publicity. He must also have worked well with Corbett who was chairman of the group of architects planning the Chicago Exposition. These projects had obviously given Hood plenty of experience with the practical aspects of office tower building, pedestrian circula-tion problems, multi-purpose structures, and unusual designs.[57] Hood had two partners, Frederick Godley (1887-1961), who ran the office's business affairs and who left the firm in 1931, and J. André

24. McGraw-Hill Building, 1931. Hood, Godley & Fouilhoux, architects.
(*Courtesy McGraw-Hill, Inc.*)

Fouilhoux (1879-1945), an excellent French-born engineer and a careful supervisor. Fouilhoux had worked for the Albert Kahn firm for several years after 1904, and had worked with Hood on the Chicago Tribune drawings.

The employment of more than one architectural firm led to "architecture by committee." None of the Rockefeller Center architects or their close associates credit any one man with contributing more than a few ideas that were used without modification by the group. John R. Todd apparently mistrusted the creative imagination of strong-willed architects like Hood, preferring those such as Reinhard & Hofmeister who executed the ideas that Todd, Robertson & Todd proposed. Group practice meant that a team of unequals would moderate the exercise of energetic architectural talents while giving the managers expertise in several specialties. But, although it is unlikely to produce buildings of profound character, "architecture by committee" need not lead to aesthetic or urbanistic failure. Washington, D.C., remains a handsome city, despite the paucity of outstanding buildings, and the Cubitts covered much of London with conventionally acceptable buildings which now form some of London's most precious surviving neighborhoods. Consensus among architects may produce buildings so well adjusted to a variety of human needs and tastes that many members of the public can find pleasing aspects of them. The committee-designed areas may then become popular and lively places. That is precisely what happened at the completed Rockefeller Center.

The use of an architectural committee also reflected practical needs of the moment. It is unlikely that any single New York firm could have executed so vast an undertaking, at least not in 1929 when architects were still busy, before commissions disappeared during the Depression. Moreover, the nature of large-scale commercial architecture had diminished the traditional importance of the single controlling designer, for a skyscraper was the joint product of the architect or a team of architectural specialists, the structural engineer, the mechanical engineer, the financial adviser, the real estate consultant, and the client. "Architecture," wrote Corbett, "has become a business as well as an art . . . to render satisfactory service these days requires a very sizable organization built upon lines of expert knowledge and business efficiency." The organization of American architectural enterprises was, in fact, more advanced than that of other countries, and it made sense for substantial clients abroad to invite Americans to design buildings in London such as Selfridge's, Devonshire House, and the Ideal House and Bush House office buildings.

The advantages of the division of labor among specialists had also appealed to the sponsors of the Chicago Century of Progress Exposition of 1933-34 (and of earlier fairs as well). Art and technology in the service of profit-making were as important to fairs as they were to business enclaves. In order to have the advice of a number of experts, the Chicago Exhibition sponsors did just what the Rockefeller managers did shortly afterward—formed a committee of architects. Hood was among the eight who worked on the Chicago committee, with Harvey Wiley Corbett as their chairman. The arrangement there was analogous to the division of a large business into departments headed by specialists who could pool their ideas.

The Exposition designers hoped to create innovative structures that would be beautiful whether seen at ground level or from the upper stories looking down (a concern Hood was to voice later at Rockefeller Center). At a fair, plants and fountains and ornamental sculpture were obligatory, and Rockefeller Center later became famous for having included them in sober business premises, even if the Center's directors long shied away from displaying flags (which fly at most fairs) for fear of giving an "exhibition character" to the development. As at Rockefeller Center, the fair's architects searched not for form, the product of rigorous aesthetic and even philosophical meditation, but for pleasing appearance, as packaging designers do. Some packages, of course, turn out to be exceptionally handsome, and even beautiful. The architects studied convenient means of access, and they planned rail, road, and water routes to make the fair easily accessible. They searched for ways of assuring convenient circulation through the fairgrounds, concentrating the buildings in a limited space and planning moving sidewalks and moving stairs, which they expected to emphasize as important architectural features. The planning experience of this committee could be applied to Rockefeller Center, where convenient access and expeditious traffic flow were among the

managers' main concerns and where the International Building lobby was given a bank of four moving stairs as its main feature.

The board of directors of the Metropolitan Square Corporation did not formally approve the arrangement with the architects until November, so that plans made before that date do not necessarily reflect Hood's or Corbett's participation. At the November 7 board meeting, Todd presented a new plot plan offering maximum financial return.[58] It was based on Reinhard & Hofmeister's plan of September 18, 1929, but included a second underground level with delivery ramps serving each building. A refined version of this proposal bears the date of November 25, 1929.

Within two weeks this cheerful progress was to be arrested, and the whole direction of the planning changed, for on December 5, after several days of courteous but chilly correspondence, the Opera group decided not to move to the Columbia property. Trouble had been coming since mid-October, at least, when the Metropolitan Square Corporation directors instructed the William A. White real estate firm to stop purchasing leases and buildings except with specific approval. The Opera group, in turn, feared that the high cost of building a new house would exceed the revenue from the sale of the old one.

There were also troublesome negotiations about a clause entitling Columbia to repossess the Opera site if the Opera House were not built. Article 18 of the lease gave the Metropolitan Square Corporation an option until April 1, 1930 to purchase the Opera site if an Opera House were built on it; otherwise, the site would revert to University possession and Columbia could rent it to the Corporation. The Opera directors wanted to build on the site in time for the November 1931 season, remaining in their old premises until the end of the previous season so that they could offer an uninterrupted program. To achieve this end, construction would have to begin in May 1930, by which time any outstanding leases on the new plot would have to be cleared. To obtain adequate funds for construction and lease-clearing, the Opera would have to sell its old house at a profit, and mortgage its new site. The Opera directors hoped Rockefeller would share the costs of clearing the leases, but he was not likely to do that. On August 17, 1929, his Underel Holding Corporation was organized to buy the properties fronting on Sixth Avenue and it would have enough expenses without clearing leases. Besides, Rockefeller thought that deciding to donate the $2,400,000 square east of the Opera House plot was generous enough.

But if the leases were not cleared, no one would grant a mortgage on the new site and the new house could not be financed. The Opera would then have to stay in its old house, and, as the Opera would not be able to build a new house on the designated new site, the land would revert to Columbia. The Opera could have closed for a season and Rockefeller could have bought the property and just waited for the Opera to be built in the future, but that would have been too risky for everyone but Columbia. The Opera would lose a season's revenue and

perhaps some of its artists and staff, as well as support from people who would find other events to patronize. And if the new house were never built, Rockefeller would own a plot encumbered with the proviso that it be used only for an Opera House. He might also be blamed for the Opera's sorry state.[59] But if Rockefeller simply leased the Opera site instead of exercising his purchase option, he could plan a business development pure and simple, as some of his real estate consultants had recommended.

John R. Todd was perfectly happy to have no opera in the development, since he could see the potential of the property even without the Opera's purifying presence. He wrote frankly that "The Opera House would be a dead spot and greatly reduce shopping values in all property facing it. I am saying this because I am hoping so keenly that the matter will not be re-opened." [60]

But Todd's relief was far from total. Could Rockefeller, with his reputation to consider, sponsor a commercial project after having begun by helping the Opera? Where was another prestigious tenant? Where, in fact, was any tenant? Here we see the first effects on the project of the October 29 Wall Street crash. Hardly any businesses were expanding and moving to larger premises; many were lucky to be solvent at all. The Todds and Rockefellers would not want failing tenants willing to move only to smaller and cheaper quarters than they occupied elsewhere.

Plainly, then, Rockefeller faced serious trouble. Existing tenants paid him $300,000 in yearly rents. He had to pay twelve times that amount to Columbia University. The longer he put off constructing new buildings, the longer he would have to support a multi-million-dollar annual deficit. New buildings might bring in a profit someday; the old buildings never would. But he had no idea what to build, or for whom.

Raymond Hood came up with a solution for the problem. He had been hired for his architectural ideas, and now he provided the critically important business idea as well. Having designed studios at 711 Fifth Avenue for the National Broadcasting Company which, with other radio broadcasters, had expanded at amazing speed in the single decade of their existence, Hood must have known that this expansion was continuing. NBC would soon need even larger corporate headquarters and studios than those which their existing eleven-story premises provided. Hood proposed that the Radio Corporation of America which controlled NBC, RKO motion pictures, and other interests be invited to rent space in the office building which would have to replace the Opera House. Wallace Harrison and Webster Todd knew a man whose wife was the niece of Edward Walker Harden, a director of RCA and chairman of its real estate and locations committee. By late December, negotiations were under way.[61]

With the focus of the development changed from culture to commerce, the architects were asked to devise new plans. Hood, for one, was happy to be working on a building linked to the future instead of on an Opera House which he saw as tied to the past. First they experimented with diagonal paths from Fifth Avenue into the heart of the property [62] which would have altered the city's street layout. These plans were soon laid aside, however, because they would have required time-consuming negotiations with city officials.

In January 1930 John R. Todd presented a key plan to the board of directors, one based on enlightened self-interest and realism rather than on the imaginative but impractical "diagonal plans" of December.[63] This plan, known as G-3 [25], established the general form of the development, although there were many changes before the original group of buildings was completed. We do not know who devised this plan. The architects certainly exchanged ideas, and they took direction from Todd and his associates, who may have been the real planners.

G-3 reversed earlier plans by placing the tallest building instead of the lowest on the western part of the center block. A fifty-story building for the radio group replaced the low Opera, and in so doing created a new skyline stepping down from the major tenants' buildings to the side blocks' buildings and then to the rest of the city. To the east of the principal building was a plaza with narrow streets skirting it, and beyond that, reaching to Fifth Avenue were two long building wings joined by an arcade. The south block had one large and two small buildings separated by two private streets.

25. Plan G-3, January 8, 1930.
(*Redrawn by Nancy Jane Ruddy*)

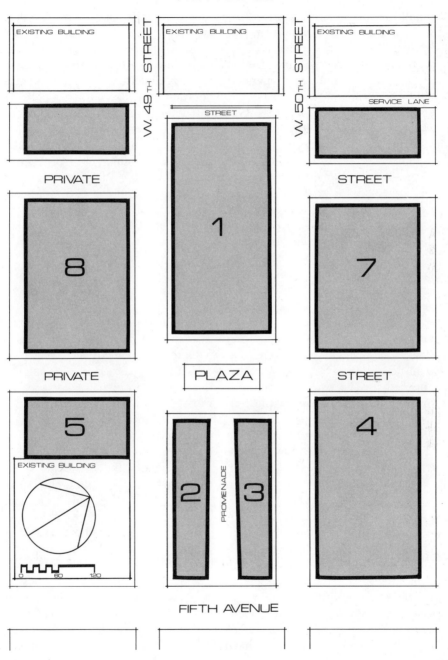

SIXTH AVENUE

EXISTING BUILDING

W. 49TH STREET

EXISTING BUILDING

W. 50TH STREET

EXISTING BUILDING

SERVICE LANE

STREET

PRIVATE

STREET

1

8

7

PLAZA

PRIVATE

STREET

5

4

EXISTING BUILDING

2 3

PROMENADE

0   60   120

FIFTH AVENUE

The north block, where Columbia owned the land all the way to Fifth Avenue, had one small and two large buildings separated by the two private streets. A narrow shipping lane like the one beside Hood's Daily News Building separated the buildings from the tenements and business premises fronting on Sixth Avenue which Todd had decided to delay buying.[64] The G-3 arrangement had several commendable features, some of which were common to most of the earlier plans. It provided for traffic circulation and delivery zones that might offset slightly the congestion caused by intensive development. The managers could offer each builder his own small block, with exposure on four sides. Symmetrical planning assured possible tenants—department store owners, for example—that neither of two similar premises would outshine the other. It also gave formal definition to an irregular site, and accorded instant stature to an area which badly needed it. The two narrow buildings on the Fifth Avenue end of the center block were not rectilinear but widened toward the west, increasing the effect of perspective recession in the promenade (or covered arcade) between them, thereby leading the visitor's eye in toward the center of the block.

G-3 and subsequent plans for the Center seem at first to be related to the generally symmetrical plans for huge building complexes focused on outstanding central buildings, which were characteristic solutions to design problems posed at the Ecole des Beaux-Arts. The Metropolitan Square architects had had that kind of architectural education and could have

been expected to design the Rockefeller project in a formalistic way. Varied silhouettes, elaborate circulation patterns including covered galleries, multi-level paths, links to transportation lines—these pleasing and functional conveniences can be found in "Beaux-Arts" projects executed on both sides of the Atlantic [13, 14]. The use of clearly defined components of a plan is another feature of Beaux-Arts training and of its offshoots in the "City Beautiful" movement, which can be observed in G-3. But, although their training left its impress on the designers of the Metropolitan Square development, the designs submitted to the owner were based on specific requirements for creating the maximum profitable rental space and were conditioned by the street pattern and the provisions of the zoning resolution and building code. Theory and artistic habit had less to do with the planning than it seems at first.

Todd emphasized to Rockefeller that these plans were not final, and that the Fifth Avenue front of the north block was only tentatively being given over to a tower building. His group was using this plan to work out income possibilities and calculate "the prices at which they could net lease the different portions to parties who might want to finance and build their own structures."

The managers had decided that the property could only be profitable if it included "more rentable floor area than was shown on the earlier plans, insofar as possible the business center of the whole three blocks must be drawn further west to increase the area of high retail values." The fifty-story building in the center block would do this. If the building were flanked by important department stores, the *Drang nach Westen* would be successful. There was another reason for the tower building: Todd's reluctance to give up the valuable center block to low-rise development when the city's Zoning Resolution permitted far more intensive development. "If we have only comparatively low buildings on the Fifth Avenue frontage, and if there is an open plaza back of these, we create important tower rights for the center block, and these tower rights cannot be transferred to the North or to the South block and therefore if we do not use them by building high buildings in the center block they simply disappear and are lost." In reply to Rockefeller's observation that putting a tall building in the center block and lower ones on the side blocks gave light and air to other people's properties adjoining the side blocks, Todd said that the Rockefeller-Todd group had "great interest" in the border streets, "and that anything which helps them (by not depriving them of light) will help our income materially in our renting values on the North side of 49th Street and the South side of 51st Street." Protecting neighborhood property values would prevent neighborhood decay and thereby maintain the value of the Rockefeller investment.[65]

There must have been a good deal of tension among the architects who had to adjust to rapidly changing plans, for in February the architects accepted Reinhard's suggestion that all the firms should "be on an equal footing as associates in the architectural work instead of having his firm as the head one." The drawings made thereafter bore the stamp of all three firms in alphabetical order.

By March 12, the architects had produced the first of the H plans which modified G-3, for use in definitive negotiations with the radio group. H-1 revised, dated May 20, 1930 [26] shows the dramatic changes which the negotiations brought about.[66] Most important was the fact that the project now extended all the way to Sixth Avenue. Underel Holding Corporation would purchase the necessary plots because the radio group planned to build theaters on the north and south blocks; if these were ever to attract passers-by, especially from the theater district a long block farther west, they would need entrances and large signs on Sixth Avenue. Only their entrances or signs needed to be situated on the Avenue, since theaters do not need daylighting and can be relegated to interior plots. The rest of the Avenue frontage would be devoted to office buildings, with those on the side blocks featuring access to air and light on all four sides. This could be guaranteed because theaters had to be low, following the Building Code's prohibition of construction above theater auditoria. The western private streets which had been projected in earlier plans disappeared in H-1 because theaters would not need maximum street frontage for display windows or for delivery access as would the department stores proposed earlier for these sites.

The changes to the eastern part of the plot were no less startling. The plaza shriveled into an area not appreciably wider than the eastern private streets, and

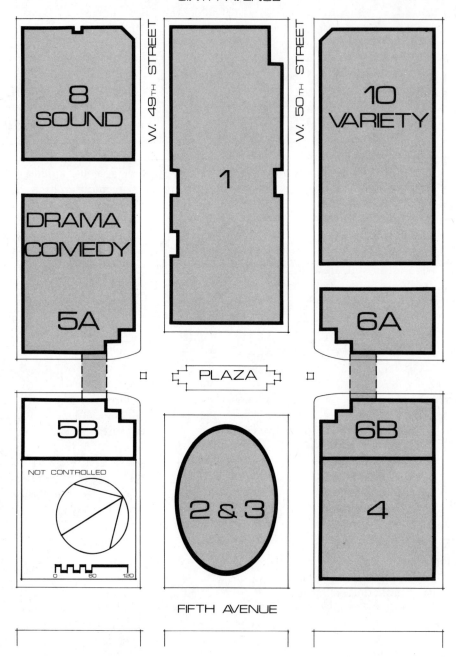

SIXTH AVENUE

W. 49TH STREET

W. 50TH STREET

8
SOUND

1

10
VARIETY

DRAMA
COMEDY

5A

6A

PLAZA

5B

6B

NOT CONTROLLED

2 & 3

4

0   60   120

FIFTH AVENUE

intensive development bordered it on all
sides. Tall buildings with a north–south
axis were to rise on the side blocks, perhaps bridging the private street. To the
east, on the Fifth Avenue front of the
central block, Raymond Hood [67] proposed
either an oval or a pyramidal building to
replace the arcaded buildings shown in
many of the earlier plans; a prospective
tenant, the Chase National Bank, needed
the working room that a unified space
would provide. The bank would occupy
the second story and others, leaving room
for shops or display windows and interior corridors below, an arrangement
found earlier at the new Philadelphia
Savings Fund Society Building. But pyra-
mids narrow quickly toward the apex,
limiting rentable floor space in the upper
parts, while ovals have floors of even
expanse throughout. Besides, the gentle
curve of an oval building, especially one
provided with attractive display windows,
will lead visitors around the structure—in
this case toward the western part of the
property. After the architects prepared a
full-size drawing of the curve in order to
convince the justifiably skeptical Rockefeller of its graceful appearance, the proposal for an oval building went forward,
and was approved by June 5, the date of
the renting agreement with the radio
group.

In less than two weeks, a plasticine
model was ready for exhibition to the
press. The *New York Times* report of it
on June 18, 1930, was as enthusiastic as a
planner could wish. The reporter rhapso-
dized about the varied heights descending
from the RCA Building, saying that "the
skyline leaped and fell . . . in a manner
usually found only in a Gothic cathedral."
David Sarnoff of RCA spoke of a "Radio
City," a name promising technological
wonders of the future.

The plans also promised a transcontinental bus terminal for the underground
area.[68] This was a response to the absence of any major transportation facilities near the development, and the managers were worried about the prospects
for attracting tenants who might prefer
locations closer to Grand Central or Pennsylvania Stations. A transcontinental bus
terminal also had a modern ring to it, for
powerful, streamlined buses driving over
routes more flexible than those of the
railroads were clearly the latest alternative to the railroads which had dominated
an earlier era.

With the heartening reactions to the
model, and the existence of at least one
major tenant, the board of directors
agreed to retain the architects jointly as
one firm instead of having one supervising
and two consulting firms. They wanted
particularly to secure the services of Reinhard & Hofmeister, Hood, Corbett and
Harrison. A supplementary agreement
with Reinhard & Hofmeister allowed them
to work on tenant layouts. At the same
time, the board also approved agreements
with Henry G. Balcom, a structural engineer, and with Clyde R. Place, a mechanical and electrical engineer—both
men of excellent reputation. Todd proposed constructing large models of the

buildings to help attract other tenants.[69]

The progress and potential scope of the development must have led the Hood and Corbett firms to reflect upon the project with which their reputations might forever be connected. While Hood and Corbett understood financial requirements they may well have been wary of tarnishing their reputations by erecting buildings which had mainly profitability to recommend them. On July 15, 1930 they proposed that the RCA building have something grander than the ordinary office building lobby. They suggested a grand lobby and promenade with corridors to the theaters of the side blocks. The idea was not simply extravagant, for it offered a publicity-generating use for the interior space on low floors which was usually difficult to rent, and the corridors would allow people to walk in all-weather shelters between the "Radio City" buildings—a convenience which could be promoted during office-rental negotiations. During the next two or three weeks all the architects gave this idea a "fling" and Hood designed a super-block embracing the entire property, with diagonal streets leading from the corners to the central plaza [27]. Like the earlier "diagonal plans," these "F" [70] plans would have required city street changes and so were dropped, but parts of the Forum idea survived, transformed into the NBC reception areas, shops and exhibition rooms.

Finding tenants and planning buildings were not the only matters to be considered. There was also the problem of financing the development. As late as the end of September 1930, Rockefeller was

27. "Fling" model, Summer 1930. Raymond Hood, architect.
(*Courtesy Walter H. Kilham, Jr.*)

still hoping to find tenants who would build (and finance) their own buildings,[71] but during the autumn everyone came to the conclusion that funds would have to be ready for immediate construction and for eventual use if tenants did not finance their own buildings. Todd dined with Frederick Ecker, president of Metropolitan Life Insurance Company, which was then the largest insurance company in the country, and with Edward Duffield of the Prudential Insurance Company of America, which was another possible source of money.[72] In November the developers and Metropolitan Life alone worked out an agreement that was made formal on March 31, 1931. It stipulated that the insurance company would purchase bonds issued by the development corporation up to a principal amount of $65,000,000. Part of the security for the bonds was the Columbia lease. The insurance company's architect, Daniel Everett Waid, would have to be retained to review the building plans and inspect the construction. It was "the largest piece of financing that the insurance company had ever done." [73] The cost of the project was $120,000,000 according to Joseph Brown's estimate of August 15, 1930, which was based on plan H-16. The actual basis of the agreement was plan F-18 for which the cost estimate was $116,312,000 dated November 18, 1930.[74] F-18 was a descendant of H-1 but included a larger plaza than H-1 and a more restricted RCA "Forum" area than earlier F plans showed. F-18 also featured an Opera House on the site of the two small comedy and drama theaters on the south block, because negotiations had been renewed with the Opera; alternatively, this Opera site could be used for a concert hall.

The most significant innovation in F-18 was the introduction of a shopping concourse under the street level [87] but above the bus station and parking level. The underground street provided a whole new layer of high-rent shop spaces, perhaps its *raison d'être*. The Rockefeller development's underground street was also meant to be linked to public transportation, in this case to the subway which would someday replace the Sixth Avenue "El," and make the project easily accessible, as the Grand Central neighborhood buildings were.

In early March 1931 the managers displayed a model of the project [28] based on F-18. The showing was meant to generate further interest among potential tenants. Todd believed that people would understand that this commercial develop-ment could not be "an adventure in pure aesthetics"; to have made it one "would have been to sacrifice useful space that we might rent. Nor could we afford to cram the center full of business property, like a Seventh Avenue loft building. To have done that would have been to cheapen the Midtown section worse than it had cheapened itself." [75]

But misunderstandings there were, loud ones. Many critics ignored the managers' statement that the model showed only the general plan. They looked at the buff-colored model with its buildings of staggered heights and noticed either the bulk or the details, forgetting that both might easily be changed. The architects had deferred a decision on the exterior appearance, and presented the buildings in the model divided into vertical strips emphasizing the structural piers, with four windows between each pier. A horizontal strip at fifteen-story intervals marked the presence of mechanical installations. Those who admired the column- or Gothic arch-bedecked skyscrapers of the recent past suggested loftily that the developers "should not experiment in modern style in so large and so conspicuous a project." [76] Ralph Adams Cram, who with his earlier partners Goodhue and Ferguson had used medieval styles in fashionable churches and at the United States Military Academy at West Point, called the Rockefeller project the staircase in Duchamp's "Nude Descending a Staircase," then a favorite target for more traditional critics. Of course, since the conservative Cram despised the motion pictures which the theaters would show, and despised radio and the idea of television as mass entertainment, he would probably not have admired anything built for their purposes. But he also represented many like-minded architects and laymen, as the "Letters to the Editor" columns of contemporary newspapers and magazines made clear.

Another group of critics had believed the press releases issued the previous June when the radio group signed the lease. The publicity referred to a "city within a city" which Todd said would typify American progress in city planning and be a center for the best type of entertainment and musical culture. The critics saw instead a model of a frankly commercial development with a huge central building and, on the side streets, two forty-eight story office buildings which would cast shadows over the development. The office buildings seemed to dwarf the open plaza which the public had expected to be more spacious. True, some of the planning was sound. In the

28. "Oilcan" model, exhibited March 6, 1931. Left to right: Webster B. Todd, John R. Todd, Merlin Aylesworth, Hiram Brown (President, RKO), Hugh S. Robertson. (*Courtesy Rockefeller Center, Inc.*)

RCA Building no office desk would be more than about twenty-eight feet from a window; the staggered heights would at least guarantee light and ventilation to many offices; the buildings stepped down to the neighboring streets and cast shadows mainly on the development itself; there was a plaza rather than complete ground coverage; the private streets would help traffic circulation, and the existing crosstown streets might be widened. But critics dreamed of lower buildings, or more open space, or admired unworkable plans for a single tower with low buildings around it.

Almost everyone loathed the oval building, soon nicknamed Rockefeller's "oilcan," as being too clumsy or too eccentric for sober Fifth Avenue.

Fortunately, the Chase National Bank could not obtain exclusive banking privileges within the development at that time, even though relatives of the Rockefeller family were bank executives. During the spring of 1931 negotiations with the bank ended. Bad as that was for the immediate rental picture, it reopened the possibility of using two low buildings on the "oilcan" site and providing a pedestrian path between the shop fronts of the buildings, an idea illustrated in plan F-19 [29], dated as early as April 3.[77] This measure increased potential shop frontage and removed the solid and oddly shaped lump on Fifth Avenue in favor of low, more traditionally shaped, and detached buildings; it thereby satisfied some of the critics as well as the management's needs. The public would be losing the delightful prospect of a roof garden on top of the oval building, but would be given a street-

29. Project in effect between mid-March and Autumn 1931, close to Plan F-19. Rendering by John Wenrich.
(*Courtesy Rockefeller Center, Inc.*)

level open promenade between the two rectangular replacements where statues and perhaps plants would adorn the center of the walk. Benches were added only later, as the aim was originally to keep people strolling near the shop fronts.

Although none of the planners voiced alarm about the criticism of the model, and although Hood vigorously maintained that they did not change the oilcan to twin oblongs on account of it,[78] they cannot have been pleased about the criticism. Hood, Fouilhoux, Corbett, and Harrison may have feared for their jobs, but Rocke-

feller said that the newspaper accounts of the Ludlow, Colorado, tragedy [79] had so upset him that he never again read press comments. The architects certainly feared for their reputations, especially when in May, the Fine Arts Federation of New York, representing sixteen artists' and architects' groups, including several of which the associated architects were members, endorsed Benjamin Wistar Morris's proposal made in April for constructing a new north–south avenue from Bryant Park at 42nd Street to Central Park midway through the Fifth–Sixth Avenue block and right through the Rockefeller development! This was a modification of his "Metropolitan Boulevarde" scheme of 1929. Morris again suggested that the Opera be located west of this new "Metropolitan Avenue" on Columbia's north block, facing St. Patrick's Cathedral across a huge public plaza.[80] Endorsement of this plan meant criticism of the existing one, and among those who endorsed Morris's ideas were Lewis Mumford and the Regional Plan Association for which Corbett and Hood had done studies. The grand proposal would supply a real, if unimaginative, urban vista of Opera and cathedral, and would help both traffic circulation and land values in the area. No one noticed, however, that this Avenue would sever the Opera from its own plaza. No one mentioned the fact that Rockefeller was already paying over three million dollars annually for the right to develop a site from which a third would be removed under this plan. He was being

asked to sacrifice the value of his land for the improvement of other people's property, as Morris knew, and no one should have been surprised when demolition for the first of the Rockefeller development's buildings began in the same month.

Once again, the investment in Raymond Hood as a man of bright ideas was repaid many times over. He generated enough favorable publicity to draw attention away from the Metropolitan Avenue project and the faults of his oilcan scheme. Hood suggested covering the setbacks below the sixteenth floor on every building with roof gardens [30]. He claimed that pedestrians looked only at the lowest three stories of tall buildings, and perhaps at their skylines, but rooftops were visible to thousands of office workers. People's view of the city, and the value of nearby office space, would be enhanced if office towers emulated luxurious apartments where setbacks were covered with plants instead of with water towers and asphalt-and-tar roofing. He confided to a member of the Chrysler family, whose own building had just been finished, that designing roof gardens was the cheapest means of beautifying the buildings. It would certainly be cheaper to put gardens on the unused roofs than to give over valuable street-level building plots to them as the civic-improvement critics of the "oilcan" model had suggested. Hood's estimate of the probable cost of all the fountains, waterfalls, pools, hedges, trees, grass, and plants ran to a figure between a quarter and a half million dollars. He thought that florists might provide flowers free or at reduced prices for the purpose of advertisement. If an additional $200,000

30. Roof garden proposed for Radio City Music Hall, 1932. Rendering by John Wenrich. *(Courtesy Rockefeller Center, Inc.)*

gardens with those atop the Music Hall and Sound Motion Picture theaters and won ready acceptance. Merle Crowell, the resourceful public relations director of the development, provided press releases that inspired the writer for *Real Estate Magazine* in February 1932 to meditate upon the "trees, thirty feet in height [which] will be transplanted to the lofty terraces, to appear as though rooted by the banks of mountain tarn" or the "sun-flecked nooks of greenery."

Fountains and foliage were not confined to the roofs and the promenade. While these were being planned, another major change in earlier proposals was under way, converting the central plaza to the sunken plaza that exists today. In the early published renderings of it made in the second half of 1931 the sunken plaza was to have been oval in shape with a long north–south axis, containing a large fountain and some planting in the center. These embellishments would keep pedestrians at the perimeter, near shop fronts— making the central space potentially profitable as well as handsome. The problem was one of getting people down there, and the solution drew on the planners' understanding of the laws of physics and human nature.

Knowing that open space would arouse people's curiosity, the planners designed a pleasant pathway to draw the public westward from Fifth Avenue [32, 33]. They made the promenade between the low twin buildings slope downward, so that the force of gravity would make people

were spent for really spectacular botanical displays, the gardens could become tourist attractions and pay for themselves through admission costs.[81] Hood may well have developed these ideas for the New York site at the same time that grand gardens and rooftop planting were under consideration for the Chicago fair. Le Corbusier had recommended planted terraces in his city plans, Frank Lloyd Wright illustrated plants hanging from the balconies of his St. Mark's Tower, the "oilcan" was to have had one, and Morris's Opera plans had planted terrace areas. The idea of gardens seemed beautiful in itself, and gardens would add a humane note to colossal modern cities.

The roof garden proposals made available to the press [30, 31] included narrow bridges connecting the RCA Building want to continue walking. Plants and attractive fountain figures by René Chambellan in the center of the path would lead eyes to the plaza and would create two lanes to keep people near shop fronts in the French and British buildings. The architects then altered their earlier plans to provide obvious access to the lower level only at the east end, by means of broad stairs leading downward from the sloping path. Since most people would not want to turn around to walk upstairs and up a slope once they had reached the sunken plaza, they would look around for another means of exit. This was provided by doors at the western side of the sunken pavement, which led to the underground shopping mezzanine. Now there could be shops from Fifth Avenue all the way to Sixth, and the plan could meet several needs—those of shoppers, of people seeking sheltered paths in rainy weather, of

32. Promenade ("Channel Gardens") between La Maison Française (left) and British Building (right), looking west toward RCA Building. Photographed August 1972. (*Courtesy Rockefeller Center, Inc.*)

the managers who needed to impress potential tenants and increase their rental revenue.

The sunken plaza plans were modified in the course of development. By early 1932 a rendering by John Wenrich (who made all the early published drawings [82]) illustrated the new concept of a rectangular plaza with a large fountain at its western end which would draw pedestrians' attention to the underground shopping concourse entrances beside the statue. Once this plan received final approval, the managers engaged Paul Manship to execute a suitable sculpture for the fountain.[83] His gilt bronze "Prometheus" [34]

was originally flanked by two smaller standing male and female figures representing mankind; these were later transferred to the roof gardens of the Palazzo d'Italia at Fifth Avenue and 50th Street. The sunken plaza was made a public attraction by staging events such as flower shows there [35].

Theater plans went forward at the same time. The radio group had earlier secured the services of Samuel Lionel Rothafel (1882-1936), known to millions as Roxy, a producer of stage shows and radio programs. Roxy had developed a series of motion picture theaters offering films and vaudeville acts which attracted enormous audiences, and his name was a household word in the 1920s. He became an adviser to the radio group in the spring of 1930 and suggested building two immense theaters, one to hold an audience of about 6300 for music-hall entertainment, and the other to accommodate about 3500 moviegoers.

Roxy was a self-made man who liked the luxurious living made possible by his gift for showmanship and understanding of the thousands of details required to make patrons happy in the make-believe environment of the theater. It was probably Roxy who thought of traveling abroad to find suitable talent for the new theater, and the managers sponsored a tour to Berlin, Moscow, and Leningrad, with brief stops in London and Paris. They sent along O. B. Hanson, the man-

33. Left to right: La Maison Française, Promenade, RCA Building, British Empire Building, International Building, looking west. Photographed c. 1936.
(Courtesy Rockefeller Center, Inc.)

ager of plant operations for NBC who held 1700 patents on radio devices, a man very famous in radio circles; Peter Clark, a brilliant inventor of theatrical machinery; Gerard Chatfield, the technical art director of NBC; Webster Todd; L. Andrew Reinhard; and Wallace Harrison, who brought his wife. They left in September 1931, intending to stay for most of October. Their itinerary offered them the chance to study "the practical working out of the German slogan 'light, sun and air,'" they said,[84] although their office building plans already provided all three. The real purposes of the tour were to look at theaters—which need only artificial light and conditioned air—to find performers, and to give Roxy a chance to confer with Max Reinhardt and Konstantin Stanislavsky. Hanson and Chatfield, who had jointly designed the technical installations in the NBC studios in New York, Chicago, and Washington, went to study the new BBC building in London, and the Reichs Rundfunk-Gesellschaft facilities in Berlin and Hamburg. They had heard of Hamburg's new acoustical and soundproofing apparatus as well as devices to increase or reduce studio size by means of moving walls, and ways to use several studios simultaneously to produce a variety of effects for a single broadcast. Hanson also visited radio installations in Dresden, Munich, and Stuttgart while most of the others went to Moscow and Leningrad. Roxy was disappointed to find that the Russians were more familiar with Peter Clark's reputation than with

his own. The others were disappointed to find that they had little to learn from the Russians except for certain effects that had no place in American entertainment, such as the film fading into a *tableau vivant* which Harrison remembers at the Kamerny Theater. They were also annoyed that someone made off with the plans that they had brought along.

In Berlin they saw the astonishing Grosses Schauspielhaus [107] which Hans Poelzig had redesigned for Max Reinhardt, visited radio stations, and probably saw other new theaters such as the Universum which Erich Mendelsohn had designed as part of a group of commercial

34. Paul Manship, *Prometheus*. Photographed *c.* 1933–36.
(*Courtesy Rockefeller Center, Inc.*)

and residential buildings. They must have heard about the suggestions made a few years earlier for developing the Alexanderplatz with high-rise buildings around open space, and may well have heard about the Luckhardt brothers' project for the Jaegerstrasse area (1927) which attempted to deal with traffic circulation problems. And they enjoyed lively dinner parties with, among others, Poelzig, Behrens, and Mendelsohn.

But they were not inspired by the advanced ideas that foreign architects described. On the contrary, they found little during their travels that could serve their needs. American theatrical machinery, they said, was at least as advanced as that available abroad. The layouts, acoustical provisions, and stage designs they had prepared before departure required no modification, and they needed only a single foreign-built stage machine for the large Music Hall.[85] The dream city of the future that Harrison, Hofmeister, and the renderer Hugh Ferriss designed, and of which pictures were published in January 1933,[86] shows rigid malls between cliffs of setback buildings and widely spaced towers that bear little relationship to advanced European work. It would have been anathema to Le Corbusier and Hilberseimer. The travelers appear to have been telling the truth when they said that the trip to Europe did not affect their work. (Of course, the emphasis on American skill made good newspaper copy, too, in a period of isolationism.)

Another trip abroad occurred at about the same time, this one with more productive results. In the spring of 1931 Hugh Robertson had conceived the idea of seeking foreign tenants for the development,[87] since American tenants were not readily available. Perhaps he recalled an unrealized project which other business interests formulated in 1929 for a Palais de France on the old Century Theater site, to house French governmental, cultural, and business premises.[88] Robertson went to France and England to find potential tenants, and found an English group interested in leasing the northern low building fronting upon Fifth Avenue in the center block. A French consortium wanted to take the southern one. The board of directors approved the necessary agreements of October 1931,[89] as these tenants would establish the desired tone of the eastern end of the development and help to attract other tenants of high quality. The press named the promenade separating the French and British buildings the "Channel Gardens."

Hugh Robertson entertained inquiries from prospective Czech, Swedish, Italian, and German tenants, and went abroad in early Spring to make further arrangements. Rockefeller wrote to Mussolini about the project, asserting that he would derive more satisfaction from the spiritual significance of international buildings than from any other aspect of the development.[90] Mussolini inspected a model of the Rockefeller buildings bracketed by models in the same scale of the Column of Marcus Aurelius and the Pantheon [37], but the Italians would not sign up immediately. Although no definite plans could be made for the north block until it had tenants, the architects revised their earlier plans to put a twelve- or thirteen-story building on the northeast corner of the Columbia property. In June, newspapers published renderings of twin nine-story buildings bordering an arcade running west from Fifth Avenue to a thirty-story tower behind them [31, 36, 37]. If specific inducements could be offered to foreign interests, they might be quicker to conclude rental agreements.

Attracting foreign tenants was made easier in July 1932, when President Hoover signed a bill giving the project's tenants special importing privileges.[91] The law and supplementary Treasury Department rulings gave foreign firms there the privilege of importing merchandise for display as samples without prepaying duty on it. Sales could be made on the basis of these displays, and only at the time of sale would duty have to be paid. Outside the project, importers had to pay duty before displaying goods, even on items that never found buyers. At the growing development, trucking costs would also be reduced since goods could be taken straight from ships to a customs office in the Center, and the merchandise could be stored in a bonded warehouse established there. Provisions for duty-free display and for a bonded warehouse were not unprecedented—generally similar concessions had been approved earlier for the Grand Central Palace which Todd had built and for fairs including the Chicago Exposition which Hood and Corbett were planning at this time. Prospective tenants would be glad to have them.

Foreign tenants could also be offered a public-relations inducement. Rockefeller said he saw the French and British Buildings as "symbols in stone and steel of the common interests, mutual understanding and good will of three great world powers. Moreover, in a larger sense, they will symbolize the spirit of coopera-

35. Sunken plaza with City Garden Club Exhibition and *Prometheus* fountain, looking southwest. West 48th Street buildings and RCA Building with trees on setbacks are in background. Photographed May 1934. (*Gottscho-Schleisner*)

tion and brotherhood among all nations—the only foundation, I am convinced, upon which enduring world peace and prosperity can be built."[92] Hugh Robertson contacted Secretary of State Cordell Hull and Secretary of Commerce Daniel C. Roper in the spring of 1933 and reported that these government officials were very much interested in the building project.[93] Pictures and models of it were displayed in the Commerce Department Building in Washington.

Robertson was also busy initiating contacts with the Amtorg Trading Corporation, representing the commercial interests of the Soviet Union, and with tenants for a Pan American Building. In March 1933 the managers announced that a

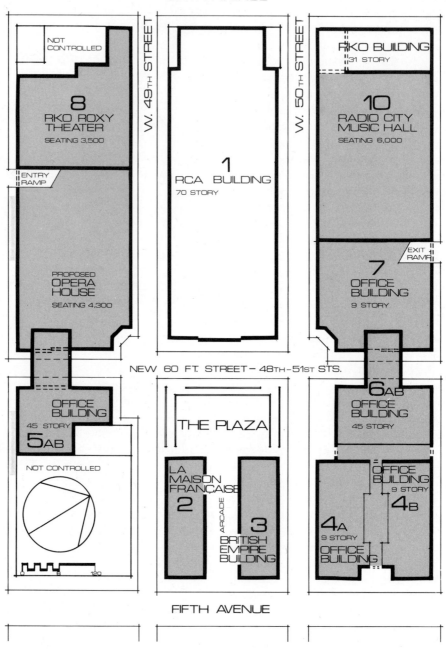

SIXTH AVENUE

W. 49TH STREET

W. 50TH STREET

NOT CONTROLLED

8
RKO ROXY
THEATER
SEATING 3,500

ENTRY RAMP

PROPOSED
OPERA
HOUSE
SEATING 4,300

1
RCA BUILDING
70 STORY

RKO BUILDING
31 STORY

10
RADIO CITY
MUSIC HALL
SEATING 6,000

EXIT RAMP

7
OFFICE
BUILDING
9 STORY

NEW 60 FT. STREET – 48TH–51ST STS.

OFFICE
BUILDING
45 STORY
5AB

NOT CONTROLLED

THE PLAZA

6AB
OFFICE
BUILDING
45 STORY

OFFICE
BUILDING
9 STORY

LA
MAISON
FRANÇAISE
2

ARCADE

3
BRITISH
EMPIRE
BUILDING

4B

4A
9 STORY
OFFICE
BUILDING

FIFTH AVENUE

company had been formed in Rome by
a group including two of Mussolini's
former ministers of state to operate an
Italian building at the development to
be known as the Palazzo d'Italia. The
managers also hoped to discuss the development with Premier Edouard Herriot
of France and Prime Minister J. Ramsay
MacDonald of Britain. Negotiations with
the Germans ended in 1934, however.[94]

The radio group directors helped in
negotiations with the Opera, still a potential tenant, because the radio group now
had a stake in the overall success of the
development in that they would have to
attract people to their theaters east of
Broadway and west of fashionable Fifth
Avenue. In September 1931 Owen Young
of the radio group, Todd, and Paul
Cravath, who had succeeded Otto Kahn
at the Opera Company in 1931, were
thinking about having NBC broadcast performances from an Opera building. They
wondered whether the Philharmonic
Orchestra would join the Opera to keep
the auditorium busy all year. They expected the musical and radio groups to
pay a total of $750,000 annual rent al-
though that was $250,000 short of the
million dollars Rockefeller wanted. In any
case, not everyone considered the Opera a
sufficiently responsible tenant since it
might not give performances even in its
old home in 1932-33. Unless Rockefeller
was willing to support the opera-produc-

ing company in case of financial emer-
gency—which he wasn't—welcoming the
Opera could only involve a serious risk to
him. The architects filed plans for an
Opera House in April 1932,[95] no doubt as
much for the sake of allocating tower
rights to other buildings on the south
block as because Todd really expected to
see the Opera erected.

It was certainly nerve-wracking to wait
for tenants to appear, but John D. Rockefeller was one of the few people in the
United States who could afford to wait.
And he was a man who knew what to do
in the meantime. So was John R. Todd.

37. Rockefeller Center model flanked by models
of the Pantheon and Column of Marcus Aurelius
in same scale.
(*Courtesy Rockefeller Center, Inc.*)

VI.

Publicity
and
Management

"There are two angles from which to consider the Rockefeller Center project. First, that of the operation itself, and second, its effect on the public and this effect subsequently on the operation itself.

As to the first, it is an investment in real estate, the return from which must be in *Rented Space*. Reactions can be set up that will defeat this end. In the boom of 1928 it was a normal, intensive operation, whose financial success would command respect as an expression of power. Success of this sort, even at the expense of others, compelled admiration and justified itself. Today the reverse is true. . . . The qualities of 1928 are the defects of 1933. The high powered methods . . . that brought success then may well bring failure now. Tolerance and generosity must replace the hard-boiled formulas of aggressive competition.
Our first problem . . . is to overcome the disadvantages of the site. Can we do it by an intensive drive for tenants that puts us in direct conflict with every building owner with invested capital in real estate? . . . . Even as long as our plots stand vacant, they are a constant threat that at the first opportunity we are prepared to throw still more space on the market. . . .
(1) Our obligation and self interest is to revise our plan to a scheme that we can finish easily and beautifully, one that fulfills our idea of what uptown New York should be. We need qualities to rent the empty space we have rather than more empty space.
(2) We should organize the land that

we leave vacant so that it is an improvement to the neighborhood. . . . We must remember that building up the district is what will ultimately create value for us.
(3) Confine our rented program to the space that is built or that we need as a minimum to complete a simplified scheme. . . .
(4) Avoid all hard business, or appearance of it. Buy close but do not chisel. We need friends even among those who work for us.
(5) No gain can ever compensate by allowing anything to weaken in the slightest degree the public good will that the Rockefellers have so carefully won over years.
(6) In a distressed condition such as to-day, a completed, beautiful group would create a public satisfaction of inestimatable value. Incomplete and active, it is a threat and an unwelcome assertion of power. To complete beautifully is a gesture of generosity to the City and to the public.
(7) A simplified scheme is possible that will provide all the space that can be filled by our efforts to-day, and it can still permit, if conditions warrant in a few years, a return to an intensive development. . . .
(8) The elements of suppleness and creative imagination are badly needed in the board of managers.

> Anonymous memorandum, typed on Todd, Robertson & Todd, Todd & Brown typewriter, February 21, 1933.
> Rockefeller Family Archives, Box 80 Todd-Robertson Cash Requirements—Estimates file

No one in the Rockefeller offices expected a horde of tenants to appear during a business depression. People had to be courted, and the planners used all the sound managements techniques they could imagine to rescue a project that was famous but failing.

The first device was the use of—one might almost say the invention of—real estate public relations. Dozens of press releases left the offices each week, to be turned with few changes into newspaper articles all over the country.

One problem of writing about the development was that it needed a permanent name. It was still called Metropolitan Square, but even if the Opera moved to the Columbia property, it would no longer occupy the central site and the name "Metropolitan" would be meaningless if the Opera never settled in the project. Radio City, the popular name for the western buildings, would not do, either, for a development which included international buildings and such corporations as Standard Oil and American Cyanamid. Rockefeller City, approved at first, or Rockefeller Center were sensible choices, and the reticent owner finally agreed to give the development his name. The question of spelling "Center" provided public relations director Merle Crowell with a good chance to issue press releases asserting that a consultant lexicographer favored "Center" rather than "Centre" because the first spelling had been the choice of Milton and Shakespeare.[96]

The name was greeted, generally, by verbal nods of approval, although the Philadelphia *Labor Record* suggested giv-

72   *ROCKEFELLER CENTER*

ing that name to Ludlow, Colorado, a mining town "where stands the monument to the nineteen women and children who were burned to death in a former effort of the Rockefeller gunmen to smash a coal miners' strike." [97] Not many spokesmen for working men were as derisive as this, for other press releases announced that about 75,000 persons would be employed in building the project, and perhaps 150,000 others would find work with the companies supplying materials and services. During the construction period there were several minor work stoppages, although they caused no serious delays because the Center's representatives could be flexible negotiators. Moreover, they had sufficient funds to pay such wage increases as would be less costly than delays in construction and renting.[98]

During the 1930s, Rockefeller Center Inc. provided elaborate health and recreational facilities for its employees. There were rooftop sports areas, an infirmary, club rooms, and social groups, often with supplies furnished by the Corporation. In 1940 they established a pension plan. Construction workers made use of new inventions such as the Kelley Dust Trap which reduced irritants during construction; the accident rate among the building trade workers was remarkable low. Members of the Rockefeller family presided over well-publicized ceremonies at

38. Sunken plaza with summer restaurant, toward RCA Building. RKO (Amax) Building in right background. Photographed Summer *c.* 1936. (*Courtesy Rockefeller Center, Inc.*)

which they gave craftsmanship awards to expert building workers. The mutually beneficial truce that prevailed between Rockefeller capitalists and labor during the Center's early years set a useful precedent for later Rockefeller family enterprises; projects which they have sponsored or helped to finance from Albany, New York, to San Francisco, California, have given years of work to construction firms and to thousands of employees.

In view of the problems of finding tenants, the planning assumed special importance. If the buildings were not designed to a very high standard, with access to air and light, and with sturdy and handsome materials, they stood no chance of attracting and retaining tenants. But high standards were not sufficient in themselves to lure tenants from existing buildings. The managers would have to offer the latest mechanical and technological refinements. One of these was the high-speed elevator, which could whisk people upward at 1200 feet per minute by 1931 and 1400 feet per minute by the time the RCA Building opened with the fastest models. Providentially, the city Building Code approved them in July 1931, in time for installation in the RCA Building. The elevators have electric-eye safety mechanisms which prevent doors from closing on passengers. Another attraction was air-cooling. Although air-conditioning was not developed to its present state, some temperature and humidity control could be achieved, and in 1928 the entire Milam Building in San Antonio, Texas, had been provided with these amenities. Theater air-conditioning techniques were already well established.

The management planned to air-condition both theaters and the underground areas and to air-cool the British and French Buildings, the international group, the RCA Building, and the RCA Building West (although not all of the RCA Building offices were actually cooled.) Offices could be kept generally free of draughts and soot by Maxim-Campbell Silencer-and-Air-Filters, which had recently been invented. Soot in the area would also be reduced by having the Center contract for piped-in electricity and steam services, a fortunate byproduct of the managers' concern that on-site electrical and steam plants required high initial costs and risked the uncertainties of fuel supply. Besides, the managers wanted to eliminate smoke and hot gases from the area, and hoped to prevent unnecessary vibrations, noise and heat.[99]

The traffic problem in this soon-to-be-crowded area could be alleviated by the city's widening of streets running through the Center and by having the Center provide off-street truck loading areas [39]. Underground ramps would lead to sub-basement-level depots, keeping thousands of vehicles from crowding the streets. This provision had long been the hope of enlightened planners, although hardly anyone had ever constructed these facilities in Midtown. The underground facilities are among Rockefeller Center's best gifts to the city.

High standards depended in part on securing proper materials. The management obtained Indiana limestone when eight banks held a chattel mortgage on the failing limestone company's supply.

The banks met the price of the only potential large customer in the country. The managers realized savings of about 20 per cent on costs because of the Depression and because their centralized purchasing branch, run by Todd & Brown, was in a position to place huge orders and obtain low unit prices.[100] Some of the savings were applied to superior materials, and to the refined craftsmanship which was honored in the workmen's award ceremonies.

Crucial to the entire undertaking was the clear organization of the huge work force required to plan and execute the project. A chart explaining the overall organization appeared in *Architectural Forum* in January 1932. In the same magazine, Wallace Harrison signed an article explaining the exemplary organization of the drafting room force and of the filing and recording procedures. Albert W. Butt was the architect directly under the three firms' members and George Johnson was the architect in charge of the drafting room.

The organization functioned admirably at all but the very top levels. For several years, the lines of authority were not clearly drawn between the board of directors and John R. Todd, a problem which led to personal disagreements. Todd could be quite high-handed about bypassing the board of directors who then set up committees to watch his activities more closely. But the directors and architects found Todd's opinion and decisions reasonable, even if they resented having a dictator in charge of the project. Todd and his partners earned the respect of

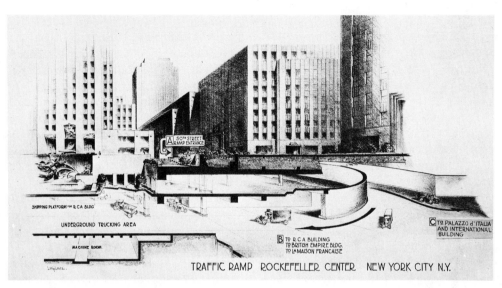

39. Underground levels, rendering.
(*Courtesy Rockefeller Center, Inc.*)

the Rockefeller personnel, who asked Hugh Robertson to remain at the Center after the Todd contracts terminated.

Hugh Robertson was the person responsible for obtaining many of the tenants. His chief assistant was Lawrence A. Kirkland, a young South Carolina lawyer who had been a personal assistant to John R. Todd and who had done some astute purchasing for Colonial Williamsburg. As an out-of-towner, he had no personal links—or, more important—obligations—to New York real estate circles. He was one of many capable men whom the Rockefeller family elevated from undeserved obscurity.

The young Nelson Rockefeller was also active in the family project. He had been elected a temporary member of the board of directors while he was still at Dartmouth in 1929. Soon after graduating in 1930, he married and traveled abroad with his bride, returning in the spring of 1931. Later that year, he joined Webster Todd and Fenton B. Turck, an employee of American Radiator and Standard Sanitary Corporation, in forming Turck & Co., "a firm that would . . . [earn] fees by setting up deals between parties who owned certain physical assets and others who wanted to buy or lease them . . ." One can imagine them encouraging Chase National Bank to buy American Radiator's radiators and their Maxim-Campbell filter-silencers, or encouraging a Rockefeller company to put its money in the Chase National Bank. After a bit more than a year went by, Nelson Rockefeller bought his partners' interest in the company and changed its name to Special Work, Inc. The corporation's task was that of publicizing and renting space at Rockefeller Center.[101]

Critics in the real estate industry worried about the fate of office building owners whose tenants were leaving, or who might find the Rockefellers subletting at lower than usual rents the space which they had taken off prospective tenants' hands. Others feared that the Wall Street area especially would suffer from competition in newly fashionable midtown. The rental department had spent a year researching names of tenants in the Wall Street and Grand Central areas and learning the terms and expiration dates of their leases. Others thought that the Center's theaters would take patrons away from older theaters on Broadway, destroying the tradition and economic life of the entertainment district. In January 1934 August Heckscher, once described as "one of the most ethical landlords in the business"[102] and proprietor of a large office building bearing his name at Fifth Avenue and 57th Street, sued Rockefeller Center, Inc. for $10,000,000 alleging unfair competition.

For their own records, the board of directors approved minutes as follows: "While in many of the above leases, Rockefeller Center, Inc. made allowances on its rental for the unexpired term of the tenants' existing leases, in only one case did Rockefeller Center assume any liability, obligation or any other part of the tenant's lease commitment as part of the transaction to induce the company to become a tenant of Rockefeller Center. This was the lease to the Industrial Relations Counselors, formerly of 165 Broadway. This transaction represented a distinct departure from general practice and was only adopted after all of the facts were called to the attention of the Rental Committee and their approval obtained." Heckscher's suit, still pending, was dismissed by stipulation on his death in 1941.[103]

Criticism did not stop the rental department, of course, whose agents signed up more and more tenants during the course of 1933 and 1934. Expensive gift boutiques moved into the sunken plaza stores, although not all the shops were successful since potential customers did not descend to the lower level in sufficient numbers. To make the sunken plaza more lively, the management installed an outdoor restaurant there in the spring of 1934, with pretty umbrellas and furniture [38].

The managers did not award contracts to incompetent firms in exchange for rental of space, but if two companies had satisfactory products, the contract would go to the firm that rented space, even if its products cost a little more.[104] Otis Elevators had been awarded some contracts at the Center when they applied for the RCA Building contract, but Westinghouse rented almost three floors in the building for several years and got that contract in exchange. As it happened, Westinghouse also offered superior elevators and safer tread designs on moving stairs.[105]

The management and Rockefeller did

not want to give exclusive renting privileges at the Center in exchange for leases, but a majority of the board of directors disagreed.[106] Accordingly, the Chase National Bank eventually received such privileges, at least for a limited time, and other companies did, too, although in decreasing numbers over the years.

John D. Rockefeller Jr. was able to influence other tenants to move to the Center—Standard Oil of New Jersey, the Rockefeller Foundation, and the Spelman Fund. These and other family interests occupying space at the Center were significant factors in the first optimistic rental reports which were issued in the second half of 1934.

Professional firms associated with the Center moved their offices to it, too, including Reinhard & Hofmeister. In 1935 Donald Deskey, the industrial designer who supervised the decoration of the Music Hall, moved there also. Wallace Harrison's firm is there today, as is the office of Francis T. Christy, the lawyer who was Secretary of Rockefeller Center, Inc. and who did much of the legal work connected with the early land acquisition.

But influence and mutual interests could go only so far. Between May and August 1933 Rockefeller tried to get Owen Young of General Electric to move to the Center. GE was a parent company of RKO which had gone into receivership and could not fulfill all its rental obligations, leaving the Center with empty space it had counted on having filled. GE itself was rumored to need more room, and it had a parent's honor to re-cover. If GE moved, Rockefeller would have bought the old GE building and applied the purchase price against rent at the Center. David Sarnoff, President of RCA, had even agreed to remove the RCA sign and change the name of the major building! All to no avail. GE moved to its jazz-modern office tower, originally built for RCA, at Lexington Avenue and 51st Street while Debevoise and Robertson—who were usually right about things—were glad that Rockefeller had not gotten deeper into a questionable real estate venture.[107]

The lobby decoration was a matter of great concern, because the public would notice it and criticize it. In August 1931 Hood told Merle Crowell that the RCA Building lobby could be a spectacular place if plans materialized. The managers expected to sign up some important tenants, each of whom would commission a large lobby mural. Apparently Hood had conceived this idea from the inspiration of the central offices of H. J. Heinz in Pittsburgh which were lavishly decorated, and Lloyd's Shipping Register offices in Fenchurch Street, London, where several artists worked including Frank Brangwyn who eventually executed paintings for the RCA Building. Hood sold the idea to the art-loving Mrs. Rockefeller and her son Nelson who were so "crazy about it" that they convinced Rockefeller himself.[108]

The planners imagined, for the French building, interior decoration "of a French type,"[109] whatever that meant, if it were not excessively expensive; no similar provision obtained in the contract with the

English group. Here lay a potential danger—that of having a dozen artists designing uncoordinated works of discordant subjects in a dozen styles within one building development. To solve this problem, Todd suggested to the board of directors that a unified art program might tie the whole development together. He estimated the cost of engaging artists at about $150,000.[110]

The management worked hard to make tenants happy that they had moved to the Center, offering a high standard of maintenance and giving proper training to the building employees. Flower shows [35], exhibits, public programs and invitations to important visitors in the city made the Center an interesting place to work and to visit. When business tenants in the RKO Building complained about the appearance and deportment of clients at theatrical agents' offices there, the Center refused to grant long leases to such agents and took other measures to get them out of the Center.[111] It was almost as important to the managers to offer tenants responsible neighbors of a high class as it was to have the offices filled.

The two theaters in the Center itself presented immediate problems for which grand future plans would not suffice. The press had focused public attention on the theater premieres, which took place during the last week of 1932—the Music Hall's on December 27, the RKO Roxy's two days later. People were especially interested in the 6200-seat Music Hall. Roxy had promised in his own sincerely hyperbolic way that this theater would offer the highest quality popular entertainment according to his formula which mixed the circus and the classics. Sixty thousand people were said to have applied for tickets to the Music Hall's opening night, and the six thousand who came were dressed elegantly for the occasion. Once inside, they saw Martha Graham, the Wallenda aerialists, and the Kikuta acrobats from faraway Japan. Titta Ruffo and Jan Peerce sang, and so did the much-admired choir of Tuskegee Institute, performing spirituals. There were so many other brilliant acts that the opening night stretched on and on. Newspaper critics were surfeited with delights, and some of their reviews suggested that they found too much of too many good things.

Fortunately, the premiere itself was so spectacular as a public event that some of the negative criticism was dissipated. Unfortunately, the public did not actually brave the winter weather in sufficient numbers to satisfy the management. After a week or so of confused operation, the Music Hall changed its entertainment policy. From mid-January 1933 onward it offered a combination of films and live stage entertainment [105], following Roxy's recipe. This change saved the Music Hall from financial failure, but it was the primary cause of the eventual closing of the RKO Roxy which opened to good reviews with the same combination of film and shorter stage show only two days after the Music Hall premiere. Although Americans somehow found enough money during the Depression to support their escapist fantasies at the movies, they simply could not sustain these two first-run motion picture theaters with a combined capacity of over nine thousand seats. The Music Hall was the more exciting of the two, which meant that the RKO Roxy led a precarious existence from the beginning. It even had to change its name in May when the old Roxy Theater owners won a suit to prevent the Rockefeller theater from using Roxy's name. The managers settled on "Center Theater" which made up in clarity what it lacked in gaiety.

Just after the Music Hall seemed to have established a sensible policy, another disaster struck, the financial failure of RKO itself. The Rockefellers took over 100,000 shares of RKO stock and an equal number of RCA shares as partial compensation for unfulfilled rental obligations, but they remained the owners of extra empty office space. And although the Center had a commanding voice in the theater operation once RKO relinquished its sole control of it, the Center's managers suddenly had to master the entertainment business.

In March 1933 the managers and directors appointed new theater administrators whose job it was to salvage what was left of the theaters' good name and to make them pay. Two of these men were particularly instrumental in the rescue operation and in making the Music Hall into a New York institution. They were W. G. van Schmus who had done publicity work and book publishing (including the children's *Oz* books) and Gustav S. Eyssell who had worked in theater management.

A year after the theaters opened, Webster Todd, van Schmus, and corporation secretary Francis T. Christy prepared a report of the theater situation, establish-

ing a basis for future action. The Center Theater attendance had suffered once the Music Hall began to show films. The Music Hall attendance itself might decline once the novelty of the building had worn off. They felt that Roxy could not or would not continue to produce the best shows—perhaps they thought that he was abandoning their sinking ship more quickly than he had abandoned his own Roxy Theater—and that he would not control costs, either. That was probably a polite way of expressing dissatisfaction with Roxy's own compensation which ran to several thousand dollars a week and included a glamorous studio suite with custom-designed furniture [98]. In January 1934 they finally got Roxy to resign,

40. RCA Building, observation roof, looking west. (*Courtesy Rockefeller Center, Inc.*)

since he would not restrain himself, although he later sought reappointment just before he died in January 1936. While keeping up the standards of the Music Hall, the new managers tried to find a use for the superfluous Center Theater. Like a handsome cat inept at catching mice, the theater had many admirers who could not find the right work for it to do. It was demolished in 1954.

In the spring of 1933 the planners considered the use of the top floors of the RCA Building. Private dining rooms and a kitchen already served corporate tenants in the building. And by the fall of 1935, an average of 1300 visitors a day paid forty cents each to visit the observation roof on the 70th floor. Provided with deck chairs and telescope, it offered something of the bracing feeling of being aboard ship, with nothing above the passengers save clouds. [40] Even now, the rooftop offers one of the best bird's-eye views of the city.

Between the dining rooms and the observation deck were several floors available for renting. One was leased briefly to an interior designers' group but customers seem not to have been eager to ascend 65 floors to the design exhibit. Aware as they were of the popularity of rooftop clubs and restaurants in the 1930s, the managers introduced restaurants, the Rainbow Room and Rainbow Grill. The former, little changed from the original decoration by Mrs. M. B. Schmidt, is still among the most elegant places to dine in the city. On leaving the elevators, patrons turn right into the lounge area facing north to Central Park, where up-

41. Rainbow Room lounge. Photographed September 1934.
(*Gottscho-Schleisner*)

holstered chairs are grouped in alcoves formed by glass enclosures containing plants [41]. The enclosures have mirrored ceilings which reflect the plants and increase the apparent amount of greenery. In the outer corners of the lounge, the city below is reflected above the plants, a brilliant decorative touch which Salvador Dali and everyone else admired. At the end of the lounge, steps lead to the Rainbow Room itself [42], a restaurant with a central dance floor marked by the recessed curved ceiling above it where colored light projections gave the room its name.[112] After several closings and reopenings, the Rainbow Room again offers entertainment, "great ceilings, immense windows, glittering chandeliers, startling views and good food." [113] The Rainbow Grill at the west end of the floor is less formal but it also offers dancing, entertainment, Picasso tapestries (added more recently) and "mind-bending views of the city." [114]

The Center could now be both businesslike and elegant. It still is.

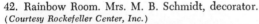

42. Rainbow Room. Mrs. M. B. Schmidt, decorator.
(*Courtesy Rockefeller Center, Inc.*)

VII.

Grand
Plans,
1934–1935

". . . the Rockefeller group should be
willing to contribute substantially toward
the construction of the Music and Art
Center, which, architecturally and otherwise, would round out the Rockefeller
Center, stabilize the development west of
the Fifth Avenue frontage, and attract
to a tax-exempt but integral part of the
Center visitors and trade which would
not otherwise be there. Let me make it
quite clear that I do not seek to create
the impression that the Rockefeller group
are interested in this subject only from a
business point of view. Rockefeller Center originated with the idea of an opera
house as the primary objective."

> Robert Moses, *Report to the Mayor
> from the Park Commissioner on the
> Proposed Municipal Art Center,*
> Sept. 20, 1938

Radio interests, theaters and international traders would attract people to the
development, but transporting them to
the three blocks was still a serious problem. Most commuters wanted to work
near railroad and subway stations. The
Sixth Avenue elevated line stopped at
50th Street, but it was not among the
most widely used transit routes in the
city. The Eighth Avenue line opened a
station in 1932 at Fifth Avenue and 53rd
Street which brought workers from
Queens. There were some Manhattan bus
lines nearby, too, including a private bus
line to the Beaux-Arts Apartments on East
44th Street which Hood had designed
with Kenneth Murchison. But these facilities could not compare with the transportation network around Grand Central
or Pennsylvania Stations.

As we have seen, the managers anticipated the widening of streets to reduce congestion on them, and they planned to construct a transcontinental bus terminal. While they waited for the Sixth Avenue "El" to be replaced by a subway. Rockefeller aide F. S. Staley suggested using the elevated structure for an attractive, quiet monorail [115]—an idea that has been echoed in other abortive plans for city transit. But more effective and practical plans were needed.

The really grand plan on which the managers were working between 1933 and 1936 was a scheme for a large rail terminal, accommodating New Jersey train lines which did not have New York terminals, and thus bringing commuters near Rockefeller Center. Commuters from Bergen County in northeastern New Jersey needed trans-Hudson train service. Real estate interests in New Jersey would benefit if the two states were linked by additional rapid transit. City officials would welcome some relief from street congestion caused by cars from New Jersey. And Rockefeller Center would benefit from proximity to a new terminal since its buildings would be near a major railway facility.

There had been earlier proposals for train access from Bergen County. The Van Sweringens' Erie Rail Road had expressed temporary interest in the Columbia leasehold site itself in the spring of 1929. Another proposal by people not affiliated with the Center for a terminal with subway connections was abandoned in 1931 because its proponents were uncertain about public demand and about the economic picture generally. Other people wanted to provide rapid transit over the George Washington Bridge at 178th Street (1931), which was originally designed, but not built, to carry it. [116]

On the advice of Major L. Alfred Jenny of Lockwood-Greene Engineers, Inc., the Rockefeller advisers chose a site at Eighth Avenue and 50th Street, extending to a main entrance at Sixth Avenue and 49th Street. Although this terminal might soon serve more passengers than either of the existing major stations, the plan had some serious drawbacks. A commuter terminal there would not solve the problem of tying Rockefeller Center into the existing subway network because the Eighth Avenue subway lines had no stop at or near the Center. The Center's managers had thought earlier of having a subway from Eighth Avenue and 49th Street running via Rockefeller Center to Grand Central. [117] Their consultants suggested a revised version of this, a shuttle subway across 50th Street, or a loop linking all the major rail stations with Rockefeller Center. To complete this plan, the city would have to offer a nominal rental and a lease long enough to warrant the expense, but the expense itself was enormous and the city was not visibly interested. Moreover, the planners were afraid that a terminal between Sixth and Eighth Avenues might engender buildings above or near it which could compete with the Center's buildings. Property owners at the freight end of the station would surely object to a noisy neighbor. Protests could damage public relations which would be important if subsidies were to be obtained from New Jersey communities or from Federal government reconstruction funds. Worst of all, no one could predict the number of commuters who would switch to buses which were cheaper and more flexible about altering their routes to serve a mobile population. The terminal plan was shelved in mid-1934, although it was not until 1939 that Debevoise drily and sensibly put a stop to further activities in connection with it. Nevertheless, a version of the terminal planned for Ninth Avenue to Broadway, 48th-49th Street, was reintroduced by government personnel in the early 1970s, only to be deferred at the end of 1973 by the Port Authority of New York and New Jersey, a bi-state group which included appointees of Governor Nelson Rockefeller.

Although the Eighth Avenue site was a problem, the Committee on Subway Connections of the board of directors pointed out that the terminal could be built on Rockefeller property just north of the Center where Hugh Robertson had quietly been buying property for the Rockefellers as an investment. Work on the Sixth Avenue subway was about to resume, and there was going to be a stop at Rockefeller Center. The committee planned to have the underground concourse connect the Center to the subway station and the terminal and hoped that the Eighth Avenue line's stop at Fifth Avenue and 53rd Street could also be connected to an adjacent terminal. The Center's planners thought of using the Sixth Avenue subway to form a connection between their terminal and Pennsylvania Station; passengers could reach the station from Sixth Avenue by walking through an underpass below 33rd Street. People might also be able to change from the Sixth Avenue subway to the Times Square-Grand Central shuttle. The proposal was attractive, but the center's planners had to turn it down. The land would have had to be rezoned, and there were other potential uses for it which would also protect the residential character of the streets, such as the apartment house and the Museum of Modern Art which the Rockefellers later sponsored there.[118]

In the spring of 1934, when the rail terminal project faced difficulties, C. O. Heydt, at least, began work on a new project which was to mature in the fall. In April he had a map prepared which showed frontages, mortgages, and ownerships on 51st, 52nd, and 53rd Streets.[119] The purpose of having the map made must have been to consider the possibilities for land acquisition and use in those blocks which lay between the Center and the Rockefeller houses. On October 13 an independent broker purchased 17 and 19 West 51st Street, for "Mr. Jr." These plots lay just north of Rockefeller Plaza, the Center's private street. This made it possible to envisage a northern extension of the street that would increase automobile access to the Center. The extension might also increase the value of the Rockefeller holdings in these blocks because north–south avenue and corner sites are usually more valuable than crosstown frontage. Heydt knew that by buying and then demolishing the houses in the private street's path, the Rockefellers could benefit more from the new corner and north–south parcels than they could from uninterrupted underutilized private houses. Access and land value considerations had influenced Benjamin Morris' and other earlier schemes for new north–south streets.

Other people were alert to these possibilities, too, including Peter Grimm of the William A. White & Sons real estate firm [120] and Lockwood-Greene Engineers, who had temporarily suspended studies on the transportation terminal. Between

1929 and 1937, the Rockefellers and their nominees (and the young Museum of Modern Art which was the object of their benefactions) added to their land holdings. By the end of 1937, they owned or controlled 17-21 West 51st Street; 11-19 and 22 West 52nd Street, 5-19, 27 and 2-24, 28 and 30 West 53rd Street; 17-23, 29 and 2-24 West 54th Street; 24-26 West 55th Street, as well as some Fifth Avenue frontage. They had bought some of this land earlier, as we have seen, but added more between 1934 and 1937 for investment, especially in case they decided to undertake the street extension. Some of the land was intended for the Museum of Modern Art.[121] The private street would link Rockefeller Center to this privately sponsored museum, rather like a modern equivalent to the Medici Palace and San Lorenzo in Florence. Drawings were prepared in 1935-36 showing this arrangement.[122] The street might, on the other hand, continue through to the block-through Rockefeller Apartments at 17-23 West 54th/26-36 West 55th Street which members of the Harrison & Fouilhoux firm designed in 1935 for construction in 1936.

But the private street extension plan came to nothing for reasons that are hard to define. With several Rockefeller Center plots still vacant and needing a large investment before they could be filled, the owner and managers may have hesitated to put even more money into an uncertain venture.[123]

The press reported that the proprietors of the "21 Club," a former speakeasy favored by fashionable patrons, refused to move from 21 West 52nd Street which lay right in the path of the street extension. It would have been possible to build a 100-foot wide street around this small

building, but that would only have rewarded the owners' obstinacy with wonderful publicity. Besides, the Rockefeller architects were planning only a thirty-foot wide street with flanking fifteen-foot sidewalks. It would have been difficult to dislodge the "21 Club" through city condemnation procedures if the extension were for a private, not a public street. Furthermore, 52nd through 55th Streets were zoned for residential use (including restaurants) and Rockefellers had supported the 1928 court action to keep those streets that way. While rezoning for commercial use was certainly possible, that would have entailed enlisting the support of other parties; enduring criticism from neighborhood retailers' present landlords (not to mention August Heckscher's supporters); going through legal proceedings; and waiting. By April 1937, the policy of the Rockefeller real estate office was to dispose of as much land as possible since the properties had not been profitable and were proving to be hard to develop.[124]

Meanwhile, in January 1935 Mayor Fiorello LaGuardia who had been elected by a Fusion Party composed of Republicans, Liberals and Democrats, promoted the establishment of a municipal art center and conservatory.[125] He hoped to have classical music offered at low prices to those who seldom could afford to go to concerts, and he wanted to provide the arts with a home and support outside the Democratic Roosevelt administration's Depression relief projects. The art center might have a symphony hall, grand opera house, a light opera auditorium, perhaps in a single hall which could also be used for conventions; a music library and a museum for musical materials belonging to the New York Public Library; space for

43. Municipal Art Center project. Harrison &
Fouilhoux, Morris & O'Connor, architects.
Rendering by Hugh Ferriss.
(*Courtesy Harrison & Abramovitz*)

the Museum of Modern Art and galleries
for modern art shows. Other possibilities
included quarters for the Guggenheim art
collection, a costume museum, and facilities for the Columbia Broadcasting System. Famous consultants to the project included Norman Bel Geddes as general
adviser, Lee Simonson as lighting expert,
and for staging advice, Robert Edmond
Jones who had put in a brief period of
employment at the Radio City Music Hall.
The Municipal Art Committee had hoped
to have the project located in Central
Park, but fortunately for the park, there
were legal obstacles to that. In the spring
of 1936 Nelson Rockefeller suggested locating the art center in the two-block area
just north of Rockefeller Center. The private street would be extended to the
north, and the art center buildings would
border its western side. The Municipal Art
Committee, which supported this project,
even offered to employ Reinhard & Hofmeister; the Rockefeller Center Directors'

Planning Committee agreed to that if the
architects' work did not interfere with
their duties at the Center. In July 1936,
however, the architects in charge were
Harrison and Fouilhoux, Benjamin Wistar
Morris and his partner, Robert O'Connor [43]. They thought the city might
even be able to condemn the "21 Club" if
it were done for a public purpose. Perhaps
there could be a wide plaza. The architects made plans for a steel and stone
opera building to cost about $6,000,000
and to seat 3500 patrons.

But the Museum of Modern Art did not
stay within the art center's 51st to 53rd
Street boundaries. It moved to the proposed northern termination of the private
street extension, for in 1936 the Rockefellers gave 15-19 on the north side of
West 53rd Street to the Museum and
traded three family-owned adjacent plots
at 9-13 for three plots, 6-10, which the
Museum owned on the south side of the
street within the art center boundaries.
Until August 1938 at least, although they
were still alert to other ways of disposing
of their landholdings north of Rockefeller
Center, members of the Rockefeller Center staff promoted the establishment of the
art center along the extended private
street probably because of civic pride
and their interest in improving the neighborhood of Rockefeller Center and the
Museum of Modern Art. There would also
have been "tremendous value" to Rockefeller Center from having such distinguished neighbors.

The Opera corporations seem to have
responded with verbal interest but with
little financial liberality. The boxholders
were no longer the same rich men and
women who had been boxholders in 1929.
Several of the earlier boxholders had died,

leaving their stock in the Metropolitan Opera Real Estate Company to estates which had the interests of heirs to consider. Other boxholders were old or in reduced circumstances. And not all of them responded favorably to LaGuardia's enthusiasm for opera for the masses. Moreover, the owners of some of the land required for this project were not inclined to sell it to the city for any but high prices.

The project had to be reduced in size if it were to be considered at all, and someone other than the busy Mayor had to coordinate the plans. Robert Moses, the Parks Commissioner and a sponsor of construction who even outdid Rockefeller in scope of his building, was appointed to oversee the plans in May 1938. Harrison and Fouilhoux sent models to interested parties, but Moses had alternative proposals prepared for the Sixth Avenue end of the two blocks by architect-engineer William Wilson and by architect Aymar Embury II who had worked for Moses earlier. A minimal plan used an interior plot on the 52nd-53rd Street block. This placed the art center buildings farther to the west than the private street, to save the expense of building a new street. A more ambitious plan [44] used parts of both 51st-53rd Street blocks for a building elevated on a plaza above a parking garage. The interior incorporated an Opera House and a symphony hall, each seating 4500 people, which could be combined by moving a dividing wall to provide a civic auditorium. At the base of the tower were a 750-seat theater and quarters for the municipal radio station. Exhibition rooms formed wings delimiting the plaza on two sides. The scheme would cost $14,500,000 for land and build-

ings. But that money was simply not to be found. By the end of 1938, no one expected to build an art center or an extended private street.

Parts of the Mayor's program were realized eventually, but in different form. In 1942, an existing auditorium, the Mecca Temple was converted into the City Center of Music and Drama to offer low-priced operas and ballets. CBS built its headquarters in the two-block site, at Sixth Avenue and 52nd Street, but not until 1965. The Rockefellers did donate 6-10 West 53rd Street for public purposes —for the admirable Donnell Branch of the Public Library. The art center itself was substantially realized at Lincoln Center, not under public sponsorship alone, but with the essential support of John D. Rockefeller 3rd.

44. Music Center project, 1938. Aymar Embury II, architect.
(*Courtesy Rockefeller Center, Inc.*)

VIII.

The Commercial Project, 1935–1940:

Filling the Gaps

By the start of 1935 the first stage of development had passed. About 80 per cent of the office space in the completed buildings was rented. The private streets, sunken plaza, and twenty-two of twenty-five shops in the underground mezzanine were in operation. By the end of April, ten buildings were up [45]. Many works of art were in place, trees grew on the setback terraces, and the public relations department had begun its program of special events at the Center which have broken the monotony of workday lunch hours for forty-five years [35, 62, 125].

Unquestionably, all this was an impressive achievement in a period of drastic economic decline. It was only disappointing if measured against the original ambitions for the' Center. The planners had hoped to have all the buildings up by the summer of 1935, but the center lots on the side blocks stood empty. There were no immediate prospects of new tenants who would rent enough space to warrant new buildings. With no new buildings, the

45. Project in effect between January 1934 and Spring 1937. Rendering by John Wenrich. (*Courtesy Rockefeller Center, Inc.*)

REINHARD & HOFMEISTER
CORBETT, HARRISON & MAC MURRAY
HOOD & FOUILHOUX
ARCHITECTS
1932

JOHN WENRICH
18766

Center was embarrassingly incomplete. The worst looking thing on the vacant plots was the exit ramp of the underground truck delivery area which was all too plainly visible on the north block. The managers thought of disguising it with minimal planting, but then decided simply to distract attention from it. Their first moves were to increase the prestige and charm of the existing buildings. The next moves were to find new tenants for whom the much-reduced architects' group could design new buildings.

Reinhard, Hofmeister, and Harrison were now the dominant architects, members of a new generation. Hood had died in August 1934, after an illness which prevented him from doing much work after January 1934. His former partner, Godley, had retired as early as 1931, having had little to do with the Center in the first place. Corbett stayed on, not as a daily working participant but as a consultant, especially on general matters of design and on the art program. Harrison left Corbett's firm in May 1935, and soon afterward entered into partnership with Fouilhoux, the remaining principal in Hood, Godley, & Fouilhoux. Although Corbett, MacMurray, and Fouilhoux appeared as architects on the plans for the Associated Press Building (1937-38), each man did only $5000 worth of consulting, not production work; two thirds of the rest of the architects' fee went to Reinhard & Hofmeister, one third to Harrison (although these three architects hired Fouilhoux to prepare specifications for an extra $5000). Fouilhoux had a larger share in the work for the Eastern Air Lines Building, and the plans for that bore his

name as well as Reinhard's, Hofmeister's, and Harrison's, but Corbett and Mac-Murray were hired only as consultants on this job.[126] Instead of the brilliant designer Hood, instead of the authoritative and progressive Corbett, the architects were now Todd's protégés and Corbett's erstwhile junior partner. These men, who had matured while working on the Center, had to complete a project of world-wide fame—if the Todds and Hugh Robertson's rental salesmen could find tenants to fill the gaps.

46. RCA Building, Museum of Science and Industry. Edward Durell Stone, architect. (*Courtesy Rockefeller Center, Inc.*)

In the autumn of 1935 Nelson Rockefeller became a trustee of the New York Museum of Science and Industry when the Museum negotiated a fifteen-year lease for premises in Rockefeller Center [46]. The Museum displays occupied the hard-to-sell, windowless interior "Forum" space on the lowest floors of the RCA Building, extending toward the RCA Building West. The long lease made the Museum a better tenant than the occasional municipal art exhibitors or the restaurateurs originally envisioned for the area. Rockefeller Center might become the cultural center that early critics had expected, but instead of having grand opera and symphony concerts, it would be a center of modern culture—modern art, radio and film, science, and industry.

The United States Post Office rented premises in the Center in January 1934, and dignified, dark-paneled facilities were designed for its original location there. The Rockefeller Center Station was convenient for the office tenants, and it was good for the Center's prestige. At the end of 1935 another government agency became a tenant. The United States Passport Office occupied space in the International Building mezzanine and decorated it with a large mosaic by Byron Browne, produced under a government work relief project for artists. Travelers would have to pass shipping and airline tenants' window displays en route to the passport bureau. The Center's renting office found a passport photographer to rent space in the underground concourse. People could then have lunch in one of the restaurants while waiting for the photographs to be developed, or they might do

47. RCA Building, eleventh floor roof. Gardens of the Nations. Dutch Garden.
(*Courtesy Rockefeller Center, Inc.*)

some impulse shopping on the premises.

The roof gardens, particularly one section run as a concession called the Gardens of the Nations [47], were an important attraction. They brought patrons near the shops and theaters by offering them the chance to see exotic plants arranged as they might be in countries of Europe and Asia.

There were already the Rainbow Room and Grill, and the RKO Gateway Restaurant on Sixth Avenue where the walls featured photomurals of historic scenes enlarged from photographs supplied by the Museum of the City of New York.[127] When the plaza shops were closed, the north and south sides of the sunken plaza were converted into restaurants, with glass walls replacing the original masonry and shop-window façades. The Union News Company leased them in July 1935, giving them names which suggested that they were really French and English and employed James Thurber and William Steig to draw some delightfully mordant cartoons on the walls. Once the shops were converted to restaurants, the entrances to the shopping concourse from the sunken plaza were closed, and a bar was installed behind "Prometheus"; the bar was later replaced by a coffee shop. This hurt the underground shops because some tourists never noticed that there were any, but it was an unavoidable move.

The sunken plaza itself, though, remained a serious problem. Several shops had failed there. Restaurateurs might well worry about the appeal of subterranean restaurants, even those with large window walls. Proposals to display flags to brighten the plaza met with a cool response from the board of directors'

48. Sunken plaza with Christmas tree; left to right: British Building, Saks Fifth Avenue, La Maison Française. Photographed December 1972.
(*Courtesy Rockefeller Center, Inc.*)

Planning Committee and from Colonel Woods, who were afraid of giving "an exhibition character" to the development.[128] No one had any useful suggestions until someone proposed a short test of an artificial ice-skating rink; a Cleveland, Ohio, inventor, M. C. Carpenter, had recently found a way to keep outdoor artificial ice-skating rinks from melting. This involved considerable alteration to the floor of the sunken plaza, but the potential rewards outweighed the expense. Besides, the managers were probably desperate for a good idea.

The skating rink opened on Christmas Day 1936 as a temporary expedient, and has been an unforgettable feature of New York City ever since [48]. Perhaps more than any other single attraction at Rockefeller Center, it has been the reason for the Center's popular success. The rink is not large, but its informality and color and motion soften the austerity of the sober limestone towers that overlook it. People can come to the Center just to pass the time, and when watching the skaters they do not look or feel like simple loiterers. The rink brings children and families to the Center, and is a merry witness to the possibility of having fun in a business district. The rink has inspired dozens of imitators on several continents, but it remains the undisputed star.[129]

Gardens of all nations, international cuisine, mail to the entire world and an office regulating departure for travel abroad; buildings identified with France and Britain and Italy (even if the foreign governments' participation was almost nil by 1935); foreign consultants; travel agencies, foreign tourist offices, air and rail and sea transportation companies; international boutiques; cablegram offices—it was not impossible to justify claims that the development was a center of worldwide activity. But the empty plots still needed buildings.

Just as the radio-based communications companies had rescued the first stage of the development, print-based communications firms represented by Time Inc. and the Associated Press rescued the second. The circulation of the young *Time* Magazine was growing rapidly, despite all the bad weekly news that it had to report during the Depression. Its owners needed larger quarters for it and for their other publications, including *Life* magazine which was inaugurated in 1936. They needed space and they needed a public image—an office building named for them. Rockefeller Center offered seven floors and a penthouse in a tall building, a promise of room for expansion, a twenty-year lease, and an up-to-the-minute, conspicuous address. The Time & Life Building, as it was christened when it opened in 1937, rises thirty-six stories high on the Center's south block, just east of the private street [49]. For a year or two, it offered space in its concourse level to the Museum of Modern Art until the Museum's own new building was completed.

When the Time & Life Building opened in April 1937, Hugh Robertson had begun negotiations with the Associated Press news agency for a home just west of the private street between 50th and 51st

49. First Time & Life Building (One Rockefeller Plaza), looking south from Rockefeller Plaza (private street). Photographed April 1937. *(Gottscho-Schleisner)*

Streets, a building that would complete the north block and leave only the south block with vacant plots [50]. The Associated Press Building's shape is different from the others at Rockefeller Center, because instead of cutting down the interior loft space, the architects had to provide a great deal of it, making a broad and bulky structure, about 200 feet by 187 feet. The building needed the large floors because newsgathering offices customarily had desks in a "pool" rather than in individual offices, and the employees also had to be near files and teletype machines. The building is only fifteen stories tall since the prime tenant needed only the fourth through seventh floors, and few other tenants were at hand; it is costly to build higher than what is necessary for a profitable return because high buildings require more elevators, and need a variety of floor plans to accommodate the setback requirements.[130]

The height of the Associated Press Building put an end to any hope of creating connected roof gardens, although as late as October 1937, Todd still thought that someday a bridge might be built over the private street between the International and Associated Press Buildings, giving the latter a Fifth Avenue address and allowing visitors to walk from one roof or setback to another. The linked gardens idea had already been damaged severely by the fact that the International Building did not bridge the private street, but was self-sufficient. The gardens were proving very costly anyhow and not all the buildings had them. Most of the Music Hall roof was used for employee recreation. At a meeting in the architect's office in January of 1938, representatives of the architects, managers, and board of directors agreed to have reinforcements for garden construction put only on the western three bays on the 13th floor set-back of the Associated Press Building. There might therefore be a garden link to the Music Hall roof some day, but not to the buildings east of the private street.

Since the new building was fifteen stories tall, it also put an end to any plans for interspersing more low buildings among the high ones at the Center. The Fifth Avenue buildings were low, of course, and so were the theaters, but hopes of developing the remaining plots west of the private street with other low buildings were defeated by economic pressure. If the Center had been built during a period of prosperity, when almost any kind of building could have found appropriate tenants, and when substantial rents per square foot meant that fewer square feet would have to be constructed, the interior plots would surely have been developed with the low buildings which are cheaper to design and build. But in 1937 the board of directors and the managers could not afford to worry about outdated plans. They built what the tenant needed and what would be most profitable. Nelson Rockefeller wrote to his father in February 1938, saying that "This is the first time that any

building in Rockefeller Center shows a profit, at 95 per cent rented at schedule, after all the charges. I think it is a real tribute to Mr. Robertson's ingenuity and persistency in cutting costs . . . and evidence of his outstanding ability." [131] If the low and shop-filled lobby reveals Robertson's intense interest in cost-efficiency, the entrance helps to disguise it, for over the door is Isamu Noguchi's stainless steel

50. Associated Press Building. Left background: RKO (Amax) Building. Left foreground: RCA Building. Right foreground: International Building with relief by Lawrie over entrance to East River Savings Bank. Photographed c. 1940. (*Courtesy Rockefeller Center, Inc.*)

relief, *News,* probably the best work of sculpture at Rockefeller Center. [51]

When the north block was taken care of, there remained the south block to fill. In the spring of 1937 Rockefeller Center opened negotiations with Dutch government officials and with a group that hoped to locate commercial operations at Rockefeller Center. A club for gentlemen of

Dutch ancestry also planned to lease space for its social activities.[132] This would have carried the theme of international ties to the western part of the Center, making the entire development more obviously integrated conceptually, with world contacts evident whether one looked at broadcasting and entertainment facilities or at commercial facilities. The sixteen-story building planned for the former Opera site just west of the private street was to have exhibition space, a dining room, a meeting room, and two-story glass-fronted shops in four-story wings that surrounded the central tower [52].

The building was also to have a garage located between the office space and the Center Theater, an idea put forward as early as November 1936, taking advantage of a Zoning Resolution amendment of the preceding year which permitted certain parking garage construction in the Midtown retail zone. The garage was built for eight hundred cars, housed on three stories underground and three above. It used space that was hard to sell, and it helped to make visiting the Center easier for those who could not use mass transit.

The building owners were not enthusiastic about the whole south block project. It was simply a response to the best current chance of building something on the property. Nelson Rockefeller wrote his opinion to his father: "I should say frankly that if we were approaching this on the basis of an outside investment, we cer-

51. Isamu Noguchi, *News.* Associated Press Building.
(*Courtesy Rockefeller Center, Inc.*)

tainly would not give this matter serious consideration; however, in view of the current carrying charges and the necessity for the completion of Rockefeller Center, the construction of the building, it seems to me, is an extremely sound step to take." [133]

The doubters were right about the financial prospects. The Dutch government maintained its consulate general there, the Dutch Indies trade commissioner had his office there, and when they moved in on March 19, 1940, they made brave speeches telling the Germans to keep hands off the neutral Netherlands. The Germans invaded their country anyway, eradicating hopes of immediate Dutch expansion in the Center, except for temporary offices of the government-in-exile.

The managers had not counted only on the Dutch interests in any case. They had entered negotiations with Eastern Air Lines, the third kind of communications industry to help pull the Center out of difficulty. Eastern, like several other airlines at the time, was expanding its services and its technology. It needed a new home and, if possible, its name on the home. As "Holland House" became less and less Dutch because of business and political conditions, it became more and more the home of the airline. Edward Rickenbacker, the famous flyer who was then president of Eastern, signed a ten-year lease for what would then be the Eastern Air Lines Building on June 13, 1940, while aloft in one of his planes. The airline agreed to provide ground transportation to LaGuardia Airport for its passengers, thereby adding at least some form of transportation terminal to the

52. Eastern Air Lines Building, looking southwest. Photographed c. 1939–40.
(*Courtesy Rockefeller Center, Inc.*)

Center. When the building was officially dedicated on October 15, 1940, the airline and Rockefeller Center managed to induce the governors of seventeen states served by the airline to pose for pictures—each, in turn, pressing the button that "started" the building machinery.

With the Eastern Air Lines Building under way, there was only one more site to fill, but in 1938 no one seemed to be eager to move to a Sixth Avenue site not yet free of four-story buildings and still fronting on the "elevated" tracks. Finally, in March 1939, the "El" demolition began at 34th Street, and at the end of a few months, Sixth Avenue was no longer gloomy. It was still seedy, though [16, 53], apart from Rockefeller Center, the Warwick Hotel, and Joseph Urban's Ziegfeld Theater a few blocks farther north at 54th Street. Office tenants would have nothing attractive to look out upon, except for a distant view of sprawling development in New Jersey across the Hudson River.

The board of directors, the management, and the Rockefellers had to provide the solution themselves, and the management was no longer at full strength. "Doc"

Todd had retired in 1937. John R. Todd retired at the end of 1938, though he, his son, and Joseph Brown were retained as consultants until April 1, 1941. Everyone admired the work of Hugh Robertson who was still vigorous and who was kept on.

Someone—perhaps Heydt—hit upon the idea of getting the U. S. Rubber Company to move from its building at 1790 Broadway. That building was near Columbus Circle at the southwest corner of Central Park which ought to be but never has been a prestigious commercial address. A few years before Rockefeller Center was begun, William Randolph Hearst, the publisher, and Arthur Brisbane, a writer who sometimes advised him on real estate, believed that the focus of Manhattan office building activity would eventually shift to Columbus Circle. They bought some of the smaller buildings there and commissioned Joseph Urban to design the Hearst Building just to the south. The area remained underdeveloped because hardly anyone else wanted to move to it, and the Depression stopped many firms from moving anywhere. Many companies who were solvent and who seemed eager to move somewhere were brought into Rockefeller Center. U. S. Rubber had been left behind. Rockefeller Center made an offer that was too good to refuse. It

53. Sixth Avenue (Avenue of the Americas), looking north, immediately after demolition of the elevated railway. Right to left: Buildings on site of U.S. Rubber Company (Uniroyal) Building, Center Theater, RCA Building West, RKO (Amax) Building, Warwick Hotel in distance. Photographed April 1939.
(*Courtesy Rockefeller Center, Inc.*)

bought 1790 Broadway, and agreed to assume the management of it by means of a new corporation owned equally by Rockefeller Center, Inc. and U. S. Rubber. Rockefeller Center, Inc. provided $125,000 for "so-called moving expenses" and an equal amount which went into the treasury of the new corporation. The architects planned the new tenant space so that the Rubber Company staff needed only eleven floors rather than the twelve they had formerly occupied and saved the rental of 35,000 square feet [54]. To celebrate the impending completion of his Center, John D. Rockefeller drove a silver rivet—the "Last Rivet" celebrated by the public relations department—into the steel framework of the building on November 1, 1939. The tenants moved in during the following spring.

The value of this move was twofold. It brought another tenant to the Center, one which remained for a long time and eventually expanded into another building which replaced the Center Theater. It also removed an important business firm from the Columbus Circle area to Rockefeller Center, thereby reducing the threat of competitive development there.

There was, in fact, a threat of rival developments elsewhere. When the "El" came down—or when its demolition was only scheduled—architects and civic groups hastened to produce plans for the Sixth Avenue of the future. Some were merely proposals for tidying up the

façades of existing buildings and planting a few trees. Some were more elaborate, and even remarkably prophetic [55].[134] Seventh Avenue was also available. It was one of the few streets left for westward expansion because the west midtown area from near Seventh Avenue to the Hudson River, from 42nd to 59th Streets had been rezoned in 1936 (with the encouragement and plans of Harvey Wiley Corbett) to

54. U.S. Rubber Company (Uniroyal) Building. Photographed *c.* 1940.
(*Courtesy Rockefeller Center, Inc.*)

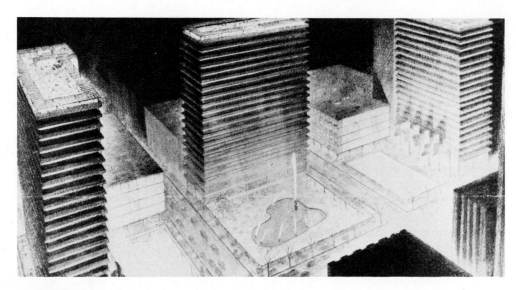

55. "Plaza of the Americas," international trade buildings proposed for Sixth Avenue, 1941. Edward Durell Stone *et al.*, architects.

increase residential, business and retail land use, with a view toward keeping unrestricted land uses clustered to the west of Tenth Avenue. This rezoning prevented scattered and uncoordinated high-rise office development in the area. But tall office buildings or new shops could be built on Broadway and on Sixth and Seventh Avenues, even though no one thought a construction boom was imminent and some even prophesied a quiet period of ten years.

Nevertheless, the rental picture was becoming brighter for building owners at the end of the decade. Some of the optimism must have been only for promotional purposes, but some of it was based on reality. Business was improving. A spokesman for William A. White & Sons said that for every 1000 square feet of space occupied by offices in 1929, there were 1100 in 1939. Low rents encouraged office expansion. And businessmen were now growing accustomed to having the larger offices which Depression prices had made possible.

By early 1940, Rockefeller Center was 87 per cent rented. In 1941, it was almost completely rented and actually began to show an operating profit. This prevented any increase in the deficit incurred during the planning and building years, a deficit which was about $26,000,000 at the start of 1935 and which had increased to about $39,000,000 in 1940.[135] John D. Rockefeller Jr. had laid out this money in cash or in pledges by corporations in which he held stock, something that few individuals in our century have been able to do since the introduction of the graduated income tax. Most huge developments are now financed primarily by large lending institutions and by governments. Although it might take years to recover the $39,000,000, at least the Center was now self-supporting from year to year. In time it might justify the total investment which had reached about one hundred million dollars at the start of 1940.[136]

With the comfort of an operating profit, Rockefeller may well have been pleased with the completed project [5]. It was not at all what he had counted on having at first, of course, but his Center had managed to weather the Depression. He could console himself, too, with the thought that probably more people enjoy watching the ice skaters than looking at the façade of an opera house. People watch the skaters while the Center's income-producing shops and restaurants are open, while opera patrons usually come when these facilities are closed. Rockefeller had safeguarded his old neighborhood, and had raised the value of his own land. Construction unions had enjoyed almost ten years of work at the worst period of America's economic history. The real estate business had been dealt a temporary blow, but it had been offered an example of the means of developing a multi-block site dedicated to many complementary uses. New Yorkers had new places to go, comfortable offices,

rooftop gardens, underground streets to use in rainy weather. There was a convenient link under the RCA Building West to the brand new Sixth Avenue subway, and Rockefeller Center helped to maintain the station. Rockefeller's project included as many paintings and sculptures as any patron could reasonably hope for.

People enjoyed working in the attractive surroundings, and they feel that way even now. As a New York museum curator said recently, "People seem to stand up a little straighter there" and look less harried. They look up at the RCA Building, down at the sunken plaza, around at the flags and flowers and strollers. If Rockefeller Center dominates the people, the tyranny is unusually agreeable.

The critics slowly began to write gentler articles. They were pleased that sheer disaster had been avoided and that the Center was not worse than it was. In fact, they began to like Rockefeller Center and its virtues began to seem substantial. There were no more *Vanity Fair* magazine covers showing dinosaurs in front of the Music Hall. After war broke out for the United States on December 7, 1941, people could think of Rockefeller Center as a model for postwar developments. When faced with this example, would not others seek to emulate it in a happier, more prosperous, more perfect world?

IX.

First Postwar Expansion, 1941–1960

"Jim said he would not mind standing all day in Radio City, where the French and British shops and the travel offices were, and the evergreens at Christmas and the tulips in the spring and where the fountains in summer sprayed ceaselessly around Mr. Manship's golden boy and where exhibition fancy skaters salved their egos in the winter. If he grew tired of the skaters, Jim said he would not mind standing and staring up and up, watching the mass of building cut into the sky. It made him know what people wanted and what they thought. It taught him more about geology and astronomy and history than he had ever learned at school."

John P. Marquand, *So Little Time*.

By 1941 the business picture was improving. Rockefeller Center benefited from the general expansion in having most of its space under leases which were good enough to provide an operating profit. Might Rockefeller be tempted to build more buildings as investments in the future? Sixth Avenue, recently cleared of the "El" [53], was ripe for redevelopment, and plans for its future had been made for the previous four years at least. Property owners there were believed to be waiting for a leader, and the leader might well be the man whose development was at the heart of any Sixth Avenue improvement.

But Rockefeller was not tempted to build anything else. He had come through a difficult twelve years, and was not eager for more of the same problems.

Nothing, in fact, was built for several years because the United States entered the Second World War on December 7, 1941. The war put a stop to most civilian construction. It put an end to Sixth Avenue plans for a while, too.

The war had two essential effects upon Rockefeller Center. The first was that any new or expanding businesses would have only existing buildings to use. The rate of tenancy at Rockefeller Center reached 100 per cent, and there were several years when the renting office kept waiting lists of prospective tenants. The Center had other troubles occasioned by the war—shortages of skilled maintenance personnel or of supplies—but finding tenants was not one of them.

Second, by bringing other construction projects to a halt for several years, the war insured Rockefeller Center a prominent position as the latest thing in office design, and the most comprehensive planning project in Manhattan—in effect, the most prominent modern commercial building group in the world. No European or Asian city was in a position to build offices and theaters and restaurants to rival it during the war years or for about a decade after.

The Center itself was host to patriotic rallies, war bond drives and visiting military displays including a two-thirds-scale ship, as well as exhibitions stressing the virtues of America's allies. "Victory gardens" replaced some of the flower beds. To celebrate the liberation of France, Lily Pons sang the "Marseillaise" at the Center. The public relations department under Caroline Hood's direction made sure that the sunken plaza became an established

base for these events, and that the Center was on the itinerary of every foreign dignitary who visited New York. The railroad men had been doing the same sort of thing at Grand Central, but Rockefeller Center could do it better and more noticeably outdoors. By steady and resourceful effort, the center's public relations staff made a collection of commercial buildings into a monument.

Of the managers and architects who had worked on the Center during the planning stage, only Robertson was left. Once the buildings were designed, the architects, except for Corbett, worked on the 1939 New York World's Fair, on which they had been active for two or three years. During the war, Harrison joined Nelson Rockefeller at the State Department where they coordinated inter-American affairs. Reinhard & Hofmeister built factories for military productions, Todd & Brown built and managed a huge ordnance plant in Indiana.

When planning for peacetime became possible again, the management had to deal specifically with the problems of leases that would soon expire, and the competition to be expected from new buildings when civilian construction began. The Esso lease, in particular, would be important.

Esso needed more space and would commission a building outside the Center if it did not get the room it needed in the Center. If such a "family" tenant moved, others might also. With the buildings filled to capacity, the only solution was that of expanding the Center itself to provide a home for Esso.[137] John D. Rockefeller Jr. owned or controlled land directly north of the private street, and by July 19, 1944 had approved the idea of erecting a building for Esso on this land. This put an end forever to any chance of extending the private street northward.

At first, the Center's board of directors and Hugh Robertson thought of a sixteen-story building on Rockefeller property. It would cost $2,000,000.

In March of 1945 Robertson informed the board of directors that in order to provide the space needed for profitable operation, the new Esso building would have to be thirty stories high. He planned to obtain the air rights over property to the east and west, which would make a larger tower practicable. The elevators already planned for a thin tower could serve a wider tower, and the Center would rent out offices in the extra space. Esso approved plans which Robert Carson and Earl Lundin (now the Rockefeller Center architects) drew up in March [57] for the first fully air-conditioned office building in New York City.

56. Rockefeller Plaza (private street), looking north from 48th Street. Left: Eastern Air Lines Building. Photographed July 1945.
(*Courtesy Rockefeller Center, Inc.*)

It is simple—a limestone-faced base and tower on a T-shaped plot with vertical accents continuing the form of the Eastern Air Lines Building in the original Center. The low base conforms to the existing building heights on 51st and 52nd Streets, and from these streets it is hard to see the tower which does not, then, alter their character. But the tall slab provides a strong terminal accent to the view north along the private street, and changes the visual configuration of the Center.

The predominant force of the original group of buildings had been that of three parallel lines running from east to west. A person standing on the side streets or on Fifth Avenue would see rows of buildings which might, for all he knew, extend straight to the Hudson River. Only in the plaza area would he be able to extend his view sidewards, but even there the most noticeable walls were those which formed part of the Center's east-west building line. The houses on 51st Street facing the private street were too low to attract the eye or form a terminus to a complex of towers [56]. But the Esso Building was emphatic enough to pull the Center visually

57. Rockefeller Plaza (private street), looking north from 48th Street. Left: Eastern Air Lines Building. At north end: Esso (Warner Communications) Building. Photographed July 1948. (*Courtesy Rockefeller Center, Inc.*)

toward the north and form a north-south axis. It is particularly strong because it extends farther north than the original three building rows [57]. A building outside the Center on 48th Street terminates the view at the south, but being just fourteen stories high and undistinguished in design, it is barely able to stand up to the job [58]. The northern boundary fixed the visual limits of the Center in that direction; anything built north of the Esso Building could not be coordinated visually with the original Center.

John D. Rockefeller Jr. approved successive increased budgets which grew in 1948 to almost six times the original estimates of 1944. The price included land worth about half a million dollars, a pedestrian passage underground which connected this building with the others of the Center, and the effects of postwar inflation.

The Center's financial situation allowed it to retire the mortgage with the Metropolitan Life Insurance Company on June 30, 1950. The mortgage had been made for $65,000,000 at 5 per cent in 1931, but Rockefeller Center had borrowed only about $45,000,000, partly because it had been able to effect many economies in planning the later buildings and purchasing materials during the Depression. But the Center's worries were not over.[138]

First, there was the matter of air-conditioning. Tenants were demanding it, and some, including Sinclair Oil, would not renew leases partly on that account. Air-conditioning would have to be installed sooner or later—sooner, preferably, to prevent tenants from moving to the new air-conditioned office buildings then going up in Midtown. But air-conditioning

58. Rockefeller Plaza (private street), looking south from 51st Street, with crowds waiting to see Christmas show at Radio City Music Hall. Photographed December 1961.
(*Courtesy Rockefeller Center, Inc.*)

would entail a large capital expenditure. Could Rockefeller Center, Inc. amortize the capital investment in air-conditioning by 1962 when the term of the Columbia lease was up? It could not. Would Columbia grant some concessions to the Rockefeller interests in exchange for having the modernization work done? It would be to Columbia's advantage, too, for if Columbia did not cooperate, Rockefeller might well decide not to air-condition the buildings, and decide not to renew his ground lease after its expiration date in 1962. He had, in fact, been thinking those very thoughts. Existing leases, and new leases terminating in 1963, might protect his own income until he turned the buildings over to Columbia. If the University then wanted to revive the Center's prestige and increase its tenancy, Columbia would have to bear the entire expense of air-conditioning the buildings. And getting tenants back into a shopworn Center would not be easy even then.

Another problem was the threat posed by television to the theaters and to radio broadcasting. Television would inevitably reduce the number of people who wanted to pay for movies and stage shows. The Center Theater had lost an average of $440,000 per year even before television became an active threat to its box-office receipts.

Adding to the Center's difficulties was the fact that other building owners had approached NBC and RCA, in hopes that these two growing corporations would move to new premises outside the Center. These firms and others, including Sinclair Oil, needed more space, which was not easy to find in the fully-rented Center. They needed different kinds of space, too —more television studios, for instance. If these firms moved, they would change the entire character of the development, and even the famous names of Radio City, or RCA Building, would be gone. Could the Center Theater be converted into permanent television studios? Not easily, bécause of the enormous investment required for conversion work, another investment which could not be amortized by the time the ground lease expired in 1962.

The problems were deferred temporarily after hostilities broke out in Korea during the summer of 1950. Technological production was diverted from such peacetime items as air-conditioning machinery to war-related products. Protracted construction of other owners' new buildings which were designed to include air-conditioning, gave the Center some time in which to work out ways to keep current tenants. Nevertheless, this was only a brief reprieve.

A partial answer to the air-conditioning problem came when Columbia agreed in 1951 to reimburse Rockefeller Center, Inc. for the unamortized balance of the cost of air-conditioning the RCA Building if Rockefeller Center, Inc. did not renew its lease in 1962.[139] RCA and NBC were also able to expand, if only for three years, into the Center Theater which was used for broadcasting space. For longer term use, the theater would have needed modifications which could not be amortized, and in 1954 it was torn down.

The theater came down because in early

1953, the U.S. Rubber Company, one of the Center's major tenants, wanted to use its space. For this firm, Harrison and Max Abramovitz (his partner since the immediate prewar period) designed an air-conditioned addition to the western end of the original U.S. Rubber Company Building [59] The form of the addition was determined by the need to provide enough marketable office space on an interior plot in a block where some of the flexibility in height and shape had been pre-empted by earlier buildings. The logical but undistinguished result is a slab on a base which has some two-story exhibition space rising from street level, a building that echoes its model, the Eastern Air Lines Building just beyond the garage to the east. The U.S. Rubber Company addition retained the limestone-clad exterior and restrained vertical articulation of the buildings designed during the first stage of construction.

In the meantime, Sinclair Oil moved out of the Center, to 600 Fifth Avenue, on the southeast corner of the Center's southern block [7]. The church of St. Nicholas had stood on the site until this office building replaced it in 1950–52, and the Reformed Protestant Church had not wanted to sell or lease the land. But church attendance in midtown Manhattan showed signs of declining permanently, and church resources could be applied to administrative and human expenses instead of to empty buildings. Massachusetts Mutual Life Insurance Company leased the church site in 1949, added three parcels on 49th Street leased from John D. Rockefeller Jr., and arranged to have its future L-shaped

building linked by an underground corridor to the Rockefeller Center concourse. 600 Fifth Avenue is a stone-faced, air-conditioned office building in a style which is simpler (and more monotonous) than the Center's style, but which does not clash with it. The Center, in fact, made its land available with the proviso that it could exercise some architectural control over the new building.[140] The Center's resident architects, Carson and Lundin, designed it. With a setback above the seventh story, it preserves the low roof line established by the four international buildings of the Center.

Unfortunate as it was for Rockefeller Center to lose an important tenant, Sinclair's move—and Esso's—freed other space in the Center for exigent tenants such as RCA and NBC. The Center did not lose as many tenants as it might have, although it lost a handsome theater and some welcome light and air on the theater site. These developments made the Rockefellers view the future of the Center with greater optimism, and in the summer of 1953, they concluded a mutually beneficial agreement with Columbia University.

Under its terms, Columbia bought for about $5,500,000 the western part of the Center's site which had not formed part of the original leasehold; Underel had bought it originally, and when Underel merged with Rockefeller Center, Inc. in 1951, the land passed to the Center proper. On the former Underel parcels rose the U.S. Rubber Company Building, the RCA Building West, and the former RKO (renamed the Americas and then the Amax) Building. The sale of this land meant that Columbia owned the land under the entire Center in the three original blocks, except for a small lot on the corner of 50th Street. On the day of the sale, Rockefeller Center, Inc. simply leased the land back and Columbia agreed to extend the lease on the entire property until September 30, 1973 in exchange for an additional $200,000 in rent each year.[141] The extra eleven years allowed the Center a longer period of time in which to amortize improvements to its buildings. To spread the cost around, the Center's management got the tenants to share some of the air-conditioning costs in exchange for extensions of their leases; this plan proved less expensive to the tenants than the costs of moving and of paying the high rents in new buildings.

When the air-conditioning work was done, the offices were fitted with recessed or surface-mounted fluorescent light fixtures which provide the increased amounts of cooler lighting customary in postwar offices. Companies could then expand to formerly dark and stuffy spaces in their own offices rather than to new space outside Rockefeller Center. The ducts for conditioned air and the light fixtures occupy space under the original ceilings, of course, and are hidden by lower, secondary ceilings. These installations can cut the height of a room substantially. The Center's engineers ordered special flatter but costlier ducts which allowed office ceiling heights to reach respectable dimensions. They had to remove other space from the rent rolls in order to install other machinery. Fortunately, the RCA Building had a never-used boiler

59. Left to right: Eastern Air Lines Building, RCA Showroom, 1947, Tom Lee, designer; Garage entrance; U.S. Rubber Company (Uniroyal) Building Addition. Photographed December 1955.
(*Courtesy Rockefeller Center, Inc., Uniroyal Company*)

110 *ROCKEFELLER CENTER*

room and a shaft extending upward from it which could house the air-conditioning equipment for that building. Because this and other buildings at the Center had been "overdesigned" with extra steel and wiring when costs were low in the 1930s, conversions could be made at lower cost in the postwar years.[142]

When Rockefeller Center and Columbia signed their 1953 agreement, they assured the continuation of the Rockefeller presence in Midtown. On this basis, Laurance Rockefeller who was then Chairman of the Board of Rockefeller Center, Inc., and Gustav Eyssell, President of Rockefeller Center, Inc., decided to enlarge the Center, this time across Sixth Avenue between 50th and 51st Streets.[143] They owned some land there already, bought more on July 31, 1953, cleared existing leases and bought still more later, often through nominee corporations one of which was named after someone's dog. Even before they purchased all the parcels, Eyssell had been in touch with prospective tenants for a building. For a while, the Center considered building a Ford automobile showroom on the property.[144] Then NBC

advised Eyssell that it could not remain any longer in the Center Theater because it needed six expensive new studios capable of handling sophisticated color television broadcasting. Perhaps NBC could work out some tax concession with city agencies responsible for keeping businesses in town. Perhaps NBC could join another major tenant in a new building, and the studio costs could be offset by the growing rents obtainable from office rentals.

The perfect building partner was close at hand. Time Inc. had been asking for more room in 1953. Their expansion program outlined in early 1954 showed that the corporation would outgrow the available area in the Center. They wanted space in a single building, too. Their management told Eyssell that they were considering moving to the suburbs or to a city in the middle west, but that they also held an option on 90,000 square feet of property at First Avenue and 48th Street, just north of the United Nations headquarters.[145] Time Inc. wanted to stay in or near the Center but would not do so without having a more commodious building of its own. That is exactly what the Center hoped to provide—a building on Sixth Avenue with NBC-TV studios at the base and Time Inc. in tower floors above.

Harrison & Abramovitz and NBC-TV's engineers worked during late 1953 and early 1954 on a suitable plan for the NBC-Time building, and with Rockefeller Center's management even produced a fifteen-minute film showing the plans and elevations and special facilities that such a building would offer. The project col-

60. Rockefeller Center, air view looking northwest, showing second Time & Life Building (center, background); 600 Fifth Avenue (left center); Hilton Hotel (top right). Between second Time & Life Building and Hilton Hotel, left to right: Equitable Building, Sperry-Rand Building, J. C. Penney Building (nearing completion), CBS Building (under construction). Photographed June 1964.
(Courtesy Rockefeller Center, Inc.)

lapsed sometime after October 1955, apparently because David Sarnoff of the broadcasting corporation would not agree to it. He had other sites in mind for cheaper, low-rise studios, although in June 1958, RCA agreed to renew its office tenancy at the Center until 1982.[146]

This left Time Inc. as the sole prospective major tenant. The suburban proposal may again have appealed to some of its executives, since building and land costs out of town would be lower than the rents of $7 per square foot which tenants of new air-conditioned midtown offices had to pay in the mid-1950s.[147] But to Rockefeller Center, Inc., losing this famous and still-growing tenant would have been almost as serious as losing Esso or the radio group. It would have been bad enough if Time Inc. moved to a suburb, but far worse if it moved elsewhere in the city. It might actually build its own building on Park Avenue which Lever House and the Seagram Building had just made an important office-building street. Rumor had it that Time Inc. owned the Marguery Apartment Hotel on Park Avenue between 47th and 48th Streets.[148]

If Time Inc. moved to a new building on Rockefeller property, the publisher's prestige and the income from his firm could be retained at the Center. If the property were directly opposite the Center, Time's building could be included in an extended Center. It could even be provided with an underground corridor link to the concourse and subway station; at the same time the owner of Saks Fifth Avenue at the Center's eastern end had asked Harrison to explore the idea of an underground extension there.[149]

The solution to Time Inc.'s and the Center's problems lay in the formation of a new corporation in 1956, Rock-Time, Inc., in which Rockefeller interests owned 55 per cent of the stock and Time Inc. the rest. The publishers could share in the income from outside tenants in the building and from rent paid by Time Inc. subsidiaries. They could also remain in the area where they had flourished for twenty years and where they had been on good terms with the landlords.

Until Time Inc. and Rockefeller Center moved across Sixth Avenue, no noteworthy building had been constructed on the western side of the street for about thirty years. In anticipation of it, the Sixth Avenue Association, a businessmen's group, succeeded in 1945 in getting the thoroughfare's name changed to the Avenue of the Americas (a mouthful of words which most New Yorkers do not use) to remove the dreary connotations of the traditional name. Nevertheless, while land parcels changed hands and appreciated in value, builders did not come. The new subway line had not tempted them. The crosstown 49th-50th Street bus hadn't either. The advice of an architects' advisory committee for the Avenue which began work in 1950 had little effect.[150] Each developer seemed to be waiting for someone else to take the risk of moving to the seedy side of the street. Only famous corporations such as Rockefeller Center or Time Inc. seemed to be logical leaders. Now they were both willing to take the chance.

Harrison & Abramovitz submitted new proposals for the Time & Life Building. They designed a broad slab rising forty-eight stories from the pavement with an eight-story wraparound building on the west and north [60]. The northern wing reached eastward to the Sixth Avenue building line, keeping the slab away from neighbors to the north and thus within the visual boundaries of the old Rockefeller Center. To let the Center build a slab as tall as this one while conforming to the requirements of the Zoning Resolution, Westprop, Inc., a Center subsidiary, had to buy the Roxy Theater immediately to the west, for its air rights. This also guaranteed that no rival tower could abut the new building in the future. In addition to the height gained from these air rights, the slab concentrated the tower rights of its own property, occupying only about

61. Sixth Avenue (Avenue of the Americas), looking northwest. Left to right: McGraw-Hill Building and plaza; Exxon Building and plaza; second Time & Life Building; Equitable Building. (*Courtesy Rockefeller Center, Inc.*)

three-quarters of its plot and leaving the rest for a plaza on the avenue and a broad pavement on 50th Street. [61, 93]

Time Inc. occupied twenty-one of the floors and Rock-Time rented out the rest after being told by any number of sages that the location would not attract high quality tenants. The roster of early tenants recalls the Rockefeller-related groups that had taken much of the non-RCA space in the RCA Building when that building was new: the Rockefeller Foundation, Shell Oil, Standard Oil subsidiaries. There were some new tenants as well.[151]

In connection with the acquisition of the Roxy site, Rockefeller Center entered into a partnership called the Rock-Uris Corporation, in which the development firm of Webb & Knapp and the Uris Buildings Corporation joined the Center for the purpose of erecting a hotel called the Zeckendorf immediately west of the Esso Building.[152] Hotel plans had figured in the earliest schemes for the Columbia property. The Center's directors and its public relations staff would have been glad to remedy the famous flaw, that one could do everything but sleep in the Rockefeller "city within a city." But Webb & Knapp experienced financial difficulties, the partners found that the site was too valuable as office space to be used for a hotel, and a Rockefeller Center tenant appeared—Sperry Rand—who rented enough office space to make the builders give the structure its name. The resulting building was at first intended to resemble the other limestone-clad buildings east of Sixth Avenue,[153] but once its future as a spec-

ulative office tower was determined, it was given the glass and precast concrete-clad steel strip form that we see today [1, 60].[154] As a result, it does not appear to be part of Rockefeller Center, even though it has an underground link to the shopping concourse. In view of the mediocre architectural quality of this bulky forty-three-story building, it is probably a good thing for the Center's reputation that the Sperry-Rand Building seems to be someone else's property. A small courtyard on Sixth Avenue, set between two projecting wings and leading to the central entrance, is the only hint of street-level amenity.

The hotel project was relocated two blocks to the northwest, where the Rock-Hil-Uris Corporation (including the Hilton Hotel chain) erected the "New York Hilton at [not in] Rockefeller Center [1, 60]." [155] The name represented an attempt to connect the two that could never be successful since two blocks, now containing more huge office towers, separate the Hilton from the Time & Life Building. The hotel is not even tied to the Center underground—although the intervening office buildings are—because the subway tunnel in crossing 53rd Street blocks the concourse extension just south of the Hilton.

There was no apparent need for the Center to grow further, and it could certainly not expand immediately to the north of the Time & Life Building because Equitable Life Assurance Society owned the property and built its own office tower there (1961). Plots on Sixth

Avenue north of the RKO (Amax) Building were filled in a building boom inspired by the construction of the Time & Life Building. CBS and ABC, the broadcasting rivals to NBC, had headquarters there, and across Sixth Avenue even Joseph Urban's Ziegfeld Theater yielded to an office building which incorporated a gaudy cinema to replace it. Construction between Fifth and Sixth Avenues was hindered by the zoning regulations governing land use, by the fact that other interests held the land, and by the visual stop that the Esso Building had given to the Center. Buildings to the south and east, while not all new, gave no sign of business failure.

The Center seemed to have been completed in a sort of Big Dipper shape when seen from the air. As if to put a seal on the development, Nelson Rockefeller's son Steven suggested erecting a monument to his grandfather,[156] and in 1962 Harrison & Abramovitz installed a granite slab with a portrait and Rockefeller's credo at the foot of the "Channel Gardens" overlooking the sunken plaza.

Not long afterward, however, the seal opened.

X.

Recent Expansion, 1960–1974

"It should nevertheless haunt the Rockefellers that John D. Jr. once did set such
a pace with a fairy tale in stone, at once
so romantic and so solid."

Douglas Haskell, *Architectural
Forum* CXXIV, January 1966, p. 46.

Rockefeller Center was not finished in 1962, as we know. It added three more buildings by 1974 and the promise of a rooftop addition between the RCA and the RCA Building West. How did this happen?

Although the Center's management gave no sign of trying to expand the Center toward the west, it joined Time Inc. in acquiring small parcels of land south of the Time & Life Building. This was only protective acquisition for a while, preventing others from construct- ing anything substantial on the streets west of the original Center. But at lunch one day in about 1963, an Esso official told Gustav Eyssell, who had become the President of Rockefeller Center, Inc., that Esso (later renamed Exxon) needed more space than the 850,000 square feet that it already occupied in the Esso and other Center buildings.[157] This was a period of business expansion when other firms grew out of their original headquarters. The rental future for new office space seemed as bright as it had to optimists before the 1929 crash. The rental office had requests for two million additional square feet of space from its own tenants alone. Eyssell thought that it made sense to consider erecting a building for Exxon, which might otherwise leave town with unpleasant consequences for the Center and for the employment and tax pictures in the city. Nelson Rockefeller, elected Governor of New York State in 1958, would be alert to the consequences, and so would the Center's management which belonged to civic development associations. The joint venture with Time Inc. had come out well; this one might, too.

The Center's and Exxon's officials conceived a larger project than one new building. In concert with Harrison & Abramovitz—especially with Harrison and Michael Harris, a younger partner in that firm—they envisioned at least two buildings. Exxon's would be placed at the western end of a plaza, and another building on the block to the south of it would stand beside a smaller plaza, closer to Sixth Avenue. Soon afterward, they planned three new buildings; there is one on each of the three blocks south of Time & Life's, forming a coordinated architectural complex with the old Center across the avenue. The Time & Life Building is a slab with a wrap-around wing extending to the north and east [93], so the southernmost of the new buildings is a slab with a wrap-around wing to the south and east. Between these parentheses, the new Exxon Building at the north and another office building at the south are slabs set far back from the building line, forming a broad plaza between the Time & Life and the southern brackets [61, 63].

Because Exxon's proposed building was to be part of a group of four buildings, the owners discreetly purchased land to make the remaining buildings possible. For the building south of Exxon's, an eminent tenant was found—the McGraw-Hill Publishing Company. Its management was impressed with the economies offered by a single location for its widely dispersed subsidiaries. A generation earlier, Raymond Hood had designed a memorable blue-green office building for McGraw-Hill at 42nd Street near Eighth Avenue [24], but this no longer sufficed for the expanded corporation. Besides, its neighborhood was growing less safe and agreeable, with derelict people and derelict buildings in the immediate vicinity. McGraw-Hill undertook the move to a sleek new corporate headquarters at Rockefeller Center, abandoning one of the city's most impressive early modern buildings for a more standardized but perhaps more efficient home [61].

Land purchases continued for the southern block where the Celanese Building was built and named for its prime tenant (which is no longer an equity partner in the building as its three northern neighbors are) [63]. This forty-five-story building was a necessary component in the plan for four buildings from Time & Life to the south, and it shares with its two northern brothers a monotonous design of stone-clad piers alternating with vertical window strips.

The overall scheme was inspired by a number of factors. Harrison & Abramovitz had long been interested in formal and classicistic planning principles. Abramovitz is said to have favored plazas and arcades along Sixth Avenue for some time. They had recently supervised the design of Lincoln Center for the Performing Arts [10] where the three major buildings are disposed around an open square in an arrangement strongly reminiscent of Michelangelo's Campidoglio in Rome. Perhaps more to the point, the old Center had been given life by its central, axial plaza; a new plaza might lend glamour and brio to the Center's extension across Sixth Avenue.

A plaza would have another advantage for the Center. It would counteract the impenetrable effect of the old Center's Sixth Avenue façades. The original Center had been designed with an approach from Fifth Avenue in mind; the planners had wanted to attract fashionable shoppers from the east side. The elevated railway which only came down after most of the buildings were up seems to have deterred

the architects and managers from creating any open space on Sixth Avenue. They were not interested in attracting anyone but theater patrons from the streets west of Sixth Avenue, for beyond the theater district lay the "Hell's Kitchen" slum (now called the Clinton area). It had been profitable to build office towers up to the limits of cost-effectiveness, particularly since the buildings rose on Underel's property. Most tenants facing the wide avenue would be above the line of sight leading to the ugly low buildings directly opposite; avenue-front offices with views of the Hudson River might be marketable if not prizewinning premises. As a result of all these factors, the old Center's western buildings are cliffs which enclose the development [62]. Now the Center proposed to add more buildings, which they wanted to have identified with the older core group. The deep plaza might give the eye a push across the street, correcting the terminal effect of the eastern wall of the avenue. Then, by providing a complementary bracket for that of the Time & Life Building, even that uncoordinated building might be related to the rest of the Center.

The great open plazas would give to the row of new towers something of the formal graciousness which might suit an Avenue of the Americas. Most of the other recent buildings on Sixth Avenue

62. Left to right: RKO (Amax) Building, Radio City Music Hall, RCA Building West, U.S. Rubber Company (Uniroyal) Buildings. Willy Brandt addressing audience from Americas Plaza of second Time & Life Building, October 1961. (*Courtesy Rockefeller Center, Inc.*)

63. Sixth Avenue (Avenue of the Americas), looking southwest from 51st Street. Right to left: second Time & Life Building, Exxon Building, McGraw-Hill Building, Celanese Building. Photographed 1974.
(*H. W. Janson*)

have cramped or awkward or formless plazas, if they have any at all (the original Center's Sixth Avenue front buildings had none). They are simply paved and provided with a few planting troughs or mediocre sculptures for the sake of minimal public relations. A powerful army of tall but unimpressive soldiers marches northward from 46th Street, its ranks broken only by the bracketed open space between the second Time & Life and Celanese Buildings [61, 63] The new Center's open space has been varied and coordinated, if rather academically. There are framing wings at the north and south, a sunken plaza containing a sundial and models of planets around a circular pool in front of the McGraw-Hill Building [61, 125] a raised pool and sitting area in front

of Exxon's tower [61]. The latter has a light-hued lobby [95] purposely varied by vast expanse of oppressively heavy purplish-red terrazzo in the McGraw-Hill lobby. Trees in east-west rows grow from planting beds on all four plazas, and the two terminal plazas have large sculptures placed upon them.

The 1961 amendment to the city's Zoning Resolution of 1916 stimulated plaza construction in selected districts. It tried to rid New York of hulking structures erected right up to the building lines with building silhouettes stepping back like the partial products of a company treasurer's multiplication problem. The amendment was therefore designed to regulate ground coverage and total height rather than bulk alone. Above a certain limit, a builder

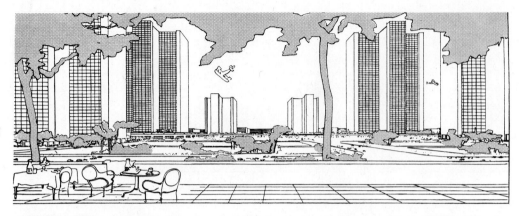

64. View from a terrace restaurant into the Ville Contemporaine, project of 1921–22. Le Corbusier, architect.
(*Oeuvre complète*)

could construct a few more floors if he provided plaza space or other street-level amenities. These provisions made compact building perimeters desirable and the use of air-conditioning and fluorescent lighting made buildings without setbacks practicable. The men who had been young when Le Corbusier designed his slab and cross-shaped towers on broad open spaces [64] were now the men who received the commissions for the new office buildings. They had all followed the fame and fortunes of the plazas and slender slabs at Skidmore, Owings & Merrill's Lever House and Mies van der Rohe's and Philip Johnson's Seagram Building. The city was soon home to dozens of tall rectilinear prisms with broad pavements beside them.

Within a few years, however, it was possible to see the adverse effects of the 1961 amendment.[158] The open spaces around the new office towers were windy and unprotected, often bare and uninviting. Few of them had intelligible shapes, and they were seldom coordinated. They were rarely aligned to provide mid-block pedestrian passages. And they led either to lobbies containing only elevators or to the formal offices of banks and airlines which were among the few tenants who could afford ground floor rents in these buildings. There were no longer the small restaurants, second-hand book stores, and specialty shops which offered useful facilities and provided human scale and human activity amid the gigantic skyscrapers.

These faults were apparent to laymen, and stood out with special clarity to city planners and others who had been reading such recent books as Jane Jacobs' *The Death and Life of Great American Cities,* Kevin Lynch's *The Image of the City,* or Gordon Cullen's *Townscape.* These authors, as well as many others, wrote about human interaction and vibrant street life on small blocks, about focal orientation points in a city, about visual variety and sensitivity in design. These writers favored such things as the original Center's private street which cut up long cross town blocks, the sunken plaza with its open space suited to varied simultaneous activities, the color given by flags, skaters, plants and shopfronts. People of like mind could see that the original Center was a focal area for the city, and that this was due to planning resulting in a mix of offices, shops, restaurants, exhibition rooms, recreation spaces, auxiliary streets, wide pavements, planting beds and special events. City planning theorists made a principle out of the successful results of the original *ad hoc* business-oriented procedure.

The Center's planners, too, thought that they understood the original complex. They would follow the economic and zoning law analysis which their predecessors had used a generation earlier. But the conditions to which they applied the procedure were different, and the results could not be the same.

The site was already attractive, unlike the decaying three blocks of old. People would not have to be lured to the new building sites as they had to be in 1930. Substantial tenants were already at hand, and could be given good buildings, but not necessarily outstanding ones. Since some key tenants were also equity partners, their architectural taste would have to be considered, dispersing the original control over decision-making. Although Shelton Fisher, then President of McGraw-Hill, is very much interested in architec-

ture, and while the Rockefeller sons inherited their father's love of building, no single person during the planning in the 1960s seems to have shared the father's passionate interest in the refinements of architecture or his consuming desire to protect his good name by building well. (An architect who knew them all observed that while Rockefeller understood architecture from the inside outward, from the plans, his sons often approached architecture from the outside inward, by looking at models.) [159] Since technology had made deep buildings as comfortable as those with 27'6" office depths, Wallace Harrison's firm could at last build the tall slabs which he had not been able to introduce at the original Center, even though this technological and architectural power might lead to an austere result. The planners would, of course, make the plazas in front of the new buildings as attractive as their own taste and maintenance budgets allowed. Symmetrical rows of potted trees, axial pools, lines of benches, sculpture—these would add color and disciplined beauty to the city.

But disciplined beauty was not exactly what critics of the Center's new additions had in mind. Nor did it appeal to the young members of the Urban Design Group a dynamic office within the City Planning Commission. Its staff was interested in the life and character of entire neighborhoods, not just in a few components, and in the needs of all classes of people, not just of corporate directors erecting corporate headquarters. The planners paid attention to the economic health of the run-down luncheonette as well as to the well-being of the giant corporations whose presence is vital to the city.

The Urban Design Group would have had little opportunity to influence men of an older generation who had other tastes in architecture and other perceptions of the city's and corporation's needs, if it were not for the fact that the Center's proposed buildings exceeded the maximum bulk permitted under the Zoning Resolution Amendment. The City Planning Commission could intervene to see that the city would get appropriate public benefits if a variance were granted to the corporations. The problem was, of course, to reconcile the two parties' perceptions of what was beneficial.

The corporate planners anticipated no trouble in obtaining a zoning variance because they were providing plaza spaces of far greater variety and extent than were the owners of nearby buildings. They planned to have varied activities in them, relying on the Center's public relations office to organize folk dance performances, concerts, crafts and historical displays, even a sheep-shearing demonstration in order to make the Sixth Avenue open areas into the popular places that they have become. The planners left the pavement on the sides of the new buildings chastely bare to provide wide walkways and unimpeded access to the building lobbies (but provided the planting tubs when they saw that the crosstown streets needed more warmth and color). But the city seized the opportunity to add amenity to the entire blockfronts between the increasingly sterile Sixth Avenue and the increasingly seamy theater area be-

yond Seventh Avenue. In exchange for permission to exceed the permissible building limits, the city planners suggested that the Center incorporate a covered shopping arcade [65] and a theater into the triad of towers. They hoped that the construction of new and up-to-date theaters would stimulate the entertainment industry on the one hand; and box-office receipts on the other, improving the city's character and economy. To facilitate this construction and make it more attractive, they authorized a special theater zoning district where builders could receive permission to build extra rental floor area provided they included theaters.

At that point, the McGraw-Hill Building was supposed to have a sort of theater developed by one of its subsidiary firms— a modern planetarium in which patrons would not have to crane their necks to see the sky as they do at older planetaria. The planetarium dome would project upward into the building's sunken plaza from the presentation space below ground, and the dome would be visible from street level in order to excite the curiosity of passers-by. Later McGraw-Hill sold the planetarium company and replaced the planetarium entrance with its bookshop at the sunken plaza level [66]. McGraw-Hill and the Center were, however, stuck with the huge sub-basement planetarium space. They filled part of it with a smaller theater for a multi-screen slide show, approached by a tall anteroom accessible from the street level through a vestibule ingeniously designed by Rambusch Associates to resemble a cheerful subway train.

The Celanese Building was to be the

65. City Planning Commission, Urban Design Group, theoretical study for mid-block *galleria*, c. 1968.
(*Courtesy City Planning Commission, New York City*)

home of the theater which the city planners advocated. Robert Whitehead undertook to run it, and Mitchell-Giurgola Associates designed it in 1968.[160] But Whitehead could not obtain sufficient financing and Rockefeller Center's management was not eager to add another theater to the Center, for they had had exhausting problems finding attractions for the Center Theater, the Newsreel (now the Guild) in the Associated Press Building, and the Music Hall. Although a legitimate theater seating 1100 was different from a film-and-spectacle theater seating 6200, or a cinema seating 450, the management was no more eager to enter the theater business, even indirectly as landlords, than John D. Rockefeller Jr. had been after RKO left the Center with the theater burden in 1933. The Center's study of existing theaters showed that of about thirty theaters in the vicinity of the Center, fifteen were closed or turned to other uses. Their study of the costs involved in adding a theater to the office showed that the construction expenses would be immense, and entirely disproportionate to the return to be received from it. Building even more floors to offset the cost—and the city would have permitted the Center to do so—would still not have been cost-effective. Besides, the building had been substantially planned before the theater idea came up. In the end, the theater plans were abandoned, but they had caused long de-

lays. During the waiting time, construction costs rose dramatically. Companies who were unsure of the completion date did not rent space in the building. During the actual construction period, building industry strikes delayed the opening even further, and, in addition, it took nine months before the Center's management could dislodge a tenant on the site who wanted some sort of philosophical revenge upon the Rockefellers (though not, it seems, any of their money). By that time a business recession made fewer firms seek to expand in the now overabundant new office buildings. For a long time, there was plenty of space available for rent in the Celanese Building.

The Urban Design Group also proposed that the Center's new buildings incorporate covered shopping arcades running through their ground floors. The designers envisioned multi-level spaces with lively contrasts of shapes and spaces, with attractive small stores catering to a broad range of users [65]. In a period of business expansion there was even a possibility that tenants might be found for the shops and that their businesses might prosper despite the off-street location. (The city planners expected that small businesses unable to pay high avenue rents could be accommodated in the arcades.) The traf-fic and commerce in these arcades might stimulate the neighborhood and cater to the needs of people in the offices and those who frequented the theater district to the west. The opening of the Celanese Building's covered passage [67] was delayed because engineers had to overcome winds caused by down-draughts from the McGraw-Hill Building across the street. These might have been anticipated if the owners had cared originally about designing a passage to be a vital, intrinsic part of the building. The Center's owners were not, however, concerned at first with planning a neighborhood, because the nearby entertainment area had acquired a reputation as the home of criminals who might

66. Section through Sixth Avenue and McGraw-Hill Building and Plaza, showing traffic circulation system, as planned *c.* 1969–71.
(*Courtesy Rockefeller Center, Inc.*)

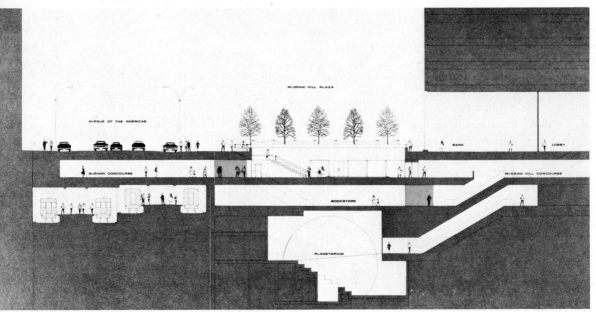

join the respectable citizens in the Center's arcades. Cafeterias inside the new buildings could serve about 60 per cent of the office tenants [161] who could also use the Center's existing restaurants, and the owners did not find it necessary to provide space for more than a few additional restaurants to replace the many small establishments demolished in the three blocks. Shopping arcades required a large initial expenditure, and their tenants might go out of business during periods of recession. Besides, the lobbies had already been planned. Inserting shopping arcades would mean redesigning the ground floors entirely, and probably the upper floors as well.

Rockefeller Center and its partners finally received permission to exceed the building limits by agreeing to purchase land for small block-through parks at the western ends of the Exxon and McGraw-Hill Buildings and for a covered shopping passage at the west end of the Celanese Building. These form staggered mid-block paths from 47th to 50th Streets.

The park behind the Exxon Building has seats that cannot be stolen easily, trees in tubs, and a waterfall [68]. Some of these ornamental features had been introduced by the landscape architecture firm of Zion & Breen at Samuel Paley Plaza.[162] This surprising little park in an elegant shopping street has plants framing the entrance which almost make one forget the buildings on three sides. Its waterfall at the far end draws the passerby into a pocket of space where an outdoor café adds to the charm of the potted trees and water. The cascade muffles street noises for those at the café tables. In contrast,

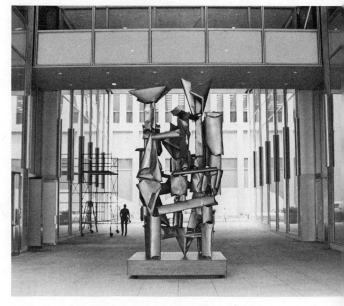

67. Celanese Building *galleria* with Ibram Lassaw sculpture, *Pantheon*. Photographed July 1974. (*Courtesy Rockefeller Center, Inc.*)

the Exxon park is a passageway as well as sitting space, so that it lacks focus. Informal design is welcome amid the formally-disposed buildings, but the park has no coherent shape. Its waterfall cannot hide street noises because it is adjacent and perpendicular to the street, not parallel to it. Its position suggests that it was placed there to be clearly visible as a sign of the builder's good will.

The McGraw-Hill minipark, however, is more successful [69]. Its shape is clearly rectangular, and it is lined with trees and hanging plants. Near the south end is a nearly circular tunnel cut into a wall which divides the park and gives the eye something attractive on which to focus. A waterfall covers the wall and purposely

68. "Minipark" west of Exxon Building. Photographed July 1974.
(*Courtesy Rockefeller Center, Inc.*)

misses pedestrians in the transparent tunnel. The arrangement must have been inspired by the waterfall and tunnel at the New York World's Fair of 1939, for which Wallace Harrison was an important designer. As soon as it opened, complete with snack bar, chairs, tables with striped umbrellas, and informally-arranged benches, the park became a busy place. People began to take the trouble to hunt for it, and increasing numbers of visitors asked friends to take their pictures in front of the waterfall tunnel. The furnishings, as well as the constant presence of guards and cleaning personnel, have made a popular public area of this pocket of space, even though it does not get much sunshine.

Perhaps designing really beautiful western additions initially promised no benefit to the Exxon and Celanese Building sponsors, beyond permission to build towers of the size they wanted. They might have known that open spaces would be used somehow in crowded New York, unless the spaces were so unpleasant as to actively discourage people, as some austere concrete platforms do. Moreover, people might steal attractive fittings, just as someone stole decorations from McGraw-Hill's sunken plaza. Corporate executives have often been less inclined than city planners to believe that busy, delightful public spaces summon virtuous users who make the areas unprofitable to criminals and inhospitable to vagrants. Businessmen may think of Bryant Park, a few blocks south at 42nd Street where such undesirable people annoy workers and students. Rockefeller Center and its partners might

have claimed that Paley Plaza between Fifth and Madison Avenues is safely distant from the haunts of the unwelcome guests, so that Paley Plaza's attractive visitors would not forcast equally attractive people in parks near Seventh Avenue. To help overcome this problem, the public relations department organized activities in the parks, thus drawing so many office workers and other welcome visitors that most disagreeable guests did, in fact, find the parks inhospitable. The original sunken plaza is king of New York's open commercial spaces, the Sixth Avenue plazas intend to be the heirs apparent, and the small stepchildren at the west are being given decent clothes and cleanliness.

With the opening of the three new buildings, there seemed to be even less room for expansion than there had been in the 1960s. There was an oversupply of office space in New York City in 1974,

69. "Minipark" west of McGraw-Hill Building. Photographed 1974.
(*H. W. Janson*)

and while optimists predicted that the offices would be filled within a few years, few developers were making detailed plans for new speculative office buildings in Midtown. Rockefeller Center cannot easily expand to the north because of existing new buildings and because of the large land assemblies made by others. Expansion toward the south beyond 48th Street is theoretically possible, although not yet under active consideration.

Expansion of the concourse toward the east has been the subject of intermittent discussion at Rockefeller Center for about twenty years. Their architects and engineers have conducted feasibility studies of underground concourse connections between the Center's concourse, Saks Fifth Avenue (49th-50th Street) and the Olympic Tower residential-retail-office building, both of these controlled by non-Rockefeller interests. It might be possible eventually to extend the underground link all the way to Grand Central Terminal, because there already exists an accessible pedestrian underground passage reaching to the station from 48th Street and Madison Avenue, a block and a half from Saks, although it is not now suitable for large-scale use. The expansion foreseen in these studies would give to tenants and to the public additional protected underground circulation space, freeing the sidewalks above from their congestion, and would make the Sixth Avenue subway line more apparently and comfortably accessible to travelers on the east side of Fifth Avenue. Such connections would enhance the prestige and convenience of both the Center and the

other commercial properties. It would tie a first-quality department store to the Center, fulfilling early plans for Metropolitan Square which included a department store. Saks has printed advertisements mentioning its location at Rockefeller Center; perhaps its owners will make the link official in the future. On the other hand, there are people who wonder aloud how long a relatively low building like Saks can afford to be the sole occupant of its enormously valuable site. Will it ever be replaced, or have a tower engineered above it?

Expansion toward the west is possible, and Rockefeller Center, Inc. has interests in several parcels of land to the west of its four grouped skyscrapers. Although development there may be affected by the provisions of the special theater zoning district where the city planners may continue to encourage the theater construction in which the Center has no interest, city planners may not press for theaters if alternative beneficial uses are proposed. The Center might, for instance, build apartment houses facing their small parks and additional green space; the apartments might be insulated from the noise of Seventh Avenue. Corporations could rent or buy these high-rent apartments for their officers and other wealthy people could occupy the apartments. If the residential units were erected, Rockefeller Center would fulfill plans abandoned almost a half century earlier. The housing might stimulate the growth of shopping facilities in the area, perhaps including some with the lively air of Ghirardelli Square in San Francisco, per-

haps including some sort of shopping area in a remodeled Radio City Music Hall, or on its site. Office buildings could also be built, since in 1974 the Center's officers correctly predicted a need for additional new business premises by the end of 1976.[163]

At the present time, Rockefeller Center includes twenty-one buildings with 17,000,000 square feet of rentable area—mainly office space with broadcasting studios and over two hundred shops and service establishments. A quarter of the total grade level area is open to broader sidewalks, parks, and plazas. There are almost two miles of underground passageways, and there are still a few roofs with plants growing on them.

Columbia University now owns the land under only 6,500,000 of the Center's 17,000,000 rentable square feet, although it owns about half the developed land. At the end of September 1973 the last extension of the original lease terminated, and a re-negotiated lease was drawn up providing a significant increase in rent and a $4,000,000 contribution to Columbia's endowment fund. For twenty-one years from October 1, 1973, the Center will pay a rent rising in $200,000 stages from $9,000,000 to $13,000,000. Since private universities are faced with enormous costs and often enormous potential deficits, the commercial Center will come to the aid of culture and learning as Otto Kahn and Mayor LaGuardia and John D. Rockefeller Jr. expected it would.

XI.

The RCA Building

"It is rational, logically conceived, biologically normal, harmonious in its four functional elements: halls for the entrance and division of crowds, grouped shafts for vertical circulation (elevators), corridors (internal streets), regular offices.
Already the skyscraper is large enough to have made it possible to spend the money necessary to do a good job."

Le Corbusier, *When the Cathedrals Were White*.

"To create luxury with simplicity, that is the modern problem, and Radio City has solved it."

Fernand Léger, "The New Realism," address given at Museum of Modern Art, New York, printed in *Art Front* December 1935.

Documents in the Rockefeller Center archives contain considerable information about the design procedure for individual buildings with the overall development.[164] Some of the structures do not require detailed discussion, although they may incorporate admirable features. The low French and British Buildings, for instance, maintained an older, smaller Fifth Avenue scale which has now become a precious asset in Manhattan's overwhelmingly large streetscape [70]. As we have seen, their example influenced the design of the low Italian and International North buildings, as well as 600 Fifth Avenue. The Esso (now Warner Communications)

70. Fifth Avenue, looking south from 51st Street. Right to left: International Building North, Palazzo d'Italia, British Building, La Maison Française, Goelet Building, 600 Fifth Avenue. Photographed September 1955.
(*Courtesy Rockefeller Center, Inc.*)

Building includes a well lighted lobby which serves as a covered pedestrian passage in mid-block, faintly echoing the unfulfilled plan for extending the private street. The U.S. Rubber (now Uniroyal) Building added what was in 1940 a welcome expanse of clear glass and uncluttered surfaces to Sixth Avenue [54] when the street's building signs, fire escapes and crumbling coarse ornaments jostled for prominence on sooty walls [16].

Other buildings at the Center deserve closer examination, either because of their intrinsic quality or because features of their design illustrate the problems that commercial planners faced and the architectural means taken to resolve them.[165]

First, of course, comes the seventy-story RCA Building [33, 47, 71-81], the most distinctive in shape and the most generous in quality—if one can forgive its enormous east-west extent which casts a shadow on more than one block to the north [5]. The linchpin in the entire Rockefeller Center scheme, it met demands for studio, shop, circulation and office space presented by the radio group, the original tenants. It is roughly rectangular in plan,[166] rising to a height of 850 feet, with a maximum width of 190 feet [72] leaving wider than usual sidewalks. The east-west length was determined by several factors. Some building had to reach eastward to the private street which no one wanted to set farther to the west, apparently fearing that the interior of the Center would look too far distant from Fifth Avenue. Something had to reach to Sixth Avenue, to make profitable use of the land which Rockefeller's Underel Holding Corporation had bought there. That "something" could have been a separate building, but there were practical reasons for making it a single structure in three parts [72]. NBC's windowless broadcasting studios took up a great deal of horizontal space on several stories. The studio area could best be set in the center

of the block, the least desirable site for office premises. To east and west, the plots fronting on the plaza and on Sixth Avenue could be given over to high quality office areas. The western offices would be built only on Underel land. The office buildings [167] had room for a spacious lobby at the east [80] and a small lobby at the west end. There was also room for wide, eastern corridors at the busier east end for entering office tenants, while studio visitors could also be admitted to NBC's own mezzanine level lobby [77, 78] through doors at the sides of the building. Above the studios no offices could be constructed because they require piers set at close intervals while studio spaces must be clear, but enough office space to compensate could be designed at the eastern end, creating a commercial building with about 2,700,000 square feet of gross floor area, more than any other in the world at that time—perhaps a dubious distinction!

The office space was designed to a high standard [73]. Purely speculative office buildings of the 1920s building boom years were often built to cover a large percentage of the ground, and designed with wide rather than narrow floors in order to have maximum rentable space with the fewest possible elevators and shafts. The floor area thus obtained was

71. View looking west from 7th floor roof garden of Palazzo d'Italia. Foreground left to right: RCA Building, International Building. Background left to right: McGraw-Hill Building, Exxon Building, second Time & Life Building. Photographed July 1974.
(*Courtesy Rockefeller Center, Inc.*)

not all desirable, though, because much of it was in the unlit, unventilated center of the building. John R. Todd and the architects, especially Raymond Hood, repeatedly emphasized the foolishness of following a similar course at the Center during a period of low demand for space. If such floors as were built could be composed almost entirely of well lighted, well ventilated, high-rent space, construction costs could be kept down while the attraction of the building would be enhanced. No one wanted to build more square footage than absolutely necessary to make a profit.

In order to avoid building much interior loft space, the elevator banks were moved to the center of the building [72, 73], a novel idea at the time, and one widely adopted later. Since new high-speed elevators had just become legal, reducing the number of elevators needed in a building, they could be used to save 30,000 square feet of construction. The elevators stand parallel to the entrance walls, leaving room for access and circulation corridors around them, and room for shops on the ground floor building perimeter. In most earlier office buildings, a corridor occupied the center with elevators grouped in recesses along the corridor's sides. This created a great deal of loft space inside the building on the upper floors—the space above the ground floor corridor, the space between the elevators. Some buildings, such as the Philadelphia Savings Fund Society Building,

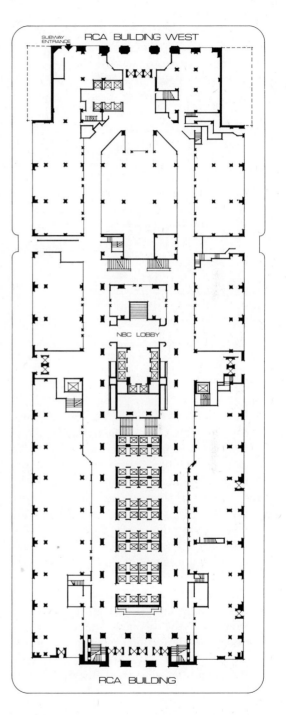

72. RCA Building, street level plan.
(*Redrawn by Nancy Jane Ruddy*)

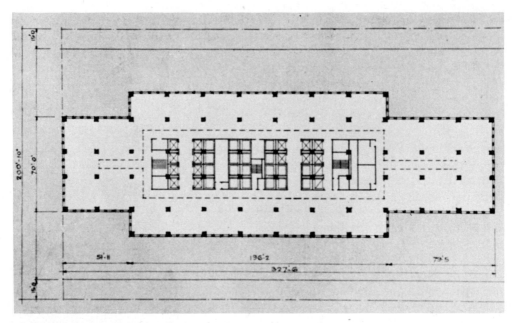

73. RCA Building, plan of 19th–31st floors.
(*From* American Architect cxxxix, *April 1931, p. 34*)

had an auxiliary wing for a row of elevators, but this meant eliminating windows from one side of the office floors. The RCA Building solution gained wide acceptance in later buildings, in part for this reason.

The interior space was designed with few of the permanent partition walls which were customarily installed in office buildings. The absence of these walls meant that a tenant could divide his space according to his needs, not the needs of the building owner. This flexibility made the RCA Building even more attractive. Moreover, the managers and architects agreed to design office floors which left no more than 27½ feet between windows and interior corridor and service areas. This was the maximum distance that would give an acceptable amount of daylight and natural ventilation to office space. This provided benefits to office workers, and it also meant that the planners would not have to air-condition the interior spaces to make them habitable. It left almost no low-rent loft space in the core of the building, while it assured decent working conditions for even the lowliest employee.

The exterior of the building was cut back to the dimensions exacted by this 27½ foot principle, making the upper parts unusually slender. The north and south sides step inward to reflect the reduced core area resulting from the progressively smaller number of elevator shafts needed for the upper floors. The idea of floor area reduction is expressed on the east façade by shallower setbacks at three levels, designed for aesthetic rather than for functionally expressive reasons and creating a gentle staggered effect of ascent. The shaved profile was the subject of intense controversy among the architects [74]. Hood had proposed it and maintained that it reflected the interior plan and functions. Harrison favored a pure slab such as he designed later above the base of the Eastern Air Lines Building and in his own firm's buildings on Sixth Avenue. It is hard to say whether this was a choice conforming to his generally spare and geometric taste in architecture—a neoclassic taste, so to speak—or whether this was partly the result of his growing interest in congenial forms of European modernism, particularly the work of Mies van der Rohe. Harrison had the architectural critics on his side for a long time. Perhaps Hood's design won out at the time because it was logical, did not destroy the plans of 27½ foot maximum working depth as Harrison's would have done, was unusual and likely to generate publicity, and required the least amount of construction (although building setbacks costs money, too). To New Yorkers now surfeited with the pure geometric slabs built after the Second World War, the stepped silhouette offers welcome variety and a distinctive appearance without tricks such as the dirigible mooring mast

on top of the Empire State Building or the more attractive curves and spire on the Chrysler Building.

The façade, then, consists of a slender central portion flanked by receding wings, all rising from a granite base which, with the eleven-story section above it, forms an anchor for the rest. The RCA Building is a more subtle three-dimensional design than the Empire State or Chrysler Buildings which have clumsier setbacks below sheer shafts rising over the quarter of the lot where Zoning Resolution height restrictions did not apply. The RCA Building differs from the prevailing wedding-

74. RCA Building, three sketch models, 1930–31. (*Courtesy Walter H. Kilham, Jr.*)

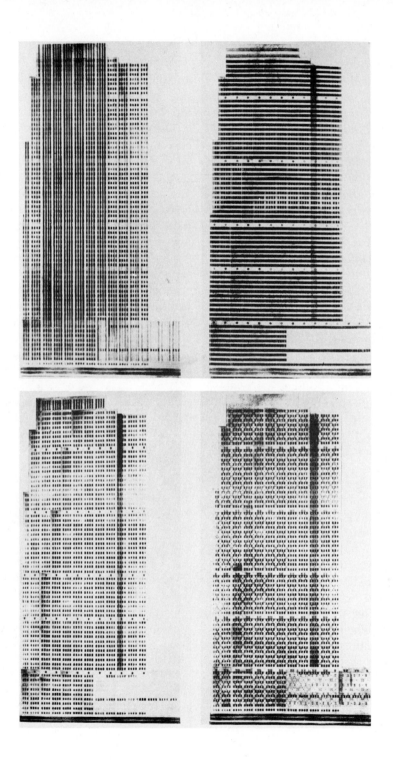

75. RCA Building, alternative exterior designs, 1931.
(*From* American Architect CXXXIX, *April 1931, pp. 34–35*)

cake designs in that its setbacks are more delicate extractions from thin parallel slabs. The RCA setbacks result from requirements for usable, appealing and marketable space. They do not come from the predominantly aesthetic considerations which determined the design of the Metropolitan Life Insurance Company's campanile headquarters (N. LeBrun & Sons, 1909) or the Foshay Tower obelisk in Minneapolis (Magney & Tusler, 1927-29) and which established the trimming on Hood's Tribune Tower. Nor do they come from almost purely financial considerations which shaped many other skyscrapers from the pre-Zoning Resolution looming rectangles (Equitable Life Assurance Building, E. R. Graham, 1913-15) to the bulky wedding cakes produced after 1916 (2 Park Avenue, Ely Jacques Kahn, 1927).

There had been thin and proportionately thin skyscrapers earlier, including Corbett's Bush Building on West 42nd Street —conditioned, as the RCA Building was, by the width of the available plot. But American architects had not commonly exploited the aesthetics of slenderness, or of thin planes that seem to slide along a building surface. Fragility and potential motion together had been presaged only by Hood's (and nominally J. M. Howells') Daily News Building, and it is no accident that of all the Center's architects, Hood was the most interested in European modernism and had the most decisive effect upon the RCA Building design.

That there are not more descendants of the RCA Building—one thinks of the Thyssen Haus in Düsseldorf (Hentrich & Petschnigg, 1957-60), or Embarcadero Center in San Francisco (John Portman, 1967-71)—is due to the advent of air-conditioning which made all interior space usable, and to an increasing and concomitant taste for slab silhouettes. The pioneer building of that type was, in fact, rising in Philadelphia while Rockefeller Center went up: Howe & Lescaze's Philadelphia Savings Fund Society Building (1929-32) which forecast the office floor of the postwar period—an uninterrupted rectangle, artificially ventilated. Although the offices were almost as shallow as those of the setback RCA Building, the PSFS Building needed no setbacks to achieve this goal because of its air-cooling devices. With interiors cooled fifteen degrees and with blinds drawn against Philadelphia's summer heat (and with a different building code, which may have helped), the PSFS Building could also be designed with proportionately more glass. The uniform floor spaces, slab silhouette, temperature control, increased use of glass, and even acoustic tile ceilings heralded later tall office design. The RCA Building did not.

The exterior treatment of the RCA Building determined that of the other buildings in the development. From the earliest consultants' opinions onward, people had recommended that the buildings have uniform external treatment. Many studies for the outer surface of the RCA Building were prepared, and although only a few are preserved, they show a wide variety of possibilities [75a-d].

Glass walls and glass spandrels were never considered because the New York City Building Code did not permit them in office buildings. Even if the law had allowed them, problems of glass supply, maintenance and repair, wind impact at heights, and excessive transmission of heat and cold would have made them poor choices. The air-conditioning equipment then available could not have overcome New York's summer heat, and the offices would have cost an enormous amount to heat during the winter. The question, therefore, was simply how to treat solid walls punctuated by windows of then-customary size.

At for the materials, the Building Code required that all steel piers be clad with masonry, and everyone agreed that limestone would be used for the lower stories. Employing even plain stone for entire buildings and all buildings would cost at least $300,000 more than using brick, and it would require extra structural support.[168] In April 1931 steel was prepared for stone facing through the twelfth floor of the RCA Building and for brick above that level.[169] The spandrels could be stone-faced, made of brick or colored tile, or faced with such metals as lead or aluminum.

John D. Rockefeller Jr. preferred historic details, and the incongruous Gothic-arched fence around the observation roof was designed to placate him. The Todds wanted a Byzantine or Romanesque style —meaning, of course, only the details. Harrison, and probably others, protested loudly against dressing up a group of skyscrapers in old-fashioned costumes. The architects generally had their way. Hood told Merle Crowell that John R. Todd was "the most conservative man in the world, and every move we make is more and more modern." [170] But the spandrels of several of the buildings of the original group terminate in elongated and slightly angular pointed leaves, late descendants of art nouveau forms, which represent a compromise between the architects' taste and Rockefeller's fondness for Gothic.

Until December 1931, the architects experimented with ornamental treatments [75a-d]. The dominant members of the exterior design staff, including Carl Landefeld and George Pauly, had come from Hood's office and produced more lively designs than did architects from the other firms. Their simplest basic design was the egregious "oilcan" model treatment. This merely revealed the existence of structural columns, floor beams, four windows and three thin spandrels between each pier, and it showed the mechanical floors clearly. This was a pure but monotonous expression of structure, and no one seems to have promoted it since it was not at all beautiful. A second, by George Pauly, provided a flashy covering for the first, varying the surface by adding four dark squares whose corners touched the corners of each window. The total effect would have been that of a seventy-story checkerboard, and while it looked lively in a magazine illustration, it was too garish to use, especially extended to fourteen buildings. A third joined the windows into horizontal bands, recalling Hood's McGraw-Hill Building [24] but this design accentuated the RCA Building's east-

76. Three-story high NBC Broadcasting studio, rendering *c.* 1931–32. (*Courtesy Rockefeller Center, Inc.*)

west extent. It would have been disastrous if applied to the entire project which had already been criticized for its bulk. A fourth scheme placed dark spandrels under the windows to create dark vertical strips between the unbroken vertical piers. The spacing was based upon that of the Daily News Building. It was this design that the planners adopted, a sound decision if we imagine the alternatives applied over twelve acres. The windows were recessed behind the piers, although for a brief time the architects considered a bay window arrangement.[171]

If brick or terrazzo were used for the spandrels, the architects could introduce a welcome note of color into the development. "Color," wrote John R. Todd later, "sells the sunrise and the sunset." [172] Terrazzo might not stand up to the New York climate, but bricks and tile would. Hood

had recently enlivened the white Daily News Building with russet and black brick spandrels, and he and Fouilhoux argued for the use of brick designs at the Center—but no garish tones, of course. In November 1931 the *General Building Contractor* (New York) published a photograph of sample bays built at full scale on the construction site with linear and geometric designs in the spandrels.

John D. Rockefeller Jr. preferred lead spandrels, but Alcoa agreed to provide cheaper and lighter aluminum ones, which gave the same sober gray tone that lead did. Restraint won over exuberance here, as usual.

The metal spandrels harmonize with the buff-colored shot-sawed Indiana limestone which was finally chosen to cover all the remaining visible surfaces, apart from Deer Island granite trim and base mold-

77. Margaret Bourke-White, photomurals showing radio transmission equipment. RCA Building, NBC visitors' reception lobby.
(*Library of Congress*)

ings. The planners were right in thinking that stone gives a more traditionally noble and costly aspect to the buildings and they were, after all, building high-quality structures which had to advertise themselves as such. Blue venetian blinds originally used on the windows also suggested unusual expense, and added subdued color to the expanse of windows and walls on the seventy-story building.

The exterior treatment was not entirely composed of broad vertical accents over the piers dominating the slightly recessed spandrels. Stretches of nearly blank wall up to the tenth floor on the sides of the RCA Building cover the National Broadcasting Company studio wing which floats free of the building structure in order to minimize vibrations.

The design development process looks like design by the process of elimination. It was not a question of "less is more," in Mies van der Rohe's famous phrase, nor was it a matter of "less is cheaper" or "less is all that I can design," at least while Hood and his designers were at work. "Less is universally agreeable" is probably the most accurate formulation here. And "less is calmer" as well as agreeable proved to be a mark of American architecture during the 1930s, distinguishing it from the work of the late 1920s which employed patterned masonry, lively color accents, and active, angular ornament.

This is not to say that a more distinctive design would have been preferable at Rockefeller Center. The one adopted is like classic white shirts which have fitted comfortably into business situations for decades, while the principal alterna-

tives might have been striking for a while before becoming outmoded or obtrusive. The simple solution adopted fitted the requirements of the building code, counteracted the horizontal spread of the buildings, and satisfied the owners' and managers' fondness for the dignity of limestone-walled simplicity. The architects could also point to well-received precedents for the smooth, flat, vertical articulation in broad stripes, including such famous Chicago buildings as Graham, Anderson, Probst & White's Mer-

78. Margaret Bourke-White, photomurals showing radio transmission equipment. RCA Building, NBC visitors' reception lobby.
(*Library of Congress*)

chandise Mart (1930) or the Carbide and Carbon Building by the Burnham Brothers (1929), the latter based in part upon Hood's own American Radiator Company Building (1924) overlooking Bryant Park in New York. Since Hood's Daily News Building [23] and Corbett's Master Apartments, both just completed in New York, had won praise for their designs which emphasized vertical stripes, there were plenty of good reasons for continuing to use this design, even though the architects risked being called lingering Gothicists by critics who hoped that the Rockefeller project would help to establish a modern style which Hood's work of the immediately preceding years had forecast.

To take care of the radio needs of the day and the television needs of the future the Rockefeller Center architects and O. B. Hanson, NBC's operating manager,

devised studios of unprecedented scope and convenience. The installations were "overdesigned;" the number of cycles which the equipment could transmit exceeded the capacity of radio receivers of 1933, but Hanson expected the industry to catch up with his engineers. Henry Hofmeister worked out ingenious floor plans. Separate elevators and corridors served the performers and the public, so that the performers would not be delayed by autograph-seekers or critics. Four studios surrounded a central control booth, permitting a single program to include sound effects created in four separate rooms or letting a single television play have four sets. Another studio was equipped for stage plays, another for child performers, another, three stories high, for a broadcasting audience of five hundred [76]. The studio areas are still in use, although their equipment has been modified. The regrettable modification occurred in the visitors' reception area, a circular lobby which once had brilliant photo murals by Margaret Bourke-White lining the walls [77, 78]; she elevated the machinery of radio transmission to stunning artistic motifs.

Below the studio area was an area which had the advantage of offering wide spans of clear space—as much as 45 feet high and 117 feet wide—but which had the disadvantage of being entirely in the unlit interior of the building. The man-

79. RCA Building. Municipal Art Exhibit, May 1934.
(*Gottscho-Schleisner*)

80. RCA Building lobby. Photographed July 1974.
(*Courtesy Rockefeller Center, Inc.*)

agers and architects labored throughout the 1930s to find a suitable use for this potentially profit-making waste space. It took until 1934 for the architects (perhaps Reinhard & Hofmeister) to design the area to provide a two-story exhibition space. It had balconies at the second floor level which led to smaller exhibition rooms. The space became the site of two Municipal Art Exhibits in 1934 and 1935 [79]. When the Museum of Science and Industry took a fifteen-year lease beginning in January 1936, Edward Durell Stone redesigned the space to create a lively display area with stepped ramps around part of a central rotunda [46], a scheme not entirely remote from that of Frank Lloyd Wright's later Guggenheim Museum, though without the latter's consistency, amplitude and dynamism. As at the Guggenheim, the public was led along a preordained path, an arrangement better suited to lively displays of basic scientific principles and technology than to the contemplation of great paintings.

Meticulous consideration to detail is apparent throughout the RCA Building. The main level flooring, for example, is both practical and exceptionally handsome [80]. It is composed of geometric

patterns of dark terrazzo outlined in thin strips of brass. The architectural detail of everything from ventilation grilles to bronze shop window trim is unusually fine in both design and quality of material.

The architects actively promoted the addition of sculpture and murals to the buildings. Lee Lawrie, who was known to them from his work on buildings by Bertram Goodhue and on Rockefeller's Riverside Church, received the most important sculpture commissions. On the RCA Building, he executed stone reliefs representing sound and light as promoters of wisdom, and a cast glass relief representing cycles of light and sound at the eastern entrance [81]. (He also executed "Atlas" [88] later, as well as doorway reliefs on other buildings.) Gaston Lachaise carved allegories of "Genius Seizing the Light of the Sun" and "The Gifts of Earth to Mankind" and similar lofty subjects on piers of the RCA Building West [82]. Leo Friedlander, a sculptor who worked with Hood at the Chicago Fair, was asked to carve "Transmission" receiving an image and sending it to "Reception" [83] as well as other themes on limestone pylons at the side entrances to the RCA Building; Rockefeller wrote to John R. Todd saying quite rightly that these were both "gross and unbeautiful." [173] No one was perfectly happy with all of this work, but as Todd said, the public seemed to like Rockefeller Center, "art work and all." [174]

81. Lee Lawrie, *Genius, Which Interprets to the Human Race the Laws and Cycles of the Cosmic Forces of the Universe, Making the Cycles of Light and Sound.* RCA Building, east façade. (*Courtesy Rockefeller Center, Inc.*)

The most famous work of art in the building was, of course, the fresco by Diego Rivera [84].[175] As if to show that his anti-capitalist themes meant less than their understanding of fine art, American industrialists commissioned pictures from the irrepressible Mexican painter. Mrs. Rockefeller was especially interested in his work, and the Museum of Modern Art had given him a special exhibition. He was asked to design a monochromatic mural on canvas for the wall immediately opposite the RCA Building main entrance which would depict "man's new possibilities from his new understanding of material things." This subject, like most of the others, was conceived by a philosophy professor named Hartley Burr Alexander who had been hired to coordinate the works of art thematically. Rivera whee-

83. Leo Friedlander, *Transmission Receiving an Image of Dancers and Flashing It Through the Ether by Means of Television to Reception, Symbolized by Mother Earth and Her Child, Man.* RCA Building, 49th Street entrance. (*Courtesy Rockefeller Center, Inc.*)

82. Gaston Lachaise, *Gifts of Earth to Mankind* and *The Spirit of Progress.* RCA Building West, façade. (*Courtesy Rockefeller Center, Inc.*)

dled permission to paint a fresco—more durable than a canvas mural—and to use gently graduated color, but he actually painted a deeply colored fresco. He departed in other significant ways from an approved sketch which he had submitted in the autumn of 1932. Most distressing to the patrons was a wholly unexpected portrait of Lenin near the center of the picture, and a number of venereal disease germs floating toward a scene of rich people playing cards. A large number of bright red flags held by people parading near the tomb of Lenin was another rude surprise. While most people would not have recognized the germs, every prospective tenant would have recognized Lenin and the flags. Nelson Rockefeller wrote to Rivera asking the artist to substitute another face, whereupon Rivera got Ben Shahn to draft a reply in good English saying that "rather than mutilate the conception, I should prefer the physical destruction of the conception in its entirety but preserving, at least, its integrity." After having the nearly completed fresco covered for almost a year and after paying Rivera the full amount specified in the contract, the managers decided that the embarrassing

84. Diego Rivera, *Man at the Crossroads,* formerly RCA Building lobby. (*Wide World*)

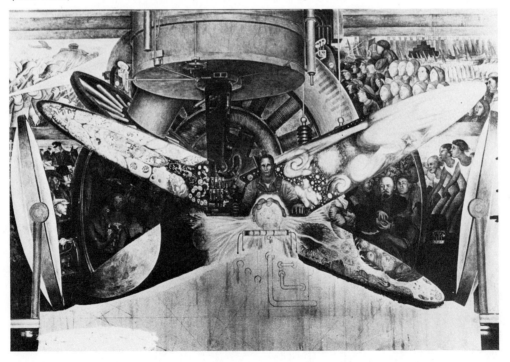

85. José María Sert, *Triumph of Man's Accomplishments through Physical and Mental Labor,* RCA Building lobby.
(Courtesy Rockefeller Center, Inc.)

and increasingly famous work had to go. Nelson Rockefeller suggested moving it to the Museum of Modern Art, where curiosity-seekers could be charged admission to see it. That proved impossible, so the planners took Rivera at his word and destroyed the fresco, a deed which has been damned as artistic vandalism and praised as a bit of common sense. In 1937 the fresco was replaced by José María Sert's bombastic murals [85] which the planners commissioned without any noticeable enthusiasm. These represented harmless lunging giants and portraits of Lincoln and Emerson rather than Lenin, and did so at a fairly economical price.[176]

Sert, along with Frank Brangwyn, had done lobby corridor murals for the building while Rivera was at work but even then Sert and Brangwyn had been second choices. The architects and managers persuaded Rockefeller to let them approach Matisse and Picasso first, but Matisse did not want to do work which would be seen only by people passing swiftly along a hallway and Picasso simply refused to meet with Hood and Todd in Paris.[177] Even later, when Picasso was offered the Rivera wall—known as the Wailing Wall because of the problem of filling it—he tried to trick Rockefeller rather than cooperate. In December 1933 Picasso agreed only to paint a picture for $32,000 but not to submit a preliminary sketch. If Rockefeller rejected the finished picture, he would have to pay Picasso only half that amount. Understandably enough, no one in New York was eager to hand out

86. RCA Management Conference Center, proposed 1974. Ford and Earl Associates, architects.
(*Courtesy Rockefeller Center, Inc.*)

$16,000 for a second unsuitable picture [178] and Picasso should have taken Will Rogers' advice to Rivera: "Never try to fool a Rockefeller in oils."

The RCA Building was not immune to other problems. The Radio Corporation itself thought of following other space-hungry firms to the suburbs. RCA had, in fact, bought land in Connecticut for this purpose. The Center worked with Cushman & Wakefield, real estate brokers, to rearrange and add to RCA's office space, and allowed RCA to plan a management conference center on the twelfth floor roof space over the broadcasting studios between the RCA Building and its western addition [86].[179]

A building erected on a pre-existing roof must limit its weight, so Ford and Earl Design Associates planned to use lightweight, prefabricated modular elements, including a great deal of glass. The glass would reduce the building's visibility—lessen "eyesore awareness" as designer Walter B. Ford II declared—and would enclose trees and plants in order to be "totally relative to the human beings" who would use it. Temperature control in a glass structure consumes a great deal of energy. As there was a fuel shortage at the time that the project was made public, Rockefeller Center was happy to announce that RCA's management center would use solar energy. Although RCA technicians and Syska and Hennessy, Inc., engineers, had not worked out the techniques, they expected the new structure to be the city's first commercial application of solar heating technology. This would help to keep the Center young in the public mind.

The streets running beneath the corridors of the RCA Building provide the backbone of the underground pedestrian system which is now about two miles in extent [4, 87]. It links all the buildings of the Center and the Rockefeller Center subway station. It also includes the Equitable and J. C. Penney Buildings to the northwest on Sixth Avenue. The clean, busy underground streets are flanked by shops selling everything imaginable for the tourist or tenant, from bird song records to rare books, with office supply stores and women's fashion shops well represented. Cobblers, cleaners, a post office, public toilets and restaurants provide services.

Attractive and weatherproof as they are, the underground lanes have not been easy to navigate. Some of the spurs to other buildings from the spine under the RCA corridors are circuitous because no paths could be cut through the Music Hall lobby or through the complex interior of the Associated Press Building with its vehicular ramp and cinema. Neat direction signs were too discreet, and there were not enough maps or directory charts. Knowing that this confusion can be costly if a visitor abandons his plans to patronize a shop that he cannot easily find, the management improved the signs in 1974 and brightened the underground area with colorful walls and plants. For inspiration, staff members visited attractive recent developments such as Place Ville Marie in Montreal or the shopping mall at Columbia, Maryland, which had earlier used Rockefeller Center's multi-level shopping areas as a model.

From the depths of the subway station tied to the RCA Building West to the heights of the observation roof, the RCA Building stands as a focal point of a comprehensive scheme of urban design. The tower is one of the best monuments of our commercial culture during two decades when Americans could concentrate on making money and not on making war.

87. Underground pedestrian concourse showing original lighting. Photographed July 1952. (*Courtesy Rockefeller Center, Inc.*)

XII.

Five Office Buildings

"So long as you keep the maximum office space above, use the ground space in any way you like to put charm and individuality into these separate buildings. It will not do just to build square buildings with straight fronts and call a piece the Spanish building and a piece the Swedish building. There must be individuality, quality and appearance."

John R. Todd letter to Henry Hofmeister, concerning proposed international buildings on the north block, October 22, 1932.
Rockefeller Center, Inc., Architects and Engineers Correspondence, 1929-1937

A cathedral may be dedicated to several saints. There is usually a principal one to whom special honor is given, and at Rockefeller Center, our secular cathedral, the RCA Building is the shrine of the first and most essential tenants as well as the finest of the office buildings. But there are other important monuments—secondary chapels, but significant ones.

The International Building [180] is less of a monument and more of a speculative structure than the RCA Building, although its materials and standards exceed those customary during the inter-war years [45, 88-90]. The earliest plans for the site included a smaller plot for the tower with a department store on Fifth Avenue [25, 26, 29]. For economic reasons, the tower was later enlarged when the department

88. Palazzo d'Italia with overdoor relief by Attilio Piccirilli, *Arte e Lavoro* (removed); International Building entrance with Lee Lawrie, *Atlas,* in front; International Building North, looking northwest from south corner of St. Patrick's Cathedral at 50th Street. Photographed *c.* 1950.
(*Courtesy Rockefeller Center, Inc.*)

store idea was abandoned, and nine-story wings flanking a galleria were designed to face St. Patrick's Cathedral across the Avenue [31]. The galleria itself shrank to a lobby by the end of 1933. The principal concession to beauty was the lowering of the wing buildings two stories so that they match the French and British Buildings to the south [1, 33]; this was done at the suggestion of Raymond Hood [181] and it was his last important contribution to the design of the Center before his final illness prevented him from working.

The wing buildings project too short a way to the east to serve as adequate em-brasures for the entranceway to a tower as tall and long as this one. The wings frame a small courtyard, again too narrow and short to complement the building, although the entranceway itself is an austerely handsome composition of three two-story rectangular openings with glass panes set within them; when the Gothic detail on St. Patrick's Cathedral is reflected in the glass, the entranceway offers a memorable mixture of simple monumentality and pleasing variety. The statue of "Atlas" which Lee Lawrie designed and which he and René Chambellan cast in 1936, crowds the courtyard but adds a third kind of form to the

89. International Building lobby, rendering *c.* 1935.
(*Courtesy Rockefeller Center, Inc.*)

entranceway. However inflated and mus-
clebound he may be, "Atlas" has become
a landmark on Fifth Avenue.

The courtyard leads to a tall, broad
lobby [89, 90] divided by thin piers from
which indirect light is cast on the copper
leaf-covered ceiling. The piers define the
center of the hall where moving stairs
lead grandly up to a mezzanine behind
the elevator banks and where other moving stairs lead unobtrusively down to the
shopping concourse. Corridors to the left
and right extend toward the central plaza
or to the private street. The walls and
piers are covered with carefully matched
slabs of green veined marble which would
give the room a warm, subdued tone if
tall, illuminated display cases did not line
the upper parts of the side walls. The
floor was to have been marble, too, but
the insurance advisors said that it had to
be made of a less slippery material.[182]

Modernist theory approved of creating the special features of a room from functional elements such as piers and moving stairs. George Howe and William Lescaze had inspired the Center's architects by emphasizing an "escalator" as an important feature of their widely-admired Philadelphia Savings Fund Society Building, completed in 1932. At the PSFS Building, the moving stairs serve an essential function, that of attracting and transporting customers from the street level, reserved for profit-making shop space, to the banking level one flight up. The bank itself was the sponsor of the entire building. Once a visitor reached the top of the moving stairs, he found himself in the building owner's grand, spacious banking hall, an appropriate functional and symbolic climax of his ascent. At the International Building, however, the visitor ascends toward a blank wall of the elevator bank which stands just a few feet from the top of the moving stairs, and he must walk left or right around the wall to find the undistinguished mezzanine-level offices. This is a puzzling and disappointing climax to the upward sweep.

Building mezzanine space to produce revenue was the underlying cause of the trouble. Had the managers not desired to squeeze rental income out of every square foot, and had not the architects been influenced by the example of an "escalator"

whose relationship to street and banking hall they could not use appropriately, they might have felt freer to design a less novel but probably more successfully integrated lobby.

The lobby lacks integration of form and function, tradition and modernity, costly display and the profit motive. The lobby is spare in form—understandably so, for a profit-seeking rental office building—but wears a marble costume and has a formal plan reminiscent of palatial entrance halls of past centuries. The marble walls and rows of piers serve as a setting only for a modern machine, while the moving stairs lead imperiously toward nothing but a blank wall for which no suggested decoration ever seemed suitable. Someone descending can look ahead

90. International Building lobby, looking out toward St. Patrick's Cathedral. Photographed 1935–36.
(*Paul J. Woolf photo, Courtesy Rockefeller Center, Inc.*)

[90] to the handsome entrance portals and through the glass to "Atlas" and St. Patrick's, which makes the passage out of the building more appealing than the passage in. By placing immense advertising cases on the north and south lobby walls in order to bring in revenue, the planners made it possible for uncontrolled and uncoordinated displays to negate the luxurious effects of the marble which might otherwise imply that no expense was spared on the building.

The desire to realize a profit from every part of the building led to a small but revealing oddity at the west end, where Reinhard & Hofmeister designed a branch of the East River Savings Bank in the autumn of 1936.[183] Because the bank wanted more unified space than the building contained, the architects had had to close part of the western lobby and all of the south entrance corridor originally provided there. In itself, this would not have been awkward, but sculptures had already been installed over the north and south corridor entrances from the private street. With one of these passageways blocked, one relief by Gaston Lachaise has no apparent reason for being where it is, and simply hangs above nothing in particular.

The planning of the first Time & Life Building [184] was impeded because the Center did not have full possession of 12 and 14 West 49th Street, and plans had to be made for the new building with and without these parcels.

In early plans for the Center, the building was T-shaped, bridging the private street, with the east-west axis predominating as it does in all but the Sixth Avenue buildings [31, 36]. In December 1935 the architects studied a project "covering the greater part of the block" between 48th and 49th Streets, including a bridge wing over the private street and containing considerable amounts of loft space. But the parcels at 12 and 14 West 49th Street would have been hard to obtain without time-consuming negotiations with the occupant who was a prominent lawyer, and with Columbia University.[185] The bridge building would have required other unwelcome negotiations with city officials. And, as usual, the managers realized that high-quality office space in salable amounts could be a better investment than loft space which brings in low rents.

By early March, the architects were at work on a slender, rectangular site on the east side of the private street, with a north-south axis [49]. Critics have praised the effect of the lone north-south axis, which varies the east-west orientation, for giving the whole development a "pinwheeling motion." [186] This result is more easily seen in an air view than from ground level; in any case, it was a happy accident rather than a conscious aesthetic decision.

On April 29, 1936, Rockefeller approved plans for a thirty-one story building with fourteen elevators. The tower could benefit from unused air rights on the site across the private street, still known as the Opera plot; plans for the Opera had been filed in 1932 primarily to allow the Time & Life plot to concentrate the air rights of both sites. For a penthouse story and on the façade, the architects suggested some modifications which would reduce the anticipated return on investment from 5.7 per cent to 5.1 per cent or 5.2 per cent. The board of directors approved the changes as they represented "the principal concessions to aesthetics. This has been done on other buildings." [187]

The building itself is as close to a pure slab as the architects had yet designed, and reflects the importance of Reinhard and Harrison as designers after Raymond Hood's death. In order to produce a building with only one setback, the architects recessed the tower from the building line, producing the simple shape that they admired and providing additional sidewalk space and room for planting boxes.

This reduced the ground floor area available for shops, a matter of great concern to Hugh Robertson. In order to keep as much space as possible for tenants who were as large as possible, Robertson was willing to sacrifice an entrance on 49th Street, the logical access point from the Center's other buildings, in favor of a main entrance on the private street and another on 48th Street to make the building accessible from outside the Center itself. The architects disagreed, being unwilling to give up an entrance from the central plaza area, and they were eventually allowed to design three doorways, each decorated with relief sculpture costing no more than $5000.

The lobby design could only be made after the access problem had been resolved. The Planning Committee decided upon a rectangular lobby two stories high, eliminating rental space immediately above the ground floor but creating a

91. Carl Milles, *Man and Nature,* first Time & Life Building (One Rockefeller Plaza) lobby. Photographed 1941.
(Courtesy Rockefeller Center, Inc.)

suitably dignified lobby. If a two-story lobby were to be covered in marble, the decorating costs would exceed the budgeted amount, but the architects preferred a higher main hall even if it were finished only in plaster. To relieve the monotony of a plaster wall, Carl Milles, who had not been able to do a sculptural decoration for the RCA Building lobby within the budget, was hired to execute three pressed-pine wood reliefs.[188] They show a rider who pauses to hear a bird's song [91], an attentive nymph and a retreating faun. The bird in question is a silver-leaf-covered Mexican nightingale, or clarino, from which recorded bird songs issue hourly.

92. Eastern Air Lines Building. View from underground pedestrian concourse level to street-level lobby. Photographed July 1974.
(*Courtesy Rockefeller Center, Inc.*)

The planning of the Eastern Air Lines Building [52] shows again the importance of financial considerations.[189] Scheduled for planning in June 1935, it was deferred just three months later for over a year. As we have seen, it was planned as Holland House originally, but became an office tower, exhibition building and garage. In June 1937 Todd showed ten alternative plans for the south block to the Art and Architecture Committee of the board of directors. They are characteristic of his careful attention to income-producing possibilities. Here, in fact, he even considered destroying the Center Theater in order to build more high-quality office space for which the renting staff had found an increased demand. Two plans were being shown to prospective tenants at that time. The first provided for ex-

hibition space, a loft building on the empty building site, preservation of the Center Theater, and an office building on the U. S. Rubber Company Building site. The second provided for exhibition, loft, and office space on the entire plot, including the theater site. Eight other proposals envisioned salvaging part of the theater, included shops on 49th Street, provided for a hotel, and combined or excluded several of the individual features.

The final plan provided for a twelve-story slab-shaped office tower on a four-story base which included one setback. Harrison had long favored a slab shape [75]. A low building gave him an opportunity to design one, because a sixteen-story building needs only one level of elevators, making unnecessary the setbacks such as those of the RCA Building which show the successive elimination of elevators. The broad lower floors were air-conditioned from the start to serve the shops, the exhibition hall, and office tenants just above them. The slab offices depended on natural ventilation.

At the western end of this building, the managers proposed building a parking garage on mid-block frontage. Early plans for the Center show on-site parking facilities created to accommodate the Opera House patrons while bringing in revenue from businessmen and visitors also. But while the Opera plans were indefinite, the managers did not press the matter of a garage, especially if they were concerned with building whatever was necessary to make a struggling development profitable and beautiful. Besides, the Zoning Resolution forbade new garages in this area until a 1935 amendment permitted exemption petitions, and the Center's planners had been eager to avoid asking the city for variances if other solutions to their problems could be found. Parking lots, however, were allowed, and the site was actually being put to this inelegant use. After deciding that their mid-block frontage would have been hard to sell as profitably without destroying their long-cherished idea of keeping interior sites as low as possible, they applied successfully in August 1937 to have their unprecedented midtown Manhattan office building-garage. Nine months later the six-story garage was open for business. Eight hundred cars fit into three underground and three above-ground levels. The Center promoted its garage as an elegant and comfortable place, including a large-windowed waiting room where patrons could sit while attendants slid down firemen's poles to reach the cars in the basement levels. The garage entrance's squat cylindrical piers, low ceilings and broad curving walls contrasted with the thin-walled glazed lounge, creating the bulky and fragile oppositions which are characteristic of the architectural taste of the 1930s.

The building lobby is low and broad compared to the tall lobbies of the RCA and International Buildings. It was designed this way in order to provide more uninterrupted rental space above it, as was the case with the earlier Associated Press Building. The standard of design is higher in the later lobby, however. The low and wide room which might seem to press down upon the observer, expands downward to the shopping concourse by means of a broad, curved flight of steps

placed in the center of the lobby. An eye moving downward is not so concerned about restricted expansion upward. Besides, this design allowed the architects to emphasize the existence of the underground facilities [92].

While the building was going up, so the story goes, John D. Rockefeller paused on the sidewalk to observe the construction activity. A supervisor of the work who did not recognize him, told him to move along, whereupon Rockefeller conceived the idea of an observer's terrace from which interested passers-by could watch the process of construction. The resulting "Sidewalk Superintendent's Club" with membership cards issued to virtually anyone was inaugurated soon afterward on a temporary terrace, providing another event which the public relations department was quick to announce. The idea was such a success that it was repeated during the construction of the second Time & Life Building, with Marilyn Monroe presiding over the inauguration ceremonies.

The second Time & Life Building [190] was, as we have seen, changed from a studio-and-office building to the latter alone when Time Inc. became the principal tenant and partner in ownership. Its new headquarters were tailor-made to its needs. Committees of important Time executives spent sixteen months formulating the plans with the Rockefeller Center officers and with Michael Harris who was the Harrison & Abramovitz partner in charge of the design and planning. They calculated the total floor space that they needed and decided to use a 4'8" square building module to achieve it; this regulated the slab-with-wrap-around shape, the overall design, and the interior partitioning. Writers, editors, and researchers required a great many interior partitions for quiet and privacy. In order to fit the greatest number of small partitioned areas into the least space, consultant office designers reduced the module to 4'8" along the perimeter by 4' into the core, confusing certain aspects of the interior arrangement and leading to some of the crowding later evident in the offices themselves (though not yet visible in early photographs). A novel plan evolved, providing for a ring corridor around the elevator and service core, with spurs leading from the ring to the building perimeter. This eliminated the usual supplementary corridors between the core and the perimeter, while it facilitated circulation to a specific destination; it also made maximum use of every inch of office space. Executives have their offices on the perimeter. There are more windowed offices in any given extent of wall than there were in buildings of the prewar Center, because the modules and the windows within them were smaller in the new building. All this allowed Time Inc. to save an entire floor of rental space.

The module was so compact that the planners specified that no structural piers should intrude upon the interior space. This helped to shape the exterior form which would have to take protruding piers into account. An early proposal to make the NBC-Time tower resemble the old Center had to be discarded, for a comparably broad limestone pier sheath-

ing would have protruded far outside the offices, forcing occupants to look out through shallow rectangular tunnels of stone. The Time Inc. officials did not want their new headquarters to blend visually into the old Center in any case; they wanted a distinctive building of their own.

They did not, however, want a patterned aluminum-faced tower of the Eastern Air Lines Building shape such as Carson & Lundin (now independent of Rockefeller Center) had just designed for the Tishman Building at 666 Fifth Avenue on former Rockefeller property, or the one which Harrison & Abramovitz had created on 42nd Street for the Socony-Mobil Corporation (1955-56). They were unwilling to accept an outside consultant's suggestion that neon lights be employed to rise upward from the base of the new building; one architect characterized this plan as akin to putting a clock in the navel of the Venus de Milo. The Time Inc. personnel then proposed a zig-zag façade. Windows sloping in and spandrels sloping out led to a design recalling superficially the Ministry of Education and Public Health building in Rio de Janeiro designed by Le Corbusier and others in 1936. Both are basically slab towers with lower wings, in both the upward direction is emphasized by uninterrupted verticals reflecting the pier and window locations, and the slanting louvered sunbreaks on the building in Rio were reinterpreted as sloping wall surfaces. The zig-zag façade design had several advantages. It could command attention; it expanded interior office space; it included a great deal of solid wall to lower temperature control costs inside by reducing large expanses

93. Second Time & Life Building, showing Americas Plaza.
(*Courtesy Rockefeller Center, Inc.*)

of glass which retain summer heat and winter cold. At the same time, occupants had ample window space admitting less glare than vertical window panes do. The design had several disadvantages, too. It would have been hard to incorporate vertical risers for air-conditioning ducts. Costs of unusual buildings tend to be high and workmen may need special training. Some internal rentable space might be lost. And the architects were not certain that the result would be beautiful. It might be bizarre. It might seem to wobble. It might be known as the Accordion Building.

The building actually executed [60, 61, 93] is divided vertically by structural piers faced with limestone to hint at a link with the old Center. Between every pair of piers are five windows, each 4′8″ wide. Bordering the windows beside the piers are the aluminum air-conditioning risers; the interior windows are separated by thin window mullions only. The rhythm given to each bay is "AbccbA"—simple without necessarily being monotonous, and reflect-

ing the structure of the building, as contemporary architectural theory required. The surface between the vertical members is all glass, with gray aluminum mesh behind the spandrel glass. The windows themselves extend down to desk-height level although the architects hoped to make them smaller and squarer to reduce the heating and cooling burden inside. Aesthetic considerations dictated the change.

In order to enhance the corporate image, the planners suggested exterior and interior improvements. On the setback area facing Sixth Avenue they installed a fountain raised in a basin surrounded by a low parapet which serves the neighborhood as a long bench. Along the south side of the building are shrubs and trees in concrete tubs as well as bicycle racks, since Rockefeller Center likes to keep up with the times. The wave-patterned gray and white pavement was Wallace Harrison's idea. He admired a similar design at the Copacabana Beach in Rio de Janeiro (and the Ministry of Education and Health Building there had a patterned tile forecourt), and thought that the pavement could modify the building's rectilinearity in a lively way. By continuing the pattern from the building line outdoors to the elevator bank indoors, Harrison hoped to link the exterior with the interior, an achievement much praised in the work of Frank Lloyd Wright (a shadowy rival to all American architects) and Mies van der Rohe (who was then working on the Seagram Building with Philip Johnson). The wide waves on Time & Life's pavement, however, have nothing to do with the planar and linear forms of the building, and they come to a dead stop at the elevator banks indoors where they clash with the works of art which Fritz Glarner and Josef Albers created for the elevator bank terminal walls [94].

Above the low wing area with its bank and varied offices, Gio Ponti designed an auditorium and dining room with auxiliary facilities on the eighth floor setback. In irregular polygonal spaces which relieved the rectilinearity elsewhere, Ponti installed bold circular and polygonal light fixtures and vividly marbleized sheet rubber floors employing the thin and sharply-jointed decorative details characteristic of the taste for angles and fins in Italian design of the period.

Below ground, the Time & Life Building was connected with the subway mezzanine. The Center's management had assumed that there would be an unimpeded passageway linking the new building with the older ones. But the new Transit Authority was trying to raise its revenues to help preserve the subway fare at fifteen cents, and could create barriers between the Center's old and new buildings unless a fee were paid to make the connection. Alternatively, the Transit Authority could lease space to concessionaires of a cheap and tawdry sort, which would lessen the attraction of the entire concourse connection. After a series of negotiations, in 1958 the Center agreed to lease the north mezzanine of the station for twenty years and to refurbish the area. The station became the best lighted, cleanest and most orderly major station in the city. The Center and the city reached informal agreements about police protection, and established a series of rights and limitations of each party, ranging from matters of default to redecoration privileges. Rockefeller Center won permission to remove the subway kiosk from the Time & Life Building street frontage (an aesthetic change which forces subway patrons to hunt for the unobtrusive entrance). The most important effect of the agreement was that it established a precedent for corporate cooperation in maintaining subway stations, a source of hope for the financially pressed transit facilities.

94. Josef Albers, *Portals*, second Time & Life Building lobby. Photographed 1961.
(*Courtesy Rockefeller Center, Inc.*)

95. Exxon Building lobby. Foreground: tapestry based on Picasso design; background: Mary Callery, *Moon and Stars*. Photographed July 1974.
(*Courtesy Rockefeller Center, Inc.*)

Several other stations now benefit from the attention of above-ground businesses and institutions, and city planners hoped to make this common in stations of the proposed Second Avenue subway.

The Exxon Corporation had a tailor-made building, too, this one becoming the leader of the Center's group of three buildings south of the second Time & Life Building.[191] The earliest plans provided about 1,000,000-1,200,000 square feet of space. The Exxon directors asked for more room and then still more until they decided to build 2,100,000 square feet for the company's needs and to produce income from other firms.

The Exxon officials and the architects—Harrison & Abramovitz & Harris with partner Michael Harris again in charge of the detailed design—decided on a fifty-four-story rectangular slab shape with a seven-story wrap-around at the western end. The elevation has window strips alternating with structural columns. As in the second Time & Life Building, there are easily-modified offices free of space-consuming intrusions made by the columns. At the Exxon Building the architects achieved this by erecting the columns close to the building core and outside the office perimeter even though this meant increasing the number and expense of the steel supports. When a mockup of the façade showed that tenants would have to peer at the world through a straight-sided passageway formed by the protruding structural columns, the architects canted the corners of the limestone-over-concrete cladding to provide a more expansive view. This added some sculptural relief to the repetitive façade strips, as it had in Eero Saarinen's nearby CBS Building.

Inside the Exxon Building, the ground floor contains the elevator banks, a lobby on two sides, and a bank which occupies the plaza front. Shops are found only in the wrap-around extension. Planting boxes with delicate-leaved trees, and a few decorative works of art add what life there is in the simple, light-filled lobby wings [95].

The decision to make the lobby primarily an anteroom to the elevator cabs was based on a combination of factors, including the architects' taste for uncomplicated shapes, the economic requirements, and the effects of the 1961 Zoning Resolution Amendment.

The tower's pure slab shape is the result of enclosing only a service core and surrounding office space. This leaves a ground floor lobby which is relatively narrow and into which shops can fit only with some difficulty. If there is no financial incentive for installing the facilities which shops require, there may be no shops. In the 1960s, unlike the 1930s, the Center had major office tenants on hand and did not need to build space for income-producing shops and restaurants. Besides, it was a bit risky to draw visitors west of Sixth Avenue because the side streets there held little promise of soon becoming a retail zone of sufficient distinction to match the corporate stature of Exxon and its neighbors.

Under the city's comprehensive Zoning Resolution amendment of 1961, setbacks were no longer required because the new rules restricted ground coverage and total height, not simply bulk. A builder could construct a few floors above those normally allowed if he provided open plazas and other public improvements. Since lateral extensions for ground-floor shops meant shrinking the plaza which entitled him to the additional rental area, a builder would not build anything on the street level besides his elevator banks and lobby, in a period of high demand for office space. Of course, he could apply for zoning variances or for permission to build additional floor area in exchange for providing additional public benefits. But no builder wants to initiate negotiations with city officials unless he has to. Besides, Rockefeller Center and its corporate partners liked the slab designs, had no consuming interest in shops, and had already planned all the office space they wanted.

The officials at the Center and at Exxon were getting a building which they all found to be attractive. The key to its appeal seems to have been its visual simplicity and perhaps its formal familiarity. Eero Saarinen's nearby CBS Building (1965) is another straight topped, vertically striped rectangle; so is Edward Durell Stone's General Motors Building (1968), then known from published renderings. Both have plazas, too, with Stone's sunken one probably partly inspired by the one in Rockefeller Center. Governor Nelson Rockefeller had also asked Harrison & Abramovitz to design the Empire State Plaza office complex in Albany, where they used a striped design for parts of the buildings [11, 12].

Simple designs are easy to understand in renderings and models, and their monotony can be obscured, perhaps unintentionally, by the renderer's varied palette or by the model-maker's trees and tiny figures. Simple designs look refreshingly clear when superimposed on photographs of a crowded city (even if the actual experience of the jumble is more agreeable to some people than clarity and order). In any case, choosing a simple form is safer than risking the repetition of an innovative mistake on three huge adjacent buildings. Cautious thinking had influenced the choice of the original Center's vertical articulation, too. Besides, the vertical strips of the new buildings might remind people of those on the older buildings to the east. The new triad might then seem to be part of the old Center as the second Time & Life Building did not—although it was a few years before newspaper articles referred to the new buildings as being in Rockefeller Center.

The group is far from perfect. The four buildings are parallel slabs, each one blocking views from the side-street windows of its companions [63]. Their massing is repetitious, unlike the varied silhouettes at the original Center. They turn their backs to their neighbors at the west, relating only to each other and to the older buildings to the east, separating themselves from one part of the city as the original Sixth Avenue façades had done, to their own ultimate detriment.

The monotony of three similar buildings lined up in a row is not all bad. Their uniform recession from the street leaves room for the plazas which could not exist otherwise. Because their design does not require much more than a glance, the buildings do not call attention away from the plaza levels, which are the places pedestrians care about. A certain amount of calm repetition and expansive space is welcome in the midst of Sixth Avenue's competing corporate monuments of glass and steel on skimpy plazas. The three buildings do not compete with each other, but form a group which punctuates the line of buildings on the Avenue. They give to the new part of Rockefeller Center something of the distinctive definition that characterizes the old part.

XIII.

Theaters

"[Roxy] impressed [me] by his simplicity, his idealism, his fine spirit and his genius, as well as his breadth of vision and grasp of practical matters . . . We were thrilled with the theatre . . . When I first saw the model of its interior . . . I said I did not know what style it was . . . but that I liked it tremendously . . . I think the great auditorium is beautiful, soul-satisfying, inspiring beyond anything I have dreamed possible . . . I liked it in every detail, the gayly upholstered seats with their black edge and black arms and the charming two-toned black carpet included. The lobby is as distinguished and unusual and truly impressive as the theatre itself. Words fail me with which to express my delight with the Ezra Winters painting. . . . I liked too the great simplicity of the wall spaces with their long brilliant mirrors flanked by the sombre velvet panels. We visited the various galleries and withdrawing rooms on each floor. These rooms are all of them interesting, unusual and distinguished to an extraordinary degree. There is a style and chic about the whole building which is impressive in the extreme."

> John D. Rockefeller Jr. to John R. Todd, November 10, 1932, shortly after meeting Roxy and visiting the almost-completed Radio City Music Hall. Box 79, Todd & Brown file.

Rockefeller Center's office buildings were planned by corporate employees with Columbia's and Rockefeller's approval, and by the architects and engineers who gave form to the space and financial program, but its theaters show the guiding hand of Roxy, the master of showmanship who all but replaced the owners and managers in the theater planning process.[192] Roxy knew almost everything about popular entertainment while the owners and managers knew almost nothing. He knew as much about creating a successful radio program as the officers of the radio corporations did, since he had made his own show one of the best known in the entire country. He knew a great deal more than most of the radio group officials about variety productions combined with motion picture presentations, for his principal career had been that of showing films in ever-larger houses, adding live performers who did everything from playing Wagner overtures to performing circus stunts.

In 1927, this remarkable entrepreneur presided over the opening of the Roxy, a theater named for him on 50th Street near Seventh Avenue (west of the Center's second Time & Life Building). Walter Ahlschlager designed the theater to seat 5920 patrons in a sumptuous setting embracing as many historic styles as possible. A low entrance area contained ticket windows set far enough away from the ticket-takers to allow customers to move freely, but near enough to discourage loitering. The low passage led to an immense circular grand lobby with colossal marble columns and an exceptionally soft round rug underfoot which had a design of four Rs in the center. Then came the ornate auditorium—its doors opened by the famous corps of ushers who lined up each day as formally as the guard at Buckingham Palace. Films and stage shows featured tal-

ented performers and the "Roxyettes" chorus girls. Roxy's ambitions were almost satisfied.

But not quite. On hearing that the radio group planned to join the Rockefeller development, he proposed that he build a rival for his own namesake. The president of NBC spoke to Rockefeller, who approved of the idea.[193]

In April 1931 Roxy announced his affiliation with the Center, having severed his ties to the Roxy Theater. He knew just what he wanted for one of the radio group's theaters—the world's biggest theater for the world's biggest stage shows. He thought that live variety entertainment was due for a revival, and he intended to present the best variety artists in the world. Since he had always been right about popular taste in show business, the radio group and Rockefeller staff apparently gave him carte blanche, something not granted even to John R. Todd, who had always been right in his work, too.

For his new theater, as at the one he had just left, Roxy wanted a low ticket lobby leading to a splendid hall and then to an even more impressive auditorium. He wanted this climactic room to be egg-shaped, with an acoustical plaster ceiling descending to the proscenium. As far back as 1922, Roxy had declared that this was the ideal shape for a cinema;[194] he also must have known about the acoustically excellent egg-shaped Hill Memorial Auditorium at the University of Michigan (Ernest Wilby? for Albert Kahn, 1914) [96]. In 1929, Joseph Urban, who had been associate architect for the Metropolitan Opera plans, designed with Shepard Vogelgesang an egg-shaped auditorium for the New School for Social Research in New York; its president asked for a room of that shape [195] which the architects created by using suspended acoustical plaster ceilings.

Roxy wanted his auditorium to be huge, seating 6200 people, but he also hoped to give the patrons a sense of being a unified group. Group unity, perhaps even intimacy, could be fostered by eliminating the large balconies which cut most auditoria in pieces and place a confining lid over the heads of half the orchestra patrons. Roxy wanted shallow balconies instead,[196] like those of the Salle Pleyel in Paris. Furthermore, if the stage extended to the sides of the room, it could link the performers and the audience, while permitting flexibility in staging grand pag-

eants. The fan-shaped Wagner Theater at Bayreuth (1872-76) had such stage extensions, and had dispensed with balconies except for a single row of royal boxes, although achieving intimacy there was easier since the seating capacity was only 1650. Poelzig's project of 1920-21 for the Salzburg Festival Theater also had stage extensions, as well as a curved ceiling which unified the space.[197] And Joseph Urban had recently published designs for a music center with a fan-shaped auditorium for 5000 people, stage extensions, and a curved ceiling to tie the auditorium sides together and make the room seem smaller [97].[198] He designed the ceiling with telescoping bands decorated with perpendicular rays like those of a sunburst, forecasting those of the Radio City Music Hall. As at the Roxy, the music center stage would have movable sections which could be raised and lowered on elevators to vary the scenery and effects, and the orchestra pit could move up and down to suite the scene designer's requirements.

Roxy ordered an even more elaborate movable stage for his new Rockefeller Center theater; the machinery was created by Peter Clark who had also designed the Roxy Theater's stage. The lights were controlled from a panel with 4305 handles, located in the orchestra space so that the operator could see the stage (this device had just been introduced at the Earl Carroll Theater). Ticket holders were admitted to this mechanical wonderland by young ushers, often chosen from church-

96. Ann Arbor, University of Michigan. Hill Auditorium, interior, 1914. Albert Kahn and Ernest Wilby, architects.
(Courtesy Albert Kahn Associates, Detroit)

97. Music Center auditorium project, sections, *c.* 1927–29. Joseph Urban, architect.
(From J. Urban, Theatres*)*

TRANSVERSE SECTION: ⑭ STORAGE SPACE ㉒ BUFFET.
㊷ PARKING SPACE ㊸ PLENUM CHAMBER ㊼ LOBBY.

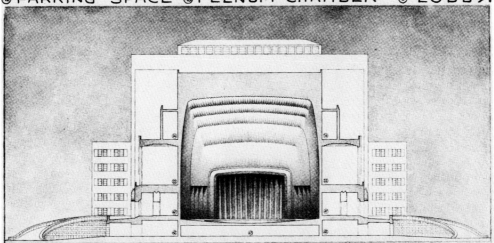

LONGITUDINAL SECTION: ① INFORMATION BOOTH ② BOX OF-
FICES ④ SUBSCRIBERS' MEETING ROOM ⑤ COAT ROOM
⑧ ORCHESTRA PIT ⑫ SCENERY STORAGE ⑬ SCENERY ELE-
VATOR ㉑ CHORUS ㉓ PROMENADE ㉕ DRESSING ROOM ㉖ OR-
CHESTRA REHEARSAL ROOM ㉞ ELEVATOR LOBBY
㉟ ROOF RESTAURANT ㊱ COSTUME DEPARTMENT ㊲ ENSEM-
BLE REHEARSAL ROOM ㊳ BALLET REHEARSAL ROOM
㊴ WORKING STAGE FOR AMPHITHEATRE ㊵ FLY GAL-
LERY ㊶ ELECTRICIANS' SHOP AND STORAGE ㊷ PARK-
ING SPACE ㊸ PLENUM CHAMBER ㊹ STAGE WORKING
SPACE ㊺ STAGE LIFT ㊻ SLIDING PROSCENIUM

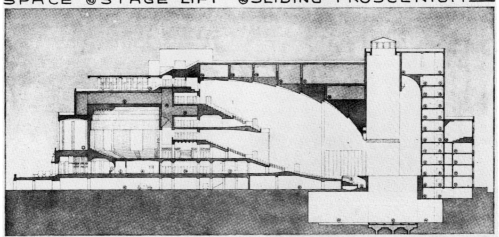

THE CENTRE AUDITORIUM IS A FURTHER DE-
VELOPMENT OF THE MEGAPHONE FORM. THE
SURFACE IS ARRANGED FOR DELICATE VARI-
ATION FROM DARKNESS TO DAZZLING LIGHT;
ONE MOOD EVOKED BY STAGE AND AUDITORIUM.

98. Radio City Music Hall, Roxy's studio, reception room. Donald Deskey, designer.
(*Helga Photograph, Courtesy* Antiques)

sponsored high schools, who were fired if they spent their rest periods in nearby saloons. The world's largest organ played as patrons settled down in extra-wide and widely spaced seats, to which an electric vacant-seat signboard directed them; this was another device borrowed from the Roxy. Latecomers could use program lights, recently installed at the Earl Carroll, to read about the fine performers and later about the new Rockettes precision dancers, rivals to the Roxyettes.

Backstage at the Radio City Music Hall, the performers' dressing rooms are as close as possible to the stage, or accessible by elevator, for Roxy believed in accommodating his employees far more comfortably than they were in most other theaters. There were a cafeteria, a dormitory, exercise space on the roof and indoors, a medical treatment room, and workshops. Roxy himself required a studio with all the comforts of home, including a reception room [98], a circular dining room, and a glass shower stall with half a dozen jets.

The architects gave physical shape to this program [99].[199] They had to place the theater on an interior site, reserving the Avenue frontage for an office building

99. Radio City Music Hall, plans and section.
(*From* Architectural Forum LVIII, *February 1933, p. 154*)

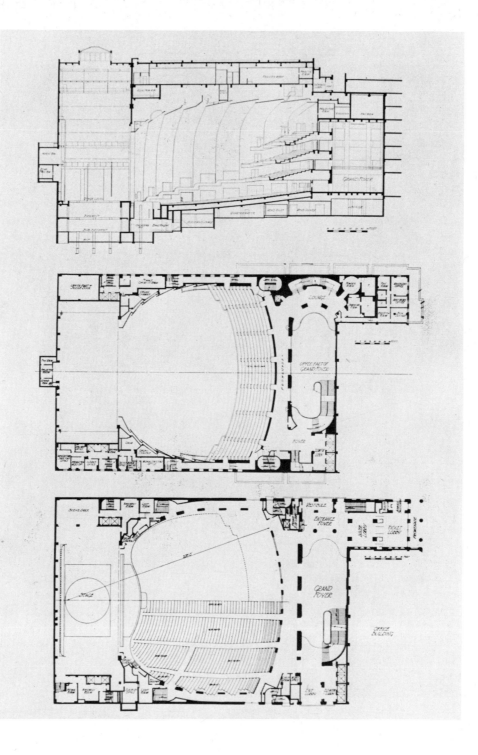

100. Radio City Music Hall, grand lobby looking north, with mural on staircase wall.
(*Courtesy Radio City Music Hall*)

mainly on Underel property, supported at its eastern end by the theater's western wall. In order to limit the theater's extension toward Fifth Avenue, they made the grand hall's axis perpendicular to that of the auditorium, forming a compact rectangular exterior with a low ticket lobby wing reaching to Sixth Avenue at the west.

The ticket lobby, low and relatively dark, is large enough to shelter many patrons during bad weather. The well spaced current performance ticket booths are aligned to establish orderly rows of purchasers, while the advance sale window is tucked out of the way at one side. As at the Roxy Theater, ticket holders move quickly to the interior entrance doors because the entrances are directly behind the ticket booths and because the distance between them is too small for comfortable lingering.

Just beyond the entrance doors, and 90 degrees to the left is a dramatically different space, a hall 140 feet long, 45 feet wide and 60 feet high [100, 101]. Toward the far (north) end, a grand staircase curves upward to the first of three superimposed corridors bordering one of the long walls; the corridors open onto

the hall on one side and into the balconies on the other side. Behind the principal staircase, a flight of steps descends to the lower and wider lounge in the basement [103] which was intended for entr'acte refreshments served at what would have been the world's largest soda fountain (which was never built). Tucked into a corridor even farther to the north are elevators to carry those who do not wish to use the softly carpeted stairs.

101. Radio City Music Hall, grand lobby looking south.
(*Courtesy Radio City Music Hall*)

Smoking lounges and powder rooms are provided at all but the main level. [112, 113, 114] as well as washrooms offering a total of 145 sinks.

Neither the lobby nor the grand hall raised any design problems. René Chambellan, a sculptor and expert model-maker, prepared clay models of the hall by early September 1931. The earliest models' wall treatment imitated an exterior pier-and-spandrel effect; the spandrels here had carved grillework decorations. Wall recesses on the staircase landing and the openings onto the upstairs corridors added patterns of shadow. In January 1932, however, the architects replaced the grillework and recesses by tall mirrors and a smooth staircase landing wall suitable for mural decoration. The final plans placed the staircase on the west wall instead of in the center as it had been, but there were no other major alterations from the January model.

The result is a high and stately hall with the great staircase of a traditional palace set against smooth and streamlined walls. The warm red and brown color scheme is given life by the sparkle of mirrors and by the light from two twenty-nine-foot chandeliers and smaller light fixtures.

102. Ezra Winter, *Fountain of Youth*, Radio City Music Hall, grand lobby. (*Courtesy Rockefeller Center, Inc.*)

103. Radio City Music Hall, basement lounge. Photographed 1932–33.
(*Courtesy Walter H. Kilham, Jr.*)

These shed a warm glow upon the golden ceiling—golden because Roxy ordered it changed at the last minute from the silver which Hood had told the decorators to execute at first. A custom-designed carpet dulls thousands of footsteps. Carefully polished metal doors with stylized reliefs of theatrical figures open into the auditorium. Alas, a candy stand on the opposite wall uses bright lights to attract attention, but a few soft bulbs would restore the architects' illusion of a splendid reception hall for the modern masses.

Warm earth colors of a mural on the staircase wall add to the harmony of the hall [102]. The painting itself is by Ezra Winter, an academic artist who decorated the Cunard Building where the Todd group, Reinhard, and Hofmeister had worked. Winter won a competition over

104. Radio City Music Hall sculptures in art studio before installation in theater. Left to right: William Zorach, *Spirit of the Dance;* Robert Laurent, *Girl with Goose;* Gwen Lux, *Eve.* Photographed 1932.
(Courtesy Rockefeller Center, Inc.)

even less distinguished rivals and represented a subject suggested by Professor Alexander. It is taken from an Oregon Indian legend, an American myth thought suitable for an American building. It warns man against trying to cross impassable frontiers—not exactly an optimistic topic for its date of 1931-32 when Rockefeller had almost three full city blocks to fill. In the picture, an old man ascends to a mountain peak, which is separated by a chasm from the fountain of youth. From this vantage point, he rieviews a "rainbow procession of the ambitions and vanities of his life"—not especially complimentary to either the aging Rockefeller or Todd, although no one noticed that. The mural is so large that it had to be painted in an unused tennis court, but it lacks force. It is decorative and undramatic, but paradoxically right for a hall which should not have been burdened with a literary subject in the first place. The results so pleased Rockefeller that words failed him.[200]

The lower lounge [**103**] is 200 feet long

by about 80 feet wide, divided into aisles by piers which support the upper foyer. The lounge is used today primarily by people going to the washrooms located on either side of a recess in one wall. But in anticipation of crowds seeking refreshments between the acts, the architects introduced three non-structural piers at the foot of the stairs to force people descending to fan out into three directions instead of crowding a single path. All the lounge piers are faced with gleaming black Carrara Glass bordered in bronze, typical of the high quality materials used throughout the building. Gunmetal mirrors add other reflections. The carpet by Donald Deskey, who supervised the interior design, is a black-on-gray plaid, complementing the ceiling design of inset concentric squares containing subdued lighting fixtures. The original draperies had geometric designs. Mural vignettes of the-

105. Radio City Music Hall, auditorium toward stage.
(*Courtesy Radio City Music Hall*)

atrical players by Louis Bouché are little more than inconsequential silhouettes and do not call attention to themselves. Even William Zorach's large statue of a kneeling nude does not stand out from its dusky surroundings because it, too, is gray—being made of aluminum—and angular [104]. The architects and designer must have wanted to create a mood of hushed refinement and understated chic, as a suitable background for the patrons.

Each corridor upstairs has slightly different decorations, and all offer views into the grand hall. Because the corridors had to be fairly narrow to leave room for the high hall, there can be unpleasant crowding when large numbers of people leave the balconies while others wait to enter.

The auditorium [105, 106] is the fitting climax for the other spaces which are tall and narrow or low and broad, and subdued in effect. Once past the metal portals and the rear transverse aisle, the theater patron approaches the great stage under telescoping bands of sunburst rays expanding from the curved proscenium arch as if they were successive layers of space. Their enormous size and their scale, which is difficult to measure, enlarge the auditorium underneath, while they tie the parts of the huge room together under their smooth curves. The rays seem to be painted in muted gold or soft beige, suggesting the rays of dawn. (A sunrise service is often held here on Easter Sunday.) The rays were actually stippled with soft tones of primary colors to avoid the stridency of white and to intensify the effects of colored lights. On request, the light orchestrator can produce an aurora borealis effect, or several thousand other patterns.

Even when the film is dull or the variety artists stale, the audience need not be disappointed. They watch the front curtain lift in any of a hundred different configurations, and see a second curtain produce openings ranging from doorway size to a frame for four five-story houses. The orchestra rises from below ground to its customary level in front of the curtain. The spectacular stage show features a corps de ballet, soloists, popular and light-classical orchestral music, singers, and circus acts. Even the Bolshoi ballerinas came

106. Radio City Music Hall, auditorium showing sides and rear mezzanines.
(*Courtesy Radio City Music Hall*)

to see the famous precision dancers, the Rockettes, who won a Grand Prix for their sixteen-minute performance at the Paris Exposition of 1937. At Christmas time a Nativity tableau features sheep, camels, donkeys, and horses. At the Easter season, another pageant transforms the stage into a church of an imaginatively ecumenical sect where Dutch-Russian-medieval maidens carry lilies and form a white cross as the orchestra plays Rubinstein's "Kamennoi Ostrow." At appropriate moments in a stage show, three parts of the stage may rise or sink or form a turntable about fifty feet wide. The stage itself can support six big elephants along with other lighter apparatus. With additional support, it can hold up a large swimming pool. Robert Edmond Jones, at one time the Music Hall art director, declared that the only stages even approaching this one were those at Max Reinhardt's Grosses Schauspielhaus in Berlin [107], and at La Scala in Milan.[201]

The stage apron extends to the side walls where platforms skirt the recesses containing the world's largest theater organ. The platforms then continue toward the rear of the auditorium stepping upward on the side walls. These extensions make splendid perches for Christmas angels and do just what Roxy said they should: surround the audience with a spectacle and make the side seats more desirable.

The design of the great auditorium was, of course, more of a problem than the design of the lounge and foyer had been. Roxy had specified its capacity, its shape, its stage, and its balconies, but not its style.

107. Berlin, Grosses Schauspielhaus. Hans Poelzig, architect.
(*Franz Stoedtner*)

108. Hartford, Bushnell Memorial Auditorium, interior. Corbett, Harrison & MacMurray, architects.
(*Courtesy Avery Library, Columbia University*)

The architects began by applying the experience of employees of Corbett, Harrison & MacMurray, for none of the other associated architects had designed a large theater. In Hartford's Bushnell Memorial Auditorium [108] the Corbett firm produced a room with stepped-back walls, an arrangement elaborating upon one which they had seen in a small theater in Paris. The steps rose to the ceiling, but stopped there, leaving a flat space on which Barry Faulkner executed a large and busy painting. At the Music Hall, the architects continued the stepped bands across the en-

110. Metropolitan Opera House project, 1927.
Joseph Urban, architect.
(*From J. Urban,* Theatres)

tire room to tie it together, providing a design in harmony with acoustical requirements and with Roxy's demand for an egg-shaped ceiling. The auditorium roof could not be made to curve, however, so that the architects had to construct a curved ceiling below it. Joseph Urban's introduction of a suspended plaster ceiling at the New School provided the model for this procedure. The lights, vents and other equipment could be tucked behind the ceiling bands, hidden from public view. The succession of curves would vary in height and shape, ranging from semicircular at the proscenium to elliptical at the rear. René Chambellan executed a series of small models to show the effect that such bands produced, in case this design did not turn out to be satisfactory, after all. Photographs made in May 1931, show that a first group of models with stepped bands was succeeded by a group of alternative models, one with a single curved ceiling with coffers [109], remarkably close to Urban's 1927 design for the Metropolitan Opera House [110]. Another model showed a square proscenium with the ceiling "steps" stretching from it to the rear of the auditorium instead of across the room. A third preserved the ceiling bands but eliminated those on the side walls. A subsequent group of models testifies to the architects' return to the transverse design of wall and ceiling bands, but the problem of detailed articulation remained, including the best method of incorpo-

109. Radio City Music Hall, preliminary auditorium model. Photographed May 1931.
(*Courtesy Walter H. Kilham, Jr.*)

OPERA AUDITORIUM. THE FLARING STAGE
OPENING IS SHAPED LIKE AN OPEN MOUTH
THE SIDES OF THE OPENING COMPOSE IN
PART THE WALLS OF THE AUDITORIUM AND
ARE OPENED AS A COLONNADE WITH SIDE
APRONS FOR ACTION AND PROCESSIONS

rating organ grilles into the wall design. Grilles following the arches seemed to be the most logical solution, but models showed that the grilles might seem to slide down the walls [111]. Edward Durell Stone who was in charge of the designs of both theaters, worked on this problem during the summer, when other models were photographed. Raymond Hood then suggested concealing the grilles behind radial lines on the ceiling and using wall bands like those which his close friend Urban had prosposed for a "Music Center" in 1929 [97], and which a renderer in Corbett's firm had sketched for the 1929 "symposium" project for the Metropolitan Square development's opera house. By September 17, a model with this arrangement was ready, complete with Stone's scalloped curtain design. Roxy later told the press and even some of the associated architects that he had thought of the radiating design after seeing a glorious sunrise or sunset while sailing to Germany and Russia, although in fact he did not even embark until six days after the model had been photographed.

This design became the final design. Chambellan built plaster models scaled at ¼" and 1", the larger one allowing the architects to enter, lie down, and look upward, to adjust details. Thereafter, they could make detailed drawings from the model. Work proceeded smoothly after that, until shortly before opening night. Roxy entered the auditorium to demonstrate its acoustic properties, and on clapping his hands found the sound totally unsatisfactory. Several stretches of auditrium wall had to be moved, and their fabric coverings rewoven in time for the opening night.

When John D. Rockefeller Jr. saw the model he said that he did not know what style it was, but liked it tremendously. After his son Nelson introduced him to Roxy in November 1932 and showed him the nearly finished theater, Rockefeller write of his admiration for both Roxy and the building. He admired Roxy's "simplicity, his idealism . . . his genius, as well as his breadth of vision and grasp of practical matters." He was "thrilled" with the theater, finding the auditorium "beautiful, soul-satisfying, and inspiring beyond anything I have dreamed possible." [202]

The room is unforgettable because its form is simple to understand and to describe, and because its size, its lack of intelligible scale, and its "celestial" shape can both exalt and overwhelm.

Gigantism was the fatal flaw of the Radio City Music Hall. The tremendous dimensions of the auditorium and of the hundred-foot-wide proscenium arch make performers look like dolls. The personalities of the people on stage do not project well to people in the orchestra, let alone to those 180 feet away in the uppermost mezzanine. The theater's depth was less than that of some other large ones of the day, but 180 feet is just twenty feet shorter than the standard length of a New York City block. Critic Douglas Haskell (who liked the theater anyway) suggested putting a giant magnifying lens over anything but massed crowd scenes. [203] The huge size of the auditorium and the comparatively small size of people on stage have led photographers to do almost what Haskell suggested. The few satisfactory pictures of the interior when it is in use are composite photographs of both the architecture and the stage. In

[105] the musicians are accurate in size in relation to the auditorium, but the Rockettes are somewhat larger than they ought to be and the performers behind them are considerably larger.

Some architectural critics have found the design bombastic, hardly worthy of comparison with Sullivan and Adler's Auditorium in Chicago. But the Auditorium was built for fewer and more cultivated patrons. Roxy said that his audiences were not ready for Bach or Beethoven or for entire operas, and he had no reason to think that they were ready for an architecturally subtle theater, either. 6200 seats had to be filled by people who could understand and enjoy their surroundings, and a simple, innovative design produced by a committee was exactly right for the purpose. Even Lewis Mumford—who did not generally admire Rockefeller Center—said that the Music Hall was infinitely better looking than the usual chain theaters which were not worthy of mention in the same breath.[204] Roxy was not, of course, as creative a spirit as Max Reinhardt, nor were the associated architects as imaginative as Hans Poelzig; the Music Hall is not equal to the Germans' Grosses Schauspielhaus in Berlin [107] which some of the American architects themselves knew. On the other hand, patrons come for the films and stage presentations, and the Music Hall does not distract from or compete with the programs.

The immense size had unfortunate economic consequences as well as aesthetic ones.[205] It was not easy to find attractions which would fill 6200 seats in a theater offering continuous performances every day of the year. The management has never been able to get all the films it wanted, and has had to show some that it did not want at all. The theater's reputation was made as a "family" theater in another generation and people still expect its attractions to be free of sex and gore. With the recent increase in "explicit" movies and with an inexact system of rating their moral content to distinguish between love and lust, the Music Hall is hard pressed to find films with which to maintain its universal appeal. The management is not eager to show only children's horse-and-dog movies.

While it is open, the theater must be staffed and heated and lighted and ser-

111. Radio City Music Hall, preliminary auditorium model. Photographed August 1931. (*Courtesy Walter H. Kilham, Jr.*)

viced. The performers must be paid even if they dance and sing for ten people. New and immense stage sets must be designed and constructed. The huge size makes the Music Hall ill-suited to conversion for other theatrical purposes; one could not possibly stage a play in it because people expect to see the expressions on an actor's face. The sound amplifying equipment which was installed after the auditorium was built does not provide perfect acoustics for grand opera or for certain kinds of rock music so that the theater can be used only for events in which the spectacle or mood takes precedence over actors' performances. Events in a theater as big as this one must be well publicized if enough people are to come to fill it, and advertising costs a great deal of money. The Music Hall also maintains its own public relations department. Nevertheless, the Music Hall generally prospered until television began to show the variety entertainment that people once could see only in person.

The original managers and the board of directors should have foreseen some of the Music Hall's problems even if Roxy's own enthusiasm and egotism prevented him from criticizing his own plans. The enormous Hippodrome spectacle hall on Sixth Avenue failed to attract sufficient numbers of people and had to close after its early heyday. Roxy was also going to compete with himself, in a way, because the old Roxy Theater with its almost six thousand seats was only one block away from the Music Hall and not much farther from the RKO Roxy (the Center Theater). There were plenty of other theaters nearby in the Broadway area which offered films

and vaudeville, singly or together. By the time that the Center's theaters were planned in 1931, someone should have thought more carefully about the effects of so much competition when fewer people had money to go to the movies. The radio group should also have assessed the potential impact of television, which it was developing at this time. The Center's planners did not do so because there was as yet no Planning or Architecture or Theater Committee; without having their own specialized working committees, the board of directors allowed the managers freedom to run the project. The managers and Rockefeller himself, however, were in no position to criticize the plans of the radio group which was rescuing Rockefeller from a loss in rent of $3,000,000 per year. No one could have known that Rockefeller Center would have to worry about operating the theaters itself, since RKO was the owner in 1931 and the Center was simply collecting the rent.

During the 1960s, when the Music Hall began to show a loss that reached about $600,000 per year in 1972, Harrison & Abramovitz prepared plans for office space to be built above the Music Hall, permitted by revisions in the theater Building Code. This might involve the destruction of parts of the world-famous interior. Subsequent plans envisioned fewer changes to the theater, but luckily (for everyone but the owners) the projects were set aside temporarily when Rockefeller Center found itself with too much existing office space and no need to build any more. Recent ways of bringing in revenue while keeping the theater open on a reduced schedule have in-

cluded midnight rock concerts which uti-
lize the theater's dazzling light effects and
draw attention away from certain acoustics problems; an ice show which recalls
the temporary solution to the Center Theater's problems; and "Art Deco" exhibitions. For a while, entrepreneurs discussed
installing an underwater show sponsored
by Jacques Cousteau which would have
required structural alterations in order to
support a huge water tank, and others
proposed building tennis courts on the
roof where Rockettes had once played
shuffleboard between shows.

The Music Hall continues to lose
money, even when 3,500,000 patrons a
year visit it. The corporate officials hope
to save it if outside funds can help to
offset the losses it sustains. It could suit
many public and private needs for as-
sembly space or it could become a convenient civic auditorium. But if that is
impossible, and if people's tastes in entertainment continue to move away from
suitable films and variety artists, the
Music Hall could turn into another sort
of theater, some sort of multi-purpose
structure, or even a department store.

The owners and managers held a limited competition in the spring of 1932 to
choose interior decorators for the two
theaters. Large department store design
staffs competed with two independent
designers, one of whom, Donald Deskey,
spent his "last $5000" to present his
winning ideas and a careful budget.
Stage designer Lee Simonson once characterized him as an artist with a good
sense of double-entry bookkeeping.

Deskey [206] is a trained architect who had
spent some time in Paris and was present
at the 1925 *Exposition internationale des
arts décoratifs et industriels modernes*—
the exhibition which is generally regarded as having established the "Art
Deco" styles in popular consciousness.
Returning to New York in 1926, he established a reputation by designing modern
window displays and furnishings. In 1930
Mrs. Rockefeller asked art dealer Edith
Halpert who was her friend and Deskey's
to engage him to remodel Mrs. Rockefeller's private print gallery. Deskey exhibited his work along with Raymond Hood's
at the American Designers' Gallery, a
group incorporated to present the decorative arts and industrial design. He also
knew the partners in Corbett's firm,
having designed new offices for them
which the architects found too advanced
at the time.

Adventurous ideas would not be out of
place in the world's largest theater.[207]
Deskey hoped to make it reflect the entire
range of American modernism, but he
had to work within a stringent budget
which he remembers as being about
$50,000. For $1500 each, he commissioned
three aluminum statues by sculptors well
regarded at the time [104]: William
Zorach, whose heavy-limbed nude "Spirit
of the Dance" kneels at the entrance to
the washroom alcove in the basement
lounge; Gwen Lux, whose "Eve" stands in
a stairwell niche; and Robert Laurent,
whose nude "Goose Girl" poses with her
superfluous pet on the first balcony corridor. The Aluminum Corporation cast
the statues free, probably for the publicity
and the experience, although a journalist

reported that at one point the casting of the goose was delayed for lack of $300. The sculptures attracted a flurry of public interest when Roxy declared that nudes were offensive to public morals, though his own lively reputation made some acquaintances doubt that Roxy himself was shocked. He ordered the statues to be removed, whereupon outraged art lovers protested and paid the statues and the Music Hall far more attention than they might otherwise have done. When the first round of news stories ended, Roxy gave his theater even more publicity by returning the three aluminum nudes.[208] It is hard to see how these bland and

112. Stuart Davis, mural, and furniture by Donald Deskey. Radio City Music Hall, men's smoking room. Photographed May 1974.
(*Helga Photograph, Courtesy* Antiques)

heavy maidens could have offended anyone's moral sensibilities.

Deskey paid the painters $1500 as well. The best composition was a 12 x 18 foot painting by Stuart Davis [209] [112] who exhibited at Mrs. Halpert's Downtown Gallery. For the basement lounge smoking room, he designed a lively semi-abstraction later entitled "Men Without Women" which incorporated barber poles, cigarettes and other "masculine" objects as part of the design. Georgia O'Keeffe agreed to paint the curved walls of an upstairs powder room, but despite the best efforts of Rambusch Decorators, part of the wall covering peeled off just when she came to inspect the room (reliable adhesives did not yet exist), and she abandoned the project. Deskey called in another exhibitor at the Downtown Galleries, Yasuo Kuniyoshi, who decorated the room within a few weeks. He painted enormous floppy flowers which alternate with round mirrors, creating a place of gentle fantasy. By a curious coincidence, if that is what it was, his use of oversized flowers recalls O'Keeffe's interest in magnified floral forms [113]. Other murals are less remarkable but agreeably decorative.

Deskey exercised particularly good judgment in choosing fellow members of the American Union of Decorative Artists and Craftsmen to work with him. Ruth Reeves designed a perfectly appropriate carpet for the grand foyer, a "synthetic cubist" arrangement of musical instruments in colors which complemented the velvet-lined wall coverings and which also hid dirt. She created another semi-abstract design of "The History of the Theater" on fireproof fabric on the rear wall of the auditorium. Henry Varnum

113. Yasuo Kuniyoshi, floral murals, and furniture by Donald Deskey. Radio City Music Hall, women's powder room. Photographed May 1974. (*Helga Photograph, Courtesy* Antiques)

Poor executed ceramic lamp bases and ceramics often in sturdy, simple shapes but with motifs often dependent upon Greek and Roman mythology. Deskey himself was a good designer and he designed some of the wall coverings, carpets, glass and wooden furniture, handsome metal lamps and light fixtures and the decoration of Roxy's studio [98]. For the walls of a men's smoking room, he designed a lively pattern with a tobacco-growing motif, executed on aluminum foil. The R. J. Reynolds Tobacco Company had recently entered the aluminum foil business, and had once asked Deskey if he could think of anything to do with the foil besides making cigarette wrappers. The DuPont chemicals corpo-

114. Radio City Music Hall, women's powder room, Donald Deskey, designer. Photographed May 1974.

(Helga Photograph, Courtesy Antiques)

ration devised a special adhesive to permit the installation of this new non-porous covering. In a polygonal powder room, Deskey installed mirrored and glass fittings, increasing the apparent depth of a small enclosure while expressing the fragility of the ephemeral tasks performed there [114]. The yellow, white and blue color scheme was appropriately light and bright, and the carpet design incorporated the geometric forms that governed the room shape. In his furniture, Deskey favored geometric, swelling shapes and tried to avoid excessive streamlining. His simple lamps, which are particularly handsome, were the products of his own taste. Roxy, however, preferred the

"Portuguese Rococo" of the Roxy Theater so Deskey applied some color accents to the case furniture and put small round ornaments on the table supports to make Roxy happier about twentieth-century design. For the tables and some other pieces, Deskey used aluminum and bakelite which were comparatively new furniture materials in the United States. They met the needs of durability and newsworthy novelty. With a feeling for economy equal to that of Todd & Brown, Deskey had his furnishings manufactured at favorable prices in exchange for the publicity which they would generate. Other materials drew attention to themselves because they seemed to be utterly impractical—ponyskin lounge chair uphol-stery, peach and silver-toned custom-designed wall coverings, hand-blocked fabrics—although some of them proved to be as durable as more prosaic materials, and the public respectfully treated them well.

In Roxy's studio [98], Deskey covered the high walls of the major room with wood paneling which conceals built-in furniture, and added free-standing pieces that provide a suitable mixture of comfort and formality to a living room used for business purposes. In the adjacent round dining room, a circular table which is the focus of the room has in its center a well which can be illuminated softly, giving the table's formal simplicity the surprising touch that mirrored Roxy's personality. Some studio rooms were remodeled in 1941 and later, but the reception/living room, dining room, pantry, kitchen, and bathroom remained virtually unchanged examples of luxurious interiors of forty-six years ago.

From the main auditorium to the hand-some metal grilles over the fire hoses or the ornamental spiral brackets under stairway handrails, the architects and decorators designed the Music Hall to an unusually high standard. It is a pity that landmarks do not always make money. The Rockettes precision dancers still sur-pass their rivals. The thousands of light combinations, the pealing organ music, the orchestra platform which rises and glides backwards, the mammoth Easter and Christmas pageants already belong to the memories of two generations of Americans. There are many families who take for granted the prospect of a four-block waiting line at holiday time [58]. The Music Hall even became the basis for two recent works of "pop" art, and for poems recited by a dancing-school teacher in front of Ezra Winter's mural.[210] It is a safe guess that more American and foreign tourists attend its performances than go to any other single entertainment attraction in New York, and they generally get their money's worth, too. If the whole Center is a secu-lar cathedral, the Radio City Music Hall is Roxy's chantry chapel.

The Center Theater always played the role of modest younger sister to big brother Music Hall, but plenty of atten-tion was lavished upon it all the same. Planning was under way by the spring of 1931.[211] In May preliminary clay models of the auditorium showed a curved ceiling over the auditorium in which the walls curved around toward a broad proscenium arch. At the rear were three shallow balconies. Beside the pro-scenium were recesses, apparently with stairs in them and perhaps mechanical equipment hidden there as well. The first model shows a ceiling decorated with concentric half-ovals. Another shows stepped-back or telescoping side walls, very much like those of the Music Hall, with spiral stairways or ramps set into the recesses. A third has side walls orna-mented in alternating plain and relief-carved strips and a stubby column appar-ently providing some support for flights of steps which replaced the spiral stair-way [115]. Another version photographed two weeks later has criss-crossed ramps

115. Center Theater, preliminary model. Photographed May 1931.
(*Courtesy Walter H. Kilham, Jr.*)

116. Center Theater, preliminary model. Photographed January 1932.
(*Courtesy Walter H. Kilham, Jr.*)

or stairways. All these projects were abandoned by August 19 when photographs were taken of a model with plain, smooth walls. The theater no longer looked like a shrunken Music Hall.

By January 9, 1932, a pair of alternative models was ready for evaluation. Both had flat ceilings, smooth walls, three shallow balconies and a large proscenium arch, but grillework on the side walls over vents and sound equipment was vertical in one study and horizontal in the model finally adopted [116]. Renderings of the theater were prepared for publication in the next few weeks.

The theater was built on an L-shaped plot, the thick auditorium leg set on an interior site within the south block, with the thin entranceway leg stretching eighty feet to the marquee on Sixth Avenue. The theater could not be situated entirely on the Avenue because the Center did not then control the adjacent building lots; besides, the managers had always planned to build an office building on the Avenue to take the most profitable advantage of Avenue frontage. A distinctive façade (principally of shot-sawn limestone on a granite base) would, they thought, attract patrons. After much study during 1931 [117a-c], the designers chose a plain rectangular front, flanked by thin rectangular towers which hid water tanks, and with a simple metal marquee below [53]. In style, the façade was a softened version of the asymmetrical geometry of

117a,b,c. Center Theater, façade and marquee studies. Photographed June 1931. (*Courtesy Walter H. Kilham, Jr.*)

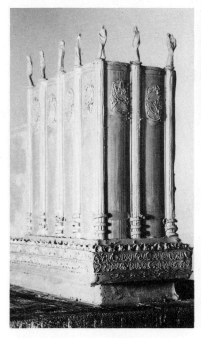  

the European circle of Josef Hofmann; there was a substantial contingent of Austrian and German architects living in New York who had been trained in that style. The theater proper,[212] east of the eighty-foot entrance corridor, consisted of the curved auditorium with three balconies which the models forecast; between the auditorium and the entrance corridor lay a lobby [118], as wide as the 158-foot wide theater but only twenty-two feet deep, providing elevator and stair access to the balconies above and to the lounge under the lobby. Five tall windows covered with beige draperies lined one side of the lobby, curving walls the other. Thick vermilion-colored piers that reminded people of steamship funnels rose above the curved walls to hold the balconies. Roxy said that his Atlantic crossing on the *Europa* had inspired this design,[213] as a sunset at sea had supposedly inspired the Music Hall auditorium design, but the Center Theater, too, was probably laid out before he saw the ship.

The auditorium seated 3500 people originally, in a room with an average

118. Center Theater, grand foyer.
(*Courtesy Rockefeller Center, Inc.*)

119. Center Theater, auditorium. Photographed 1932.
(*Wide World*)

height of sixty-five feet [119]. The walls were covered in ribbed mahogany veneer over steel, maintaining the red-brown-beige color scheme of the entire theater. The high stage wall was never good for film patrons because those in the upper balcony who looked straight ahead had a view only of a blank wall above the movie screen; these people would have to look down at the screen, an uncomfortable arrangement which also distorted the pictures. Much of the ceiling was covered by a gigantic chandelier, twenty-five feet in diameter, weighing six tons and incorporating four hundred hot floodlights which required their own special ventilating system. René Chambellan and Oronzio Maldarelli decorated it with un-

distinguished classical figures; a lighting specialist firm, Cox, Nostrand and Gunnison executed the light fixtures. The installation occasioned a strike because the plasterers wanted to install the chandelier since it was almost an entire ceiling, while the electricians claimed it as their own.

Although Donald Deskey won the competition for the position of interior decorator in both theaters, he could not do that much work, and yielded here in favor of Eugene Schoen who was also interested in contemporary design. Schoen provided colorful upholstered chairs with simple lines for the lounges. He designed a lively women's lounge with mirror-lined walls which repeatedly reflected the fur-

120. Center Theater, women's lounge. Eugene Schoen, designer.
(*Courtesy Radio City Music Hall*)

niture [120]. In an adjoining room, Maurice Heaton created a semi-cubist glass relief commemorating the transatlantic flight made by Amelia Earhart [121], a favorite heroine of both Roxy and John R. Todd. This also complimented women, who were not included among the sketches of those who left "Footprints in the Sands of Time" on the third mezzanine walls. These were Roxy's heroes of invention and adventure such as Edison, Marconi, Admiral Byrd, Charles Lindbergh, and Eadweard Muybridge.

The men's lounge had its curving walls entirely covered with memorable photomurals by Edward Steichen [122, 123], representing the Wright Brothers' first flight, Lindbergh as a mail pilot, British and American aerial photographers, and other aspects of aviation history.[214] If the patrons' taste seems curiously able to have

encompassed Steichen's brilliance and the weakness of some of the decorative painters, it must be admitted that the patrons probably leaned more toward the latter than the former. Steichen seems to have been Schoen's choice, and a photographer was invited to do the work because he could produce about 150 feet of seven-foot-tall mural in three weeks, faster than a painter could. Art critics outdid each other in praising Steichen's achievements, with only a few crotchety dissenters failing to understand how photography could produce works of art.

Critics found the whole building appealing, in fact. They found a 3500 seat theater to be "the intimate drawing room that advance publicity had proclaimed it" and said that it had "intimacy of scale . . . gained by the use of oversize ornament combined with great simplicity of scheme." Its modernism came from "finding a natural beauty in materials themselves." [215] It was not old-fashioned, not an expressionist experiment, not formally or intellectually challenging. It was dignified and cheerful and commodious. But it could not make a profit.

The managers asked Walter Damrosch, the eminent musician, to find out whether or not it could be used for live music, including opera or Philharmonic concerts. It couldn't, having been so carefully prepared for sound movies that acoustical reverberations for concerts would be inadequate. Later in the year, the managers installed a movable, revolving stage, lowered the high proscenium arch and added new cooling equipment to make it suitable for stage shows. It became a second-run cinema for a while. At one point, Max Reinhardt expressed interest in using the theater, but nothing came of that owing to conflicting commitments that the Center had made to the film industry. In 1936 the architects extended the stage by removing sixteen feet of orchestra space, again in order to mount several successful spectacular musical shows.

In 1940 the roof of the theater was rented to Simon & Schuster, publishers, for twenty offices and reception rooms.[216]

121. Maurice Heaton, *Amelia Earhart Crossing the Atlantic, Harbor Grace to Ireland, May 1932* and furniture by Eugene Schoen. Center Theater, women's lounge. (*Courtesy Radio City Music Hall*)

Harrison & Fouilhoux, Reinhard & Hofmeister designed a one-story building there with a flat slab roof cantilevered over thin piers [124]. Much of the building perimeter was made of 250 feet of plate glass, but the roof overhang of about three or four feet was great enough to shield the interior from the unpleasant effects of summer sun and winter wind. The tenants loved their rooftop perch and the charming views, through glass walls, of planting on the pavement around them. They admired Edward Durell Stone's simply-designed furniture which was finished in carefully-oiled natural

122. Edward Steichen, *Story of Aviation*. Center Theater, men's lounge.
(*Courtesy Radio City Music Hall*)

123. Edward Steichen, *Story of Aviation*. Center Theater, men's lounge.
(*Courtesy Radio City Music Hall*)

tones of wood; such fittings were novel in corporate directors' offices at the time.

In the same year, Norman Bel Geddes directed the removal of even more seats from the interior of the theater and made an even larger stage suitable for ice shows.[217] This gave the theater distinctive identity, but in 1950 NBC's need for more studio space outweighed the importance of ice shows. Eight more rows of seats came out, this time at the back of the orchestra, so that a television control booth could be added when the theater was used for television broadcasting. Three years later, NBC's requirements outgrew the theater's ability to satisfy them, just when the U. S. Rubber Company needed room to expand. Harrison & Abramovitz designed an extension to the U. S. Rubber Company Building which replaced the Center Theater in 1955 [59].

The demolition men who wrecked the theater in 1954 sold its stage to Bob Jones University in South Carolina; its lighting fixtures and equipment to the Steel Pier in Atlantic City, New Jersey; its seats to Bowdoin College in Maine, to the Grand Teton National Park Theater in Wyoming, and to a synagogue in Lakewood, New Jersey; and its organ to a man in Pennsylvania who built a new wing on his house for it. The wreckers sent the world's largest chandelier to be scrapped for the steel it contained. All this represented a sacrifice of architecture, of Edward Steichen's photomurals and of other works of art and decoration, but these things may have seemed to the owners little more than trappings on a white elephant.

124. Center Theater, roof. Simon & Schuster offices, 1940. Photographed 1940 or 1941.
(*Courtesy Condé Nast Publications, Inc. Copyright © 1941–1969 by The Condé Nast Publications, Inc.*)

XIV.

A Future Half a Century Old

"By and large, we can be very thankful indeed for what remained in the Center as conservatism. Both the fact of the uniform material . . . and the fact of the lingering symmetry of Beaux-Arts composition, turned out to be highly useful in giving the Center a distinct sense of place and letting you feel, in terms since made familiar by Kevin Lynch, that you know where you are within the scheme, where you have been, and where you are going."

Douglas Haskell, *Architectural Forum* CXXIV, January 1966, p. 46.

Rockefeller Center is symbolically satisfying. Unlike Walt Disney World's fantasyland and unlike an academically-conceived civic building complex focused on a latter-day Roman temple or Palladian villa, Rockefeller Center does not pretend to be what it is not. It was a business development first of all, and the appropriate focus is on the RCA Building [33], the seat of the companies that saved Rockfeller from losing over three million dollars a year. The owner, who was interested in the maximum beauty consistent with profitability, also got a balanced and intelligible, profit-generating plan.

The relationships between buildings are clear, and yet the plan is not dull. The sunken plaza forces visitors to diverge from the main visual axis, and the varied sequences of ground-level spaces, enclosures, and openings from Saks Fifth Avenue to the Exxon minipark is comparable to that of the Forum of Trajan, or even to Michelangelo's project which

125. McGraw-Hill sunken plaza during concert performance. Photographed 1974. (*Courtesy Rockefeller Center, Inc.*)

linked—at least in plan—the Campo dei Fiori with the Palazzo Farnese and the Villa Farnesina. Rockefeller could enjoy looking at the limestone towers and the works of art, the flags and skaters and plants which both tourists and town planners find memorable, too.

Current tendencies in architecture and planning help to explain a renewed interest in Rockefeller Center. Many younger architects have abandoned the ideal of the soaring white rectangle on the spacious plaza. It seems a sterile ideal now, although it was refreshing and inspiring a half century ago, making a belated entry into New York planning through the zoning amendment of 1961. Plazas often isolate buildings, making them objects placed on concrete trays rather than integral stitches of a city's fabric. Outside Rockefeller Center, Sixth Avenue's irregular pockets of concrete and planting tubs beside high glass towers look as brittle as the promises of a more sensitive urban environment. The wind sweeps people and rubbish across open pavements and some people fear that criminals lurk behind the bushes in the landscaped spaces.

New York City's Master Plan of 1969, the zoning amendments of 1973, and proposals made in 1974 foster a different sort of development. The Master Plan lists desirable features "for the midtown and lower Manhattan areas where highly complex uses are concentrated . . .:

Extra usable space for pedestrian movement or for public use, including bridges over streets and concourses under streets, [87]

Direct connections from buildings to the subway system, [4]

Underground truck access to new buildings, so that service and supply vehicles will not block congested streets, [39]

Mid-block pedestrian arcades that provide rental space for smaller shops and businesses which cannot afford avenue frontage, [67]

Housing for a wide range of income levels." [218]

All but the last have already been done at Rockefeller Center, the fourth feature included under city pressure at the Celanese Building, but the other three incorporated by the original planners. Housing, but for high-income tenants, may be built in the future.

The new zoning admendments favor retail shops placed at the building line instead of bank offices recessed in windy plazas. There will be covered pedestrian passageways, too. Planners want to see chairs and trees in the plazas. These features are all meant to add color and convenience and interest to the experience of being in the city. Exciting density has returned to favor. So has an interest in retaining the strong building line as a characteristic physical feature of Manhattan, which is kept at Rockefeller Center for profit and for the sake of an intelligible design. Transportation planners envision a network of underground pedestrian passages in midtown like those of the Center

—attractive, well lighted, and well patrolled, lined with shops and connected to mass transit facilities. The combination of office work and ice-skating, progressive planning and traditional limestone, advanced communications and vaudeville acts, international trade and colorful retail shops, cost-efficiency, and a Christmas tree provide the varied urban experiences congenial to current planning ideas.

Insofar as New York is the laboratory city of the western world in this century, Rockefeller Center has been a critical experiment, testing ideas for city development. The worst results reveal significant problems of the twentieth-century, such as the glorification of corporate business while man, diminished, stands in the shadow of his own creations. The best results also incorporate the best experience of urban life—the multitude of exciting experiences available in a concentrated location [125, 126], man's ability to control aspects of technology, the provisions made for a humane working environment in the earliest buildings, consideration for both pedestrians and drivers, and the combination of work and rest.

In 1969, the American Institute of Architects recognized the achievement of the original group of buildings, by awarding its Twenty-Five-Year Citation for architectural excellence:

To a lesson in land use which devotes such large areas to air and space, but also for human enjoyment

To a group of high structures . . . which offered a new approach to urban planning . . .

To an exemplary composition of building masses . . . not only delineating the boundaries of the project but integrating building, malls and plazas into a uniform design solution

To one of the first . . . circulation concepts which separated pedestrians from vehicular traffic . . . and purposely relates to public transportation systems

To an . . . effort of integration of all the arts, including landscaping . . .

To the vision and foresight of an enlightened client . . .

To the selection of an architectural idiom which due to the simplicity of its design and the quality of its material remains a timeless and enduring example of its era

To a project so vital to the City and alive with its people that it remains as viable today as when it was built.

126. Rockefeller Center, Christmas, 1940.
(*Courtesy Rockefeller Center, Inc.*)

Notes

(All box numbers refer to Rockefeller Family Archives, Business files, except as noted.)

1. For the functional and symbolic analogies between Rockefeller Center and the Forum of Trajan, see my article "Rockefeller Center," *Antiques* CVII, March 1975, pp. 478–86.

2. In passing, we may note that crucifixes were sold in 1940 which had medallions of Rockefeller Center below the body of Christ; Box 69, General file, Memo E. Phillips to N. Lavender, 6/7/40. They were not made or sold by the Center. The Woolworth Building had been nicknamed the "Cathedral of Commerce" but that referred to its tall tower ornamented in a Gothic style.

3. Rev. Joseph Sizoo of St. Nicholas Reformed Church formerly at Fifth Avenue and 48th Street, quoted in *Rockefeller Center Magazine* III, April 1940, p. 7.

4. W. Hegemann, *City Planning. Housing*, New York, 1938, p. 31, fig. 197.

5. J. Barnett and J. Portman, *The Architect as Developer*, New York, 1976.

6. P. Blake, "Downtown in 3-D," *Architectural Forum* CXXV, September 1966, pp. 31–51; "Place Ville Marie," *ibid.*, CXVIII, pp. 74–89. The cliffhanger story of Place Ville Marie's financing and of the resolve exhibited by the project's developer, William Zeckendorf, in the face of distress are also reminiscent of the Rockefeller Center situation. Zeckendorf had worked for Rockefeller Center for some years.

7. See S. Stephens, "Chicago Frame-Up," *Architectural Forum* CXL, Jan.–Feb., 1974, pp. 75–79; M. W. Newman, "Oh Oh Calcutta In the Sky," *Inland Architect* XVIII, December 1973, pp. 12–16.

8. P. Blake, "Walt Disney World," *Architectural Forum* CXXXVI, June 1972, pp. 24–41; P. Goldberger, "Mickey Mouse Teaches the Architects," *New York Times Magazine* 10/22/72; "Review of Disney Impact," *Florida Trend*, November 1972, pp. 45–90.

9. The successive projects are illustrated in C. Moore, "The Establishment Invites You . . . ," *Architectural Forum* CXXV, September 1966, p. 72. For the earlier "arts center" proposal which is part of its background, see volume of the Regional Plan cited in note 39 below. In 1949, Harrison designed a new Opera House, concert hall, television studio and garage for a site south of Washington Square and in the autumn of 1953 worked on a combination Opera House and office building for Broadway and 64th Street; an ancestor of this is the proposal by Benjamin Wistar Morris, see below, p. 28 ff. For a chronology of the Lincoln Center development, see the *New York Times Index*, 1955 ff.

10. "The Chase: Economics of a Big Invest-

ment," *Architectural Forum* CXV, July 1961, pp. 86–87; "Want to be a Rockefeller?" *ibid.*, pp. 63, 65. Architects: Skidmore, Owings & Merrill, 1960.

11. For this project, formerly known as the South Mall, see *New York Times Index,* and articles especially of 8/21/66, 2/15/71, 1/25/73, 10/9/73, 2/20/74; my essay "St. Petersburg-on-the-Hudson," in *Festschrift* for H. W. Janson (forthcoming). E. Carruth, "What Price Glory on the Albany Mall?" *Fortune* LXXXIII, June 1971; "Too Much at Any Price," *Architectural Forum* CXXXVI, May 1972, p. 7. Nelson Rockefeller estimated the cost at $985,000,000 plus interest, see *New York Times* 1/26/75. Other estimates are $1.1 to $1.5 billion.

12. At various times in the past the stock of Rockefeller Center has been held by holding companies such as Midtown Development Corporation and Rockefeller Plaza, Inc. The family members have been sole stockholders in these corporations. Concerning the ownership of the land and buildings, see C. Kaiser, "The Truth Is, Columbia Owns Rockefeller Center Buildings, Too," *New York Times* March 2, 1976, VIII, pp. 1, 6.

13. A convenient summary of his family's building activities is in "The Rockefeller Touch in Building," *Architectural Forum* CIX, March 1958, pp. 86–91.

14. For the history of the Columbia site, see C. Klein, "Columbia and the Elgin Botanic Garden," *Columbia University Quarterly* XXXI, December 1939, pp. 272–97; *idem*, "The Rockefeller Center Property," *ibid.* XXXIII, February 1941, pp. 59–75.

15. A succinct account of skyscraper growth including more than the analysis of architecture is given in *The Skyscraper,*

a large pamphlet published by the American Institute of Steel Construction and produced by the editors of *Fortune,* New York, 1930, esp. pp. 37–38.

16. See M. Scott, *American City Planning Since 1890,* Berkeley, 1969.

17. T. E. Tallmadge, *The Story of Architecture in America,* New York, 1927, p. 294.

18. For Grand Central, see D. Marshall, *Grand Central,* New York, 1946; "The Lost New York of the Pan American Airways Building," *Architectural Forum* CXXVIII, January–February, 1968, pp. 48–55; D. Haskell, "Futurism with its Cover On," *Architectural Review* CLVII, May 1975, pp. 300–304; J. M. Fitch and D. S. Waite, *Grand Central Terminal and Rockefeller Center,* Albany, 1974. For Terminal Park, I have used a telephone interview with the late Ralph Walker, correspondence with William Holabird, old plans and photographs.

19. Box 82. Metropolitan Square Corporation Sale to Opera Company file.

20. Metropolitan Opera Association archives.

21. Box and file: See note 19. Harry Hall to C. O. Heydt, 12/3/29.

22. For these early Opera plans, see archives in note 20; W. Weisman, "Towards a New Environment: The Way of the Price Mechanism; The Rockefeller Centre," *Architectural Review* CVIII, December 1950, pp. 398–404; *idem.* "The First Landscaped Skyscraper," *Journal of the Society of Architectural Historians* XVIII, May 1959, pp. 54–59; *idem,* "Who Designed Rockefeller Center?" *ibid.* X, March 1951, pp. 11–17.

23. New York County Register (records of land transfers).

24. *New York Times* 5/11/28.

25. John D. Rockefeller, Jr. Real Estate In-

terests, Box 27. 22–24 West 53rd Street file: On June 25, 1928, Heydt wrote to Rockefeller suggesting that he buy 22, 24 and 28 West 53rd Street to block a sixteen-story apartment hotel that was being planned; it would be very noticeable from Rockefeller's house at 10 West 54th Street. Heydt also thought it advisable to buy all properties between 4 and 22 West 53rd Street since prices were comparatively reasonable because of the unpleasant subway work going on. The purchase would also stave off anticipated efforts to rezone the streets. "In view of the possible development of the Columbia property, all of these properties will be greatly increased in value and the whole area within three or four blocks of the Columbia University development will take on new life. I feel especially concerned about those buildings in 53rd Street which are directly opposite Mrs. Prentice's house and the empty lot at 9 West 53rd Street."

26. Box and file: see note 19.
27. The suggestion is in Box 70, B. W. Morris Correspondence file. Drawings he made for the opera project are at the Avery Library, Columbia University.
28. See archives and file in notes 20 and 27.
29. Francis T. Christy, *History of Rockefeller Center,* unpublished typescript at Rockefeller Center, Inc., 4th draft, 1950, p. 11. The people interested were Herbert L. Satterlee representing Walker & Gillette, architects, with the National City Company and U.S. Realty Investment Company, Inc. Former employees of Walker & Gillette, and Poor & Swanke, successors to Walker & Gillette, have no records concerning this project.
30. Some people who knew Heydt say that he did the preliminary work on new projects and only brought to Rockefeller's attention those which were promising. Other people think that Rockefeller's staff never did anything without telling him about their activities. In the present case, "Mr. Jr." may have given his approval for the initial steps, but he only heard the results in May.
31. Box and file: see note 19. Ivy Lee to Rockefeller 5/25/28.
32. Box and file: see note 19. Heydt to Rockefeller 6/1/28.
33. Box 72, 1933–1945 file. Heydt to Rockefeller 3/24/36; it was actually to be between $3.3 and $3.8 million. On June 1, Hall had prepared a map showing the assessed valuation on each lot; Box 84, Miscellaneous map and data file.
34. All the real estate consultants' opinions are contained in Box 77.
35. For Todd, see his autobiography, *Living a Life,* New York, 1947, ed. William Vogel; G. Hellman, "The Man Behind Prometheus," *The New Yorker* 11/14/36, pp. 35–38, 11/21/36, pp. 23–26; for Todd, Robertson and Todd, see "A Phenomenon of Exploitation," *Architectural Forum* LXI, October 1934, pp. 292 ff.; *The Boulevard* I, November 1931, pp. 25 ff.
36. Todd, *Living a Life,* pp. 78–80.
37. For Reinhard and Hofmeister's careers, I rely on the memories of Mrs. Reinhard, Walter Kilham, Jr., Wallace Harrison, and Earl Lundin. Mrs. Reinhard prepared an unpublished biography of her husband shortly before his death and kindly allowed me to read it.
38. A short form of the lease, the only version recorded, is in Liber 3810, p. 172 of Conveyances in New York County. Articles 18 and 21 of the lease are

addressed particularly to the opera and plaza sites. The lease was eventually extended to September 30, 1973 when it was renewed for a higher rental.

39. *Regional Plan Association of New York and its Environs, II The Building of the City,* ed., Thomas Adams *et al.,* New York, 1931, passim; "The Problems of Traffic Congestion and a Solution," *Architectural Forum* XLVI, March 1927, pp. 201–208; *New York Times* 2/27/31; "Architecture Has Become a Business," *The American Architect* CXXXVII, # 2579, January 1930, p. 46.

40. For Harrison, see A. Churchill, "Architect for the World," *This Week* III/23/47, pp. 11, 26; *Time* 9/22/52, pp. 78–84; H. W. Wind, "Architect," *The New Yorker* 11/20/54, pp. 51 ff.; 11/27/54, pp. 51 ff.; 12/4/54, pp. 55 ff.; J. Greenfield, "Curtain Going Up for Wallace Harrison," *New York Times Magazine* 8/21/66, pp. 37 ff.

41. Corbett's copy of the program is at Avery Library, Columbia University. For these projects, see W. Weisman, *The Architectural Significance of Rockefeller Center,* unpublished dissertation, Ohio State University, 1942, pp. 21–24; *idem,* for a briefer summary in articles cited in note 22 above. Charles A. Platt never submitted a proposal.

42. For the Mayor's cultural center, see below, pp. 85 ff.

43. Morris' blueprint, dated March 18, 1929, is in Box 84, Miscellaneous Maps and Data file. Heydt obtained them in early April (Box 70, B. W. Morris Correspondence file).

44. Box 70, B. W. Morris Correspondence file. 4/26/29.

45. Minutes 5/15/29.

46. Box 84, Miscellaneous Maps and Data file.

47. *Ibid.,* and Box 79, Todd & Brown file. Morris' early proposals in this series are dated 7/2/29. Heydt's authorship of the unsigned letter to Rockefeller is confirmed by internal evidence.

48. Todd, *Living a Life,* pp. 83-84.

49. Box 79, Todd & Brown file. Rockefeller memo 8/28/29.

50. Box and file: see note 49. John R. Todd to Debevoise 8/28/29.

51. Rockefeller memo cited in note 49; another copy in Box 84, Misc. Maps and Data file.

52. Box and file: see note 49.

53. Box and file: see note 46.

54. For Reinhard, Hofmeister, Hood and Corbett, see board of directors' minutes 10/22/29; for Morris, see Proposed Resolution of board of directors, 11/4/29. Rockefeller Center, Inc., file 7-1-1, Corporate Matters, General Correspondence.

55. Todd, *Living a Life,* pp. 88–89.

56. For the same company, Hood designed Ideal House (now Palladium House) in London, with R. Gordon Jeeves (1928); the ground floor has recently suffered a lamentable remodeling.

57. For Hood, see W. H. Kilham, Jr., *Raymond Hood, Architect,* New York, 1974; A. T. North, *Raymond Hood,* New York, 1931; A. Talmey, "Man Against the Sky," The New Yorker 4/11/33, pp. 24 ff.; for Todd's remark, see Hellman article cited in note 35.

58. Todd resigned from the board of directors on November 4. Nelson Rockefeller, aged 21, replaced him. For details of the plot plan, see Weisman dissertation cited in note 41, p. 25.

59. Box and file: see note 19. Letters of

12/3 and 12/6/29; Box 69, General file, Rockefeller memo 6/2/33, Rockefeller speech 9/30/39.

60. Box and file: see note 19. Todd to Winthrop Aldrich 12/4/29. Todd, *Living a Life,* pp. 90–92 gives a more diplomatic version of this opinion.

61. *Ibid.,* pp. 119–120. Harden wrote to Rockefeller on 12/27/29.

62. Weisman dissertation cited in note 41, p. 31 and his figs. 23–25; illustrations in *Architectural Forum* LVI, January, 1932, pp. 2–3.

63. Minutes 1/8 and 1/21/30. An amended version of the January 21 plan was presented on February 3; Weisman's dissertation gives excerpts from it on pp. 32–33.

64. Board of directors' minutes 1/8/30.

65. Box and file: see note 49. John R. Todd to Rockefeller 2/11/30.

66. The revision of May 20 was the basis of the agreement with the radio group of June 5, 1930, approved by Columbia University on August 13, 1930 with the proviso that buildings on Underel property be separable from those on the Columbia leasehold.

67. For Hood as originator and Rockefeller as critic of the oval: interview with Earl H. Lundin 12/19/73.

68. Later this was abandoned because the City required more entrances and roadway space than the developers wanted. Earlier ideas for having two levels of shops—at grade level and above—were dropped because the arcades in front of the lower shops would have obscured the display windows and entrances.

69. Minutes 6/24/30.

70. The plans known as F plans come after the G and H plans. Weisman's dissertation, cited in note 41, discusses them on

pp. 41–42. The Rockefeller Center staff threw the sketches away several years ago.

71. Box 80. Todd-Robertson Cash Requirements file. Rockefeller memo after 9/15/30.

72. This occurred by 9/15/30.

73. Todd, *Living a Life,* p. 110.

74. The yearly gross income from F-18 was calculated at about $19,000,000 and the net at about $11,000,000 before interest and return on the investment. Christy, *History,* p. 52. Cost estimates varied. On February 26, 1935, Hugh Robertson wrote to the Financial Information and Budget Committee of the board of directors that the total estimated cost was $74,875,000.

75. Todd, *Living a Life,* p. 87.

76. *New York Herald-Tribune* 3/31/31.

77. But apparently planned on March 24 and revised on April 16. Christy, *History,* p. 53.

78. Transcript of conversation between Hood and Merle Crowell 8/19/31.

79. For the Ludlow incident, see below p. 73 and note 97. Rockefeller's comment and architects' fears: interview with Wallace Harrison 6/18/73.

80. Box and file for Morris' viewpoint: see note 27.

81. See note 78.

82. None of Wenrich's renderings were drawn to scale. Information from Morris Weiss, architect at Rockefeller Center.

83. Board of directors' minutes 7/22/32 approving employment of Manship. The present sheet of water behind Prometheus and the present lighting were designed by Abe Feder in 1958. A preliminary sketch for Prometheus is illustrated in E. Murtha, *Paul Manship,* N.Y., 1957, pl. 80. A small gilt bronze

sculpture of two figures, one in Prometheus' pose, is in the Rockefeller Center, Inc. art collection. For Manship's opinion of his work and for his earlier ideas, see K. Andrews, "What Paul Manship Thinks of Prometheus," *Rockefeller Center Weekly* II, 1/17/35, pp. 5, 22, 23.

84. *Theatre Management* XXVI, October 1931.

85. Harrison interview, see note 79; Mrs. Reinhard interviews.

86. *New York American* 1/25/33.

87. Christy, *History*, p. 61.

88. *New York Times* 8/13/29.

89. Minutes 11/13/31.

90. Box 70, Sol Bloom file. Rockefeller to Mussolini 3/10/32. Mussolini's visit and the new twin buildings are described in the Rockefeller Center press release of 6/1/33 which all New York papers printed on that day or the next.

91. 72nd Congress, Public Act 296, signed 7/19/32.

92. Rockefeller letter to Lord Southborough in Rockefeller Center, Inc., *The British Empire Building*, New York, 1933.

93. Board of directors' minutes 4/21/33.

94. Box and file: see note 49. Woods to Rockefeller 6/22/33.

95. Box and file: see note 19. See also archives cited in note 20, and plans as described in *New York Times* 4/9–10/32, 7/16/32. Only in 1937 did Todd announce an end to the Opera plans, but Rockefeller criticized his statement about the "opera house that . . . until your article day before yesterday we had all assumed would ultimately be built." Box and file: see note 49. Letter dated 5/13/37.

96. Press releases 2/23/32.

97. The Ludlow tragedy in which the victims suffocated in a cave blocked by a burning tent, is still discussed in labor union circles. It affected Rockefeller profoundly and he remained grateful to C. O. Heydt, then an aide to the senior Rockefeller, for accompanying him to Ludlow where Heydt did much to improve a bitter situation. Friends and services Box 126, Heydt Retirement file, Rockefeller to Heydt 11/6/41.

98. For their handling of labor matters, see board of directors minutes 1/20/33; also box and file cited in note 49, Nelson Rockefeller to his father 8/13/32.

99. The actual need for fuel was hard to calculate because broadcasts and theater productions might increase their power requirements in the future. For climate control measures, see *Heating and Ventilating Magazine* XXIX, May 1932, pp. 18–31 and June 1932, pp. 47–51.

100. Interview with Webster Todd, 10/25/72; Todd, *Living a Life*, p. 111; board of directors' minutes 11/18/31.

101. J. A. Morris, *Nelson Rockefeller*, New York, 1960, pp. 93–94.

102. *Business Week* 1/20/34, p. 14; *New York Times* 1/11/34; Box 70, Heckscher file.

103. There were other minor suits. Two, which were dismissed, were for patent infringement in machines used at the Music Hall. The only successful suit was brought by the Roxy Theater management which stopped the Rockefeller Center cinema from using Roxy's name.

104. Box and file: see note 49. Letter to Joseph O. Brown 3/8/32.

105. Todd, *Living a Life*, p. 121; Webster Todd interview. The Board of Directors did not agree immediately to use Westinghouse products; Minutes 12/18/31.

106. Box 69, General file. Letter to F. S. Staley stating that Rockefeller did not

want exclusive privileges given, even to the Chase National Bank of which his brother-in-law was president.

107. Box 69, General file. Documents between May and August 1933.

108. See note 78.

109. Board of Directors Minutes 11/13/31.

110. Minutes 11/20/31.

111. *Variety* 2/2/38.

112. Early plans had fewer mirrors, no wine storage vaults, and a single-level floor, Box 80, Nelson Rockefeller to his father 7/9/34. Changes are discussed in board of directors Minutes 10/26/34.

113. *New York Magazine* VII, 12/9/74, p. 34.

114. *Ibid.*, p. 37.

115. Box 96, Terminal File. Staley to Heydt 8/10/33.

116. All material about the terminal proposals comes from Box 96, Terminal file, except where specifically indicated.

117. Board of directors' minutes 9/23/31.

118. *New York Times* 2/21/68, 12/28/73. Real Estate Interests, Boxes 26–29.

119. Box 70, A. C. Marks file. Heydt to Debevoise 6/29/36.

120. Box 69, General file, 10/26/34 although Grimm had been making inquiries about this property since July 31.

121. For the Rockefellers and the Museum of Modern Art, see pertinent files at the Rockefeller Family Archives. Sketches for the private street extension are in the Architecture and Design Department of the Museum.

122. R. Lynes, *Good Old Modern,* New York, 1973, p. 175.

123. Real Estate Interests, Box 27, 14 West 53 Street file. Heydt to Real Estate Committee 4/19/37; Real Estate Interests, Box 29, West 53–54 Street Development file, Staley memo 5/3/35; Real Estate Interests, Box 33, Apartment House file, Gumbel to Nelson Rockefeller 8/1/38.

124. A number of other New Yorkers also proposed north–south routes, e.g. a real estate man, A. N. Gitterman who suggested an unrealistic version of Morris' "Metropolitan Boulevarde" to the Manhattan Borough President; see *New York Herald-Tribune* 1/5/36.

125. For the municipal art center, see Cultural Interests, Box 89. See also Robert Moses, *Report to the Mayor from the Park Commissioner on the Proposed Municipal Art Center* 9/20/38; Planning Committee Minutes 8/17/35. Other information from interview with Wallace Harrison. J. A. Morris, *op. cit.*, p. 106 says that Nelson Rockefeller originated the Municipal Art Center project.

126. Architects' contracts and responsibilities information is in Rockefeller Center, Inc. file L, Contracts and Agreements, Architects Group file, and Architects and Engineers Office 1-1 file of Architects and Engineers' Correspondence.

127. Illustration in *The Boulevard* I, October 1934.

128. Planning Committee Minutes 8/7/35, 9/5/35.

129. Perhaps the most perceptive appreciation of the central plaza is that of Gerald Allen, "High Rise Buildings: The Public Spaces They Make," *Architectural Record* CLV, March 1974, pp. 128–137.

130. Box 80, Building No. 7 file. 1/28/38 for the meeting. Letter dated 2/16/38.

131. *ibid.*

132. Interview with Bertram Hegeman,

Vice-President, Renting Office 6/28/74. *New York Times* 11/2/38.

133. Box 80 Garage file. 9/22/38.

134. For the U.S. Rubber Co. (Uniroyal) Building: Box 94, Rockefeller Center leases, letters of 12/1 and 12/19/39. See *New York Times Index* 1939–41 s.v. Sixth Avenue, New York City. Other New York newspapers carried similar articles. For a particularly striking vision of Sixth Avenue in 1939 and in an architect's dreams, see *New York Mirror* 8/13/39 with drawing by Caleb Hornbostel.

135. Testimony submitted to the Temporary National Economic Committee, summarized in *New York Times* 2/28/40.

136. Merle Crowell speech to Real Estate Board of Newark, N.J., reported in *New York Sun* 3/7/40.

137. For the development of the Esso Building, see documents dated 1941–48 in Box 81, Esso Building file.

138. For these problems, see Box 72, 1947—file, especially Nelson Rockefeller, Summary of Problems Facing Rockefeller Center . . . 6/20/50 and his memoranda to the Board of Directors of 8/15/50 and 8/22/50.

139. Caroline Hood, *Outline of a Report on the Decade at Rockefeller Center 1949–1959,* unpublished typescript at Rockefeller Center, Inc., p. 151.

140. *ibid.,* p. 153. Rockefeller Center bought 600 Fifth Avenue in 1953.

141. *ibid.,* p. 152.

142. Interview with Louis C. Schoeller, retired Executive Vice-President and an engineer in charge of all operating functions at the Center.

143. For the development of the NBC and Time Inc. project, see Rockefeller Center, Inc., Corporate Matters, General Drafts and Duplicates, 7-1-1, Mrs. Louise Boyer file.

144. Information about the nominee corporation's name and the Ford showroom proposal from interview with Remsen Walker, Vice-President, Subsidiary Projects.

145. Information about Time Inc.'s possible move from interview with Gustav S. Eyssell.

146. Hood, *Outline* . . . , p. 48.

147. "A Tall Tower for Time Inc.," *Architectural Forum* CVIII, January 1958, p. 96.

148. Remsen Walker interview.

149. For the Saks proposal, see Box 69, General file 1951–62, memorandum of 10/18/54.

150. H. W. Corbett, chairman; Members Leopold Arnaud, Edward Durell Stone, Hugh Ferriss, Wallace K. Harrison, Walter H. Kilham, Jr., Stephen Voorhees, Ely Jacques Kahn.

151. Interview with G. S. Eyssell.

152. Interview with Bertram Hegeman. A rendering of the project is in *Progressive Architecture* XL, March 1959, p. 160. Harrison & Abramovitz prepared the design.

153. The photograph files of the Avenue of the Americas Association contain a photograph of the building. Harrison & Abramovitz were the architects.

154. Sperry-Rand Building 1962: Emery Roth & Sons, architects; Harrison & Abramovitz, consultants, Mr. Hegeman asserted that Harrison & Abramovitz suggested changes from the building's original design which was based purely on economic considerations.

155. Hilton Hotel, 1962: William Tabler, architect; Harrison & Abramovitz, con-

sultants. Rockefeller Center, Inc. sold its interests in the hotel in 1960.

156. Box 69, General file 1951–62, letter of 5/12/60.

157. For the origin of the project for the three new buildings, I rely on interviews with Messrs. Eyssell and Hegeman. For the architectural development: interviews with Mr. Walker and with Michael Harris, partner in Harrison & Abramovitz (which has also been known as Harrison & Abramovitz & Harris). See also *New York Times* 11/28/67 showing McGraw-Hill Building rendering no. 2127 of a building 645′ tall with 1.8 million square feet; *ibid.,* 8/6/71 with rendering no. 2227 showing the building finally built.

158. Lauren Otis, former Deputy Director of the Mayor's Office of Midtown Planning and Development provided insights into contemporary planning theory, with particular reference to midtown Manhattan. See above, note 129 for excellent critique of the Rockefeller Center plazas on Sixth Avenue.

159. Interview with Earl Lundin, 12/19/73.

160. Additional information from Mitchell/Giurgola Associates, Architects. The project was published in A. H. Kemper, *Drawings by American Architects,* New York, 1973.

161. For the cafeteria designs, see "The Many Facets of Exxon's New Domain. Highlights of Welton Becket/New York's Vastest and Most Challenging Interiors Endeavor Begin with the Employee Cafeteria in a Romantic Subterranean Garden," *Interiors* CXXXII, January 1973, pp. 74–84.

162. Another excellent small park, designed by Sasaki, Dawson, and DeMay is Greenacre Park on East 51st Street

(1972), the gift of Abby Rockefeller Mauzé.

163. Interview with Alton F. Marshall, President of Rockefeller Center, Inc.

164. The project and design supervisors' names do not appear in the records of Rockefeller Center, and most participants in the project have forgotten them. As far as Wallace Harrison, Walter Kilham, Jr., Earl Lundin, William Delehanty, Edward Durell Stone, Morris Weiss, and Gunnar Svalland can remember, the supervisors were: RKO Building: Earl H. Lundin, job captain. RCA Building and RCA Building West: T. Somers Newman, job captain, Carl Landefeld, design supervisor. NBC Studios: Bert Deer, job captain. Radio City Music Hall: Edward Durell Stone, design supervisor, William Delehanty, job captain. Center Theater: Edward Durell Stone, design supervisor, Galen White, job captain. Architects and draftsmen from Reinhard & Hofmeister's office were Newman, Deer, A. W. Butt and George Johnson. Landefeld, Svalland, Pauly, Kilham, H. V. K. Henderson (a specialist in ornament), Frank Roorda and Oscar Wiggins had worked for Hood. Delehanty came from the Corbett firm and was one of the few Corbett employees to work for a considerable length of time at the Center. Other architectural staff members were Robert Carson and Earl Lundin who later became resident architects at Rockefeller Center before starting an independent firm, Richard Granelli, and men named Denz, Griffin, and Ferrari. Ralph Calder was a specialist in ornament, especially dense symmetrical vine scrolls and plant forms. Other participants' names are now lost. I have

heard several architects wish that they had a nickel for every job applicant who claimed to have helped design Rockefeller Center.

165. In chapters XI and XII, I discuss the original designs rather than the subsequent interior remodellings which have been so thorough that Louis Schoeller said that there are no old buildings at the Center; see *Real Estate Forum* October 1960, also June 1973 with Mr. Schoeller's remark. J. Wilson, "An Office Address That's Constantly Redressing," *Buildings* LXVIII, June 1974, pp. 73–83.

166. Two old four-story buildings still stand on the Sixth Avenue corners, testimonials to the profitable stubbornness of their owners who must have understood that the development would benefit their businesses. Rockefeller Center recently bought one of them, housing a genuine old saloon, and converted it into an artificially old "pub."

167. For the design of the RCA Building and the RCA Building West, see Weisman, reference in note 41, pp. 48–49; H. H. Dean, "A New Idea in City Rebuilding," American Architect CXXXIX, April 1931, pp. 32–35, 114, especially for the four early fenestration schemes shown in our illustration 75a–d; "Rockefeller Center Has World's Largest Office Building," *Architecture and Engineering* CX, August 1932, pp. 49–56; "RCA Building, Rockefeller Center, New York," *Architectural Forum* LIX, October 1933; pp. 273–277; drawings in the Architectural Department, Rockefeller Center, Inc.; photographs of early schemes and models by Walter H. Kilham, Jr. Interviews with Messrs. Kilham, Harrison, Lundin, and Webster

Todd supplemented these sources. For the NBC Studio designs, see O. B. Hanson, *The House that Radio Built*, New York, 1933; *idem*, "The Plan and Construction of the NBC Studios," *Architectural Forum* LVII, August 1932, pp. 153–59; "The Radio City Broadcasting Studios," *Architectural Record* LXXV, January 1934, pp. 73–92.

168. Board of directors' minutes 5/1/31.

169. *Ibid.*, 4/7/31.

170. See above, note 78.

171. Rockefeller Center, Inc., Architects' Department, Drawing Tube no. 279. It was done for plan F-18M and is dated 11/11/31.

172. Todd, *Living a Life,* p. 116.

173. Box 94, Theme and Decoration file. 9/29/33.

174. Box 94, Theme and Decoration file. John R. Todd to Rockefeller 10/24/35.

175. For Rivera's career and for the Rockefeller Center commission, see Box 95, Rivera file, and the biography and published correspondence in B. Wolfe, *The Fabulous Life of Diego Rivera*, New York, 1963, pp. 317–334. For Rivera's own version of the events, see D. Rivera (with B. Wolfe), *Portrait of America*, New York, 1934, pp. 21–32, and pp. 40–47 for illustrations of the Rockefeller Center mural. Rivera's sketch is reproduced in "The Stormy Petrel of American Art: Diego Rivera on His Art," *London Studio* VI, 1933, pp. 24–25. For Shahn's role, see Archives of American Art, Shahn papers, under letter R, Microfilm roll D 147. See also G. Hellman, "Profile" of Rivera, *The New Yorker*, 5/20/33. The "Wailing Wall" proposals are discussed in Planning Committee Minutes and Supplementary Records between 10/18/35 and

11/14/36, as well as in correspondence in Box 94, Theme and Decoration file.

176. Box 95, Sert file.

177. Box 94, Theme and Decoration file.

178. Box and file: see note 49. John R. Todd to Rockefeller 8/2/33.

179. *New York Times* 1/17/74.

180. For the International Building, International Building North and Palazzo d'Italia, see Weisman reference in note 41, pp. 49–53, 83–86, 93–94; *New York Times* 6/1/32 for rendering with nine-storey wings; "International Building," *Architectural Forum* LXIII, November 1935, pp. 456–68.

181. Box 79, Todd & Brown file: Rockefeller to Hood, 2/3/34.

182. Box 69, General file: R. W. Gumbel to Rockefeller 12/27/34.

183. Minutes of the Planning Committee 9/17/36; Weisman dissertation cited in note 41, p. 119.

184. For the first Time & Life Building, see "Operation Rejuvenation," *Real Estate Forum* X, October 1960, pp. 16–37.

185. The houses at 12 and 14 West 49th Street may be seen beside the completed office building in our illustration 49; they were later destroyed when the land became the site of a wing on the Sinclair Oil Building (now 600 Fifth Avenue). The December 1935, plans are described in the Planning Committee Minutes 12/4/35 and the problems *ibid.*, memorandum to the Committee 11/21/34, among the Supplementary Records.

186. AIA citation, see below, pp. 198–199; S. Giedion, *Space, Time and Architecture*, Cambridge (Mass.), 1941, pp. 576–577, seems to be the source of these ideas.

187. Board of directors' Minutes 4/27/36.

188. For all these decisions, see planning committee minutes between 11/22/35 and 11/10/36, including the Supplementary Records related to meetings held between those dates. Production work began on 5/1/36.

189. For the Eastern Air Lines Building and garage, see "Building No. 11, Rockefeller Center, New York," *Architectural Forum* LXXII, January 1940, pp. 23–27; Reinhard, Hofmeister, Harrison and Fouilhoux were the active architects and Corbett and MacMurray were available for consultation. See Rockefeller Center, Inc., Contracts and Agreements—Architects Group file, especially letter from Rockefeller Center, Inc. to the architects 7/26/38.

190. See above, notes 144–148, and "Time & Life Building Presages the Renaissance on the Avenue," *Real Estate Forum* XIV, June 1959.

191. For the Exxon Building and its neighbors, see above, notes 157–161, and "How Rockefeller Center Stays Young," *Real Estate Forum* XXVIII, June 1973; C. Harman, *A Skyscraper Goes Up*, New York, 1973 (an account of building construction meant for teen-aged readers); S. Cavander, "Lobbying in Midtown Manhattan," *New York Times* 11/11/73, X, pp. 1, 12; letter by P. Goldberger, *ibid.*, 11/25/73, X, p. 4. The McGraw-Hill Building has granite-faced columns which intrude into the office space; such columns are cheaper to build than those of the Exxon Building. Intruding columns produce a flatter façade; granite could have been added to make the exterior column faces more robust, but granite was very expensive and the planners did not want to make Mc-Graw-Hill and Exxon Buildings identi-

cal. The McGraw-Hill interior module is 5′, Exxon's and Celanese's is 4′6″. For the McGraw-Hill Building, see J. Morgan, "A Tale of Two Towers," *Architecture Plus* I, October 1973, pp. 42–52, 82–83; "Designing an Office Building for a Particular Client and His Needs," *Architectural Record* CXLV, April 1969, pp. 186–191. The Celanese Building resembles its northern neighbors but is the cheapest and flattest of the three. It uses flat limestone panels to sheathe the intruding columns. Its *galleria*, from which Ibram Lassaw's sculpture, "Pantheon," provides a welcome distraction, is undistinguished in design and detail. See also E. Carruth, "The Skyscraping Loss in Manhattan Office Buildings," *Fortune* XCI, February 1975, pp. 78 ff.

192. For Roxy, see Rothafel scrapbooks, New York Public Library Theater Collection, and S. L. Rothafel as told to J. C. Fistere, "The Architect and the Box Office," *Architectural Forum* LVII, September 1932, pp. 194–196; S. L. Rothafel, "The Heart Is the Target," *Woman's Home Companion,* July 1932, pp. 13–14; K. Macgowan, "Profile" of Roxy in *The New Yorker* 5/28/27, pp. 20–22; B. Hall, *The Best Remaining Seats,* New York, 1961, pp. 121–23 and insert by J. Alicoate, "The Romance of the Roxy."

193. B. Mantle, column in the *Chicago Tribune* 1/8/33.

194. *New York Times* 6/11/22, VI, p. 2.

195. A. Johnson, *Pioneer's Progress,* New York, 1952, pp. 320–24.

196. See above, note 194.

197. Paul David Pearson brought this to my attention.

198. J. Urban, *Theatres,* New York, 1929.

The "music center" may well represent Urban's ideas for the Metropolitan Opera House on the 110th Street site.

199. The design process can be traced through photographs by Walter H. Kilham, Jr., and in drawings in the Rockefeller Center, Inc. Architects' Department. My information is also based on interviews with Messrs Harrison, Lundin, Deskey and Harold Rambusch, and on telephone interviews with William Delehanty and Edward Durell Stone. See also E. D. Stone, *The Education of an Architect,* New York, 1962, p. 30. Models are illustrated in H. Hofmeister, "The International Music Hall," *Architectural Forum* LVI, April 1932, pp. 355–60. Although the Center's architects designed the theaters, RKO engaged George L. and C. W. Rapp as consulting architects for the Music Hall and Thomas Lamb for the cinema. Metropolitan Life Insurance Company sent two of Daniel Everett Waid's assistants to examine the theaters. None of these outsiders had any discernible effect on the theater development. The Rapp correspondence at the New York Public Library Theater Collection contains no information about the Music Hall.

200. Box 79, Todd & Brown file. Rockefeller to John R. Todd 11/10/32. Elaine Evans Dee told me that Winter's preliminary sketches are at the Cooper-Hewitt Museum. The subject is described in Rockefeller Center, Inc., *The Art Program of Rockefeller Center and its Contributing Artists,* Typescript, rev. ed., 1972, p. 14.

201. G. Britt column in *New York World-Telegram* 12/20/32.

202. See above, note 200.

203. D. Haskell, "Roxy's Advantage Over God," *Nation* CXXXVI, 1/4/33, p. 11.

204. L. Mumford, "The Sky Line," *The New Yorker* 1/14/33, pp. 55–56.

205. For problems facing the Music Hall and plans for its future I have interviewed Messrs. Marshall, Eyssell and Harris, and Mrs. Patricia H. Robert, Director of Public Relations for the Music Hall.

206. Interviews with Donald Deskey. Articles about him include G. Seldes, "Profile" in *The New Yorker* 2/25/33, pp. 22–26; *New York Herald-Tribune* 7/9/32; "The New Decoration in America," *London Studio* V, January–June 1933, pp. 22–30. Deskey also designed rooms in the apartment of Abby Rockefeller, then Mrs. David Milton, and a dressing room and bathroom for her mother.

207. For illustrations of the Music Hall interior, see "Radio City Music Hall, Rockefeller Center, "*Architectural Forum* LVIII, February 1933, pp. 153–160; "With the Gentlemen in Mind," *Arts and Decoration* XXXVIII, January 1933, pp. 27–29; P. G. Whiting, "Rockefeller Center Debut," *American Magazine of Art* XXVI, February 1933, pp. 83–84.

208. Zorach's autobiography, *Art Is My Life*, New York, 1967, pp. 89–93 tells the story from the artist's viewpoint and gives information about his *Spirit of the Dance*.

209. The painting was moved to the Museum of Modern Art in 1975. Hilton Kramer wrote: "Its removal signifies the loss of a civic ideal—a belief in the viability (and durability) of first-rate public art, and a resigned acceptance of the museological segregation of high art." *New York Times*, 4/13/75, II, p. 29. A study for it was offered for sale at Sotheby Parke-Bernet, New York, Sale no. 3520, 1973, from the O'Donnell Iselin estate; see catalogue no. 35C with illustration. Deskey owns another study for it, as well as a study for Kuniyoshi's paintings described below.

210. L. Alloway, "Art," *Nation* 6/19/72, describing works by Ira Joel Haber and Brigid Polk. For Mary Bruce's poems set to music, see E. Leogrande, "At the Radio Mural Hall," *New York Daily News* 3/27/73.

211. The design process can be traced through photographs by Walter H. Kilham, Jr. G. Schutz, "The Motion Picture in Rockefeller Center," *Motion Picture Herald* 2/13/32, pp. 13–15 has illustrations of preliminary designs for the interior.

212. The completed theater was described in "RKO Roxy Theater," *Architectural Forum* LVIII, February 1933, pp. 160–64; "Radio-Keith-Orpheum Theatre," *American Architect* CXLII, December 1932, pp. 41–54.

213. E. Gilligan column, *New York Sun* 12/9/32.

214. N. Ház, "Steichen's Photo-Murals at New York's Radio City," *American Photography* XXVII, July 1933, pp. 404–08. See also "Mural Photographic Decoration—A New Industry," *Photography* (London), December 1933; "Nyheter fra Amerika," *Meddelelser fra Oslo Fotografforening* I, February 1934, pp. 1–2.

215. R. Watts, cited in "World's Biggest Playhouse Opens," *Literary Digest* CXV, 1/14/33, p. 17; T. Hamlin, *Forms and Functions of Twentieth Century Architecture*, New York, 1952, p.

119; Schutz, *op. cit.*, p. 15 respectively.

216. J. O'Connor column in *New York Journal-American* 1/29/40, when other New York newspapers carried stories about it; *House and Garden* LXXIX, March 1941, pp. 26–27. Mr. Leon Shimkin, Chairman, Simon & Schuster, Inc., offered his comments about the building.

217. For the later history of the theater, see G. Freedley, *The Stage Today*, typescript copy of article about New York theaters, New York Public Library Theater Collection; "Last Word," *The New Yorker* 8/21/54.

218. New York City Planning Commission, *Plan for New York City, I: Critical Issues*, New York, 1969, p. 33.

Bibliography

Background

For the history of the Rockefeller Center site, see Claire Klein, "Columbia and the Elgin Botanic Garden Property," *Columbia University Quarterly* xxxi, December 1939, pp. 272-97, and *idem*, "The Rockefeller Center Property," *ibid.* xxxiii, February 1941, pp. 59-75.

General Works

The tendencies in American commercial architecture in the years just before Rockefeller Center was inaugurated can be gauged from Thomas Tallmadge, *The Story of Architecture in America*, New York, 1927, and Francisco Mujica, *History of the Skyscraper*, New York, 1930.

While the Center was rising, the following works were published, reflecting historians' reactions to it: Sheldon Cheney, *The New World Architecture*, rev. ed., New York, 1935, and Walter Curt Behrendt, *Modern Building*, New York, 1937.

A recent work which reflects current interest in the decorative aspect of New York architecture between the World Wars is Rosemarie H. Bletter and Cervin Robinson, *Skyscraper Style: Art Deco, New York*, New York, 1975.

Accounts
of Rockefeller Center

The fundamental study of the first phase of Rockefeller Center is that of Winston Weisman, "The Architectural Significance of Rockefeller Center" (unpublished dissertation, Ohio State University), 1942. Professor Weisman later published the following studies, several of which are based on material in his dissertation: "The Way of the Price Mechanism: The Rockefeller Centre," *Architectural Review* cviii, December 1950, pp. 399-405; "The First Landscaped Skyscraper," *Journal of the Society of Architectural Historians* xviii, May 1959, pp. 54-59; "Who Designed Rockefeller Center?" *ibid.* x, March 1951, pp. 11-17; "Slab Buildings," *Architectural Review* cxi, February 1952, pp. 119-23; "A New View of Skyscraper History," *The Rise of an American Architecture*, E. Kaufmann, Jr., ed., New York, 1970, pp. 115-60.

David Loth, *A City Within a City: The Romance of Rockefeller Center*, New York, 1966, a popular account based on the work of Weisman and other authors, is the only book-length treatment of the Center. An unpublished corporate *History of Rockefeller Center, 1928–1975*, by Francis T. Christy Esq., and by Caroline Hood and Rita Gallagher, successive Vice-Presidents for Public Relations, is in typescript at the offices of Rockefeller Center, Inc.

The Center publishes frequently-revised editions of a booklet, *A Digest of Facts about Rockefeller Center* which contains brief historical remarks and basic statistics. Samuel Chamberlain, ed., *Rockefeller Center, a Photographic Narrative*, another of the Center's publications, has also been issued in several revised editions. Other publications of Rockefeller Center, Inc., are: *The Story of Rockefeller Center,* New York, 1932, a completely new work with the same title, New York, 1939, and Merle Crowell, ed., *The Last Rivet,* New York, 1940.

Specifications for several of the buildings are at Columbia University, Avery Library, and those for the Music Hall are also at the New York Public Library, Theater Collections. Documents of 1927-62 concerning the Center may be consulted by qualified persons upon prior application by mail to the Rockefeller Family Archives, Room 5600, 30 Rockefeller Plaza, New York, N.Y. 10020. The Corporation's documents are not normally accessible, but I have used them for this book.

Extensive photographic documentation of the Center exists in the Gottscho-Schleisner photographic negative collection, Jamaica, Queens, New York City; in the collection of Walter H. Kilham, Jr., AIA; at Wide World Photos; and at the *New York Times* which incorporates the photographic resources of the defunct *New York Herald Tribune; inter alia.*

Important Shorter Accounts of the Center

An excellent description and summary history of the first stage of development is in Lou Gody, ed., *New York City Guide* (Federal Writers' Project, American Guide Series), New York, 1939, pp. 333-41. Sigfried Giedion, *Space, Time and Architecture,* Cambridge (Mass.), 5th ed., 1967, pp. 845-56 offers a stimulating interpretation of the Center. Douglas Haskell, "The Super-Block as a Core: Unity and Harmony at Rockefeller Center," *Architectural Forum* CXXIV, January 1966, pp. 42-47 is an unusually valuable article. Lewis Mumford's criticism appeared regularly in his "Skyline" column in *The New Yorker* during the 1930s; see especially those of 1933 and of May 4, 1940. William H. Jordy, in a chapter called "Rockefeller Center and Corporate Urbanism" in his *American Buildings and their Architects: The Impact of European Modernism in the Mid-Twentieth Century,* Garden City, 1972, pp. 1-85 presents a critical and comprehensive account of the pre-1940 Center from the perspective given in the subtitle of his book.

There are constant references to Rockefeller Center in the press, often stimulated by press releases issued by the Center, but sometimes originated by the publications themselves. The *New York Times Index, s.v.* Rockefeller Center; John D. Rockefeller Jr.; Metropolitan Opera; provide a continuous outline narrative and summary indication of the Center's critical fortunes. Periodical articles on the Center number in the thousands; many can be located through references to the Center and the Opera in the standard art bibliographies and periodical indices.

Biographies and Autobiographies

For John D. Rockefeller, Jr., see Raymond B. Fosdick, *John D. Rockefeller, Jr., A Portrait,* New York, 1956; Rockefeller Center, Inc., *John D. Rockefeller, Jr., Founder of Rockefeller Center,* New York, 1961.

For Nelson Rockefeller, see Joe Alex Morris, *Nelson Rockefeller; A Biography,* New York, 1960; Michael Kramer and Sam Roberts, *"I Never Wanted To Be Vice President of Anything,"* New York, 1976.

For the family, see Peter Collier and David Horowitz, *The Rockefellers*, New York, 1976.

For John R. Todd, see his autobiography written with William C. Vogel, *Living a Life*, New York, 1947, and Geoffrey Hellman, "The Man Behind Prometheus," *The New Yorker*, November 14, 1936, pp. 31-34, November 21, 1936, pp. 23-26. For biographical information on James B. Todd and Hugh S. Robertson, see their obituaries of January 6, 1939, and June 25, 1951, respectively in major New York newspapers; also "A Phenomenon of Exploitation," *Architectural Forum* LXI, October 1934, pp. 292-98, and "The Builders and Contractors of Radio City," *The Boulevard* I, November 1931, pp. 25, 27.

The principal biographical accounts of the architects are: For Hood, Walter E. Kilham, Jr., *Raymond Hood, Architect*, New York, 1973; A. T. North, *Raymond M. Hood*, New York, 1931; J. B. Schwartzman, "Raymond Hood, The Unheralded Architect" (unpublished M.A. thesis, University of Virginia School of Architecture), 1962; Allene Talmey, "Man Against the Sky," *The New Yorker*, April 11, 1931, pp. 24-27. For Harrison, Herbert Warren Wind, "Architect," *The New Yorker*, November 20, 1954, pp. 51-77, November 27, 1954, pp. 51-84, December 4, 1954, pp. 55-82; J. Greenfield, "Curtain Going Up for Wallace Harrison," *New York Times Magazine*, August 21, 1966, pp. 37 ff. For Reinhard, L. Andrew and Ruth R. Reinhard, *Not the Impossible*, unpublished typescript owned by Mrs. Reinhard.

For "Roxy" Rothafel, see Kenneth Macgowan, "Deus ex Cinema," *The New Yorker*, May 28, 1927, pp. 20-22; clippings scrapbooks at New York Public Library Theater Collection; *New York Times Index s.v.* Rothafel, S. L.

For Deskey, see Gilbert Seldes, "The Long Road to Roxy," *The New Yorker*, February 25, 1933, pp. 22-26; Sheldon and Martha C. Cheney, *Art and the Machine*, New York, 1936, esp. chapter 9 and pp. 184-86.

Information pertinent to Rockefeller Center and its successors can be found in the autobiographies of William Zeckendorf, *The Autobiography of William Zeckendorf*, with E. McCready, N.Y., 1970; and Robert Moses, *Public Works: A Dangerous Trade*, New York, 1970, and in the biography of Moses by Robert Caro, *The Power Broker*, New York, 1974.

For the architects' opinion about the nature of their work, see H. W. Corbett, "Architecture Has Become a Business," *The American Architect* CXXXVII, January 1930, p. 46; idem, "High Buildings on Narrow Streets," ibid. CXIX, June 1921, pp. 603-8, 617; *idem*, "The Skyscraper and the Automobile Have Made the Modern City," *University of Pennsylvania Bicentennial Conference: Studies in the Arts and Architecture*, ed. C. W. Blegen et al., Philadelphia, 1941, pp. 107 ff.; "Many Criticize Architectural Design of Rockefeller 'Metropolitan Square'," *Theatre Engineering* II, May 1931, p. 26. See also L. A. Reinhard, "The Young Architect Must Be Versatile," *The Architect and Engineer* CXV, December 1933, pp. 41-42; idem, "What is the Rockefeller Radio City?" *Architectural Record* LXIX, April 1931, pp. 275-81. See also R. M. Hood, "What is Beauty in Architecture?" *Liberty Magazine* VII, December 1929, pp. 65-66; *New York Times* December 23, 1928, XI-XII, p. 2; February 3, 1929, XI, p. 8, April 26, 1931, p. 7; October 25, 1931, XI p. 6; November 10, 1931, p. 27; November 30, 1931, p. 17; M. J. Woolf, "Architect Hails the Rule of Reason," *New York Times Magazine*, November 1, 1931, p. 6. See also A. Keller, "Leading Architects [Harrison and Fouilhoux]," New York *World-Telegram*, February 16, 1938; Wallace K. Harrison, "Office

Buildings," *Forms and Functions of Twentieth Century Architecture,* ed. T. F. Hamlin, New York, 1952, IV, pp. 140-68.

Architectural Design

For the architecture in general, see "Design Reference for Office Buildings," *Architectural Record* LXXXIV, December 1938, pp. 86 ff, esp. pp. 87-89. For the individual buildings, see references cited in notes and the following basic articles: RCA Building—"RCA Building, Rockefeller Center, New York," *Architectural Forum* LIX, October 1933, pp. 273 ff.; A. W. Knecht, "Heating and Ventilating the 70-Story Skyscraper," *Heating and Ventilating* XXIX, May 1932, pp. 27-31. French and British—E. de Morsier, "La Maison Française à New York," *La revue mondiale,* September 1932, pp. 146-50; Rockefeller Center, Inc., *The British Empire Building in Rockefeller Center,* New York, 1933. Center Theater—clipping file, New York Public Library Theater Collection; "Radio City Music Hall and RKO Roxy Theater," *Architectural Forum* LVIII, February 1933, pp. 160-64. Music Hall—Douglas Haskell, "Roxy's Advantage Over God," *Nation* CXXXVI, January 4, 1933, p. 11; Henry Hofmeister, "The International Music Hall," *Architectural Forum* LVI, April 1932, pp. 355-60; "Radio City Music Hall, Rockefeller Center," *ibid.* LVIII, February 1933, pp. 153-60; E. A. Jewell, "In the Realm of Art," *New York Times,* January 1933, II, p. 9; P. G. Whiting, "Rockefeller Center Debut," *American Magazine of Art* XXVI, February 1933, pp. 77-86; Ralph Flint, "Fine Architectural Grouping . . . ," *Art News* XXXI, December 24, 1932, pp. 3-4. There have been several revised editions of the souvenir booklet, *Radio City Music Hall.*

Economic Aspects

Articles which include particularly useful information on the economic viability of the Center are: "A Phenomenon of Exploitation," *Architectural Forum* LXI, October 1934, pp. 292-98; "Rockefeller Sued," *Business Week,* January 20, 1934, pp. 14, 16; "Rockefeller Center Now Threatens to Climb out of the Red; a View of its Changing Reputation," *Fortune* XIV, December 1936, pp. 139-53; F. L. Allen, "Look at Rockefeller Center," *Harper's Magazine* CLXXVII, October 1938, pp. 506-13; Frank Fogarty, "The Earning Power of Plazas," *Architectural Forum* CVIII, January 1958, pp. 106, 168; Eleanore Carruth, "Manhattan's Office Building Binge," *Fortune* LXXX, October 1969, pp. 114-25; Glenn Fowler, "Rockefeller Center Reaching its Final Form," *New York Times,* October 4, 1970, VIII, pp. 1, 9; Eleanore Carruth, "The Skyscraping Losses in Manhattan Office Buildings," *Fortune* XCI, February 1975, pp. 78-83, 162 ff.

Index

Individual buildings are listed under the cities in which they are found, apart from the Metropolitan Opera and Rockefeller Center, which have their own listings.

Abramovitz, Max, 7, 108, 111-12, 115, 117, 158, 162, 182, 195, n.152-155
Ahlschlager, Walter, 165
Air-conditioning, 16, 73, 104, 120, 134, 137-38. *See also* Rockefeller Center, air-conditioning.
Albany, Empire State Plaza ("South Mall"), 8, 73, 162
Albers, Josef, 160
Aldrich, William T., 36
Alexander, Hartley Burr, 145, 174
Ann Arbor, Hill Auditorium, 165
Architects. *See* Abramovitz; Ahlschlager; Aldrich; Behrens; Bel Geddes; Bennett; Carson; Corbett; Cram; Cross & Cross; Delano & Aldrich; Embury; Flagg; Ford & Earl; Fouilhoux; Gilbert; Godley; Goodhue; Harris; Harrison; Hofmeister; Hood; Howe & Lescaze; Kahn, A.; Kocher & Frey; Le Corbusier; Luckhardt; Lundin; MacMurray; Medary; Mendelsohn; Mies van der Rohe; Mitchell/Giurgola; Morris; Murchison; Pei; Platt; Poelzig; Ponti; Pope; Portman; Reinhard; Rockefeller Center, architects; Saarinen; Stone; Urban; Waid; Wright; York & Sawyer.
"Architecture by committee," 47, 121
Artists. *See* Albers; Bouché; Brangwyn; Browne; Chambellan; Davis; Faulkner; Ferriss; Glarner; Heaton; Kuniyoshi; Léger; Matisse; O'Keeffe; Rivera; Sert; Shahn; Steig; Thurber; Wenrich; Winter. *See also* Craftsmen; Designers; Photographers; Sculptors.

Ashforth, Albert B., 31, 32, 40
Atlanta, 6, 7

Balcom, Henry G., 55
Bayreuth, Wagner Theater, 166
Behrens, Peter, 66
Bel Geddes, Norman, 86, 194
Bennett, E. H., 36
Berlin, 7, 64-65, 177, 181. *See also* Mendelsohn; Poelzig.
Bouché, Louis, 176
Bourke-White, Margaret, 142
Brangwyn, Frank, 77, 147
Brown, Joseph O., 33, 57, 98
Browne, Byron, 91

Carson, Robert, 104, 108, 158
Chambellan, René, 63, 151, 172, 178, 180, 191
Chase National (later Chase Manhattan) Bank, 55, 59, 75, 77, n.106. *See also* New York City, Buildings.
Chatfield, Gerard, 65
Chicago, 7, 17, 141-42
    Auditorium Building, 181
    Century of Progress Exposition, 1933–34. *See* World's Fairs.
    Terminal Park project, 20-21, 46
    Tribune Tower, 39, 45, 47, 137
Christy, Francis T., 77, 79
City Planning and building development theory, 5-7, 9-11, 19, 20, 41, 47, 52, 53, 57-58, 70, 74, 119-22, 124, 126, 197-99
Clark, Peter, 64-65, 166

Cleveland, Businessmen, 24
  Union Station, 20, 21
Columbia University, 16, 18, 22, 23, 27, 29, 48-50, 52, 107-9, 129, 154, 164, n.12, n.66
Concourse. *See* Rockefeller Center, underground streets; Streets, multi-level.
Corbett, Harvey Wiley, 36, 38-41, 45-48, 56, 61, 67, 90, 99, 103, 137, 142, 178, 180, 183, n.150
Craftsmen. *See* Chambellan; Poor; Rambusch Associates; Reeves.
Cram, Ralph Adams, 45, 57
Cravath, Paul, 69
Crowell, Merle, 62, 71, 77, 138
Cross & Cross, 36
Cutting, Robert Fulton, 23, 26, 28, 30

Davis, Stuart, 185, n.209
Debevoise, Thomas, M. 23, 27, 28, 33, 42, 77, 84
Delano & Aldrich, 36
Depression, 1929, ff. 16, 26, 44, 49, 75, 78-79, 85, 98, 100-101, 106, 111
Designers. *See* Bel Geddes; Deskey; Jones; Schmidt; Schoen.
Deskey, Donald, 77, 175, 183, 185, 191
Disney World. *See* Orlando.

Elevators, 73, 76, 94, 104, 133, 135, 142, 156
Embury, Aymar II, 87
Engineers. *See* Balcom; Place; Todd & Brown.
"Escalators." *See* Moving stairs.
Esso Corporation. *See* Standard Oil.
Expositions. *See* World's Fairs.
Exxon Corporation. *See* Standard Oil.
Eyssell, Gustav S., 79, 111, 116

Fairs. *See* World's Fairs.
Faulkner, Barry, 178
Ferriss, Hugh, 66, n.150
Flagg, Ernest, 21
Ford & Earl Associates, 148
Fouilhoux, J. André, 46-47, 85-87, 90, 139, 194
Friedlander, Leo, 144

Garages, 32, 156-57
Gilbert, Cass, 36
Glarner, Fritz, 160
Godley, Frederick, 46, 90
Goetze, Frederick A., 31

Goodhue, Bertram Grosvenor, 39, 45, 57, 144
Grimm, Peter, 31, 84

Hamburg, radio installations, 65
Hanson, O. B., 64-65, 142
Harris, Michael, 117, 156, 157, 161, n.157
Harrison, Wallace K., 7, 38-39, 40, 45, 55, 65-66, 74, 77, 85-87, 90, 103, 108, 111-12, 115, 117, 121, 126, 135, 138, 155-56, 158, 159, 162, 178, 182, 194, 195, n.9, n.150, n.152-155
Hartford, Bushnell Auditorium, 178
Haskell, Douglas, 21, 116, 180, 196, n.18, n.157
Heaton, Maurice, 192
Heydt, Charles O., 23, 27, 31, 33, 41-43, 84, 98, n.30, n.47, n.97
Hofmeister, Henry, 35, 42, 48, 55, 66, 77, 86, 90, 103, 142, 143, 154, 173, 194
Hood, Caroline, 103
Hood, Raymond M., 20, 21, 35, 36, 39, 45-48, 50, 55-56, 61, 67, 77, 82, 90, 117, 133, 135, 137-42, 144, 147, 155, 173, 180, 183, n.56, n.67
Howe & Lescaze, 137, 153
Hull, Cordell, 67

Ice-skating rink, Rockefeller Center. *See* Plazas.

Jones, Robert Edmond, 86, 177

Kahn, Albert, 47, 156
Kahn, Otto, 23, 31, 69, 129
Kirkland, Lawrence A., 75
Kocher & Frey, 38
Kuniyoshi, Yasuo, 185, n.209

Lachaise, Gaston, 144, 154
LaGuardia, Fiorello H., 5, 85-87, 129
Lassaw, Ibram, n.191, fig. 67
Laurent, Robert, 183
Lawrie, Lee, 144, 151
Le Corbusier, 14, 36, 62, 66, 120, 130, 158
Lee, Ivy, 30-31
Léger, Fernand, 130
Lhasa, Palace of the Dalai Lama. *See* Albany.
Lockwood-Greene Engineers, Inc., 83-84
London, 47, 65, n.56
Luckhardt brothers, 66
Ludlow, 61, 73

Lundin, Earl H., 104, 108, 158, n.159
Lux, Gwen, 183

MacMurray, William, 38, 90
Manship, Paul, 64, 102, n.83
Matisse, Henri, 147
McGraw-Hill Publishing Co., 117, 121, 122
Medary, Milton, 36
Mendelsohn, Erich, 65
Metropolitan Life Insurance Co., 16, 56-57
Metropolitan Opera, 16, 22-24, 26-27, 31, 42, 48-
    49, 61, 69, 71, 86-87, 101, n.95
  Buildings, at Broadway, 23
    Unexecuted projects, 23-24, 28-29, 39-42,
        57, 61, 154, 178, n.9, n.27, n.198
  Garage, 29, 156
  Plaza. See Plazas.
  Stimulus of to commerce, 28, 32, 33, 44, 49,
      n.25
Mies van der Rohe, Ludwig, 7, 36, 120, 135, 140,
    159
Milan, La Scala, 177
Milles, Carl, 155
Miniparks, 124, 127, 196, n.162. See also Plazas.
Mitchell/Giurgola Associates, 123
Montreal, Place Ville Marie, 6, 7, 149
Morris, Benjamin Wistar, 23, 24, 26, 28-32, 35,
    36, 39-42, 61, 62, 84, 86, n.9, n.47
Moscow, 65
Moses, Robert, 82, 87
Moving stairs, 48, 76, 153
Mumford, Lewis, 21, 61, 181
Murchison, Kenneth, 20, 82
Mussolini, Benito, 66, 69

NBC (National Broadcasting Co.), 50, 65, 69,
    109, 194
New York City
  Building Code, 16-17, 52-53, 73, 138, 141, 182
  Buildings, 18
    ABC (American Broadcasting Co.), 115
    American Radiator Co., 46, 142
    Architects', 32
    Beaux-Arts Apartments, 20
    Brooks Brothers, 32
    Bush, 137
    CBS (Columbia Broadcasting System), 86-
        87, 115, 162
    Chanin, 20

Chase Manhattan Bank, 8
Chrysler, 6, 20, 35, 135
City Center (formerly Mecca Temple), 87
Cloisters, 15
Columbus Circle area, 98
Cunard, 32, 173
Daily News, 46, 52, 137, 139, 142
Dunbar Apartments, 15
Earl Carroll Theater, 166, 168
Empire State, 6, 135
Equitable Life Assurance (1915), 137;
    (1961), 115, 148
GE (General Electric), 77
GM (General Motors), 162
Goelet, 33
Grand Central Terminal and vicinity, 19-21,
    33, 55, 57, 67, 82, 103
Graybar, 33, 35
Guggenheim Museum, 86, 143
Hearst, 98
Hilton Hotel, 114, n.155
Hippodrome, 182
International House, 15
Lincoln Center, 7, 87, 117-18
London Terrace Apartments, 21
Master Apartments, 38, 142
McGraw-Hill (42nd St.), 46, 117, 138
Metropolitan Life Insurance, 137
Metropolitan Opera. See separate listing.
Municipal Art Center, 5, 82, 85-87
Museum of Modern Art, 15, 84-86, 93, 145,
    147
NBC (National Broadcasting Co., 711 Fifth
    Ave.), 50
New School for Social Research, 165, 178
Olympic Tower, 128
Riverside Church, 15, 144
Rockefeller Apartments, 25, 84, 85
Rockefeller Center. See separate listing.
Rockefeller University, 15
Roxy Theater, 113-14, 165-66, 171, 186,
    n.103
Saks Fifth Avenue, 128, 196
St. Mark's Tower project, 62
St. Nicholas' Church, 3, 108, n.3
St. Patrick's Cathedral, 3, 61, 151, 154
Socony-Mobil, 158
Standard Oil, 32
Tishman (666 Fifth Ave.), 158

Tudor City Apartments, 20, 21
Two Park Avenue, 137
United Nations, 15
Ziegfeld Theater, 98, 115
Fire safety code, 32
Master Plan, 197-98
Streets, new, 20, 32, 33, 40-42, 50, 52-53, 59, 61, 84-86, 103, 121, n.124
Transportation facilities, 25, 26, 41, 82-84, 97, 112, 118, 160-61. *See also* Rockefeller Center, links to transportation facilities.
Zoning, 5, 17-19, 21, 24, 28-29, 52-53, 84, 85, 96, 99-100, 113, 115, 119-22, 128, 135, 156-57, 162, 197-98
Noguchi, Isamu, 95-96

O'Keeffe, Georgia, 185
Orlando, Walt Disney World, 7, 196
Osborne, John A., 31, 32

Paris, 6, 64, 166, 178
Pei, I. M., 7
Philadelphia, 7, 55, 133-34, 137, 153
Photographers. *See* Bourke-White; Steichen.
Picasso, Pablo, 81, 147, fig. 95
Place, Clyde R., 55
Platt, Charles Adams, 36, n.41
Plazas, 5, 7, 119-20, 162. *See also* Miniparks.
Metropolitan Opera, 22, 24, 26, 28, 29, 31, 39-41, 49
At Rockefeller Center, 50, 53, 57-59, 61, 129
Ice-skating rink and sunken plaza, 8, 10, 62-64, 76, 92, 101, 102, 121, 127, 196, 198
Sixth Avenue, 10, 114, 117-19, 121, 127, 159, 163
Poelzig, Hans, 64-65, 166, 181
Ponti, Gio, 160
Poor, Henry Varnum, 185
Pope, John Russell, 36
Portman, John, 7, 137

Rambusch Associates, 122, 173, 185
RCA (Radio Corporation of America), 50, 77
Realtors, 31, 75-76, 83, n.124. *See also* Ashforth; Edwards; Grimm; Osborne; Tonnelé; Webb & Knapp; White; Zeckendorf.
Reeves, Ruth, 185
Regional Plan Association, 14, 36, 40, 61, n.39

Reinhard, L. Andrew, 35, 42, 47, 48, 53, 55, 65, 77, 86, 90, 103, 143, 154, 155, 173, 194
Reinhardt, Max, 64-65, 177, 181, 193
Rio de Janeiro, 158, 159
Rivera, Diego, 145-48
RKO (Radio Keith Orpheum) Corp., 50, 77, 79
Robertson, Hugh S., 33, 66-67, 75, 77, 84, 93, 95, 98, 103-4, 155
Rockefeller Center, 21, 130, 164-65. *See also* Artists; Depression; Miniparks; New York City, ' Building code, Fire safety code, Streets, Zoning; Plazas; Wars.
Air conditioning, 73-74, 107, 109, 156
Architects, 10, 47, 53, 55, 59, 74, 108, 133, 138, 140, n.54, n.164
Art and decoration, 9, 77, 101, 119, 144, 155
Buildings at
Associated Press, 90, 93-95, 149, 157
British Empire (later: British), 74, 130
Celanese, 117, 122-24, 126, 198
Center Theater (earlier: RKO Roxy), 78-80, 99, 107, 156, 187-95, n.103, n.164
Eastern Air Lines, 90, 96-97, 105, 108, 135, 156-57
Esso (later: Warner Communications), 104-6, 115, 130-31
Exxon, 119, 126, 161-62
Garage, 32, 96
International and International Building North, 48, 67, 74, 130, 150-54, 157
Maison Française, 74, 130
McGraw-Hill, 117, 119, 122, 124, n.157
NBC Studios, 107, 111, 131-32, 140, 142, n.164. *See also* NBC; New York City, NBC.
Palazzo d'Italia, 64, 130
Radio City Music Hall, 35, 66, 78-79, 94-95, 129, 149, 164-87, 189, n.103, n.164
RCA and RCA Building West, 49, 73, 74, 76, 77, 91, 107, 108, 131-49, 150, 157, n.164
RKO (later: Amax), 35, 108, 115, n.164
Sinclair Oil (600 Fifth Ave.), 108, 130
Sperry-Rand, 114
Time & Life (first, One Rockefeller Plaza), 93, 154
Time & Life (second, Sixth Ave.), 26, 112-13, 117-18, 157-61
U.S. Rubber (later: Uniroyal) and U.S.

Rubber (Uniroyal) Addition, 98, 108, 131, 156, 195

Financial matters, 49, 52, 56-57, 74, 76, 100-3, 106, 108-9, 129, 133, 153, 155, 156, 162

Goals, 30, 40, 42-43, 52, 70, 71, 88, 95, 128, 150, 161, 180-83, n.74

Ice-skating rink. *See* Plazas, at Rockefeller Center.

Industrial relations, 73

Lease, 31, 48-49, 107-9, 129, n.66

Links to new streets, 5, 40, 61, n.124

Links to transportation facilities, 5, 25, 26, 32, 40, 43, 55, 57, 82-84, 96, 97, 101, 112, 128, 160, 198, 199

Metropolitan Square Corp., 15, 35-36, 41, 48, 101.

Name, 55, 71, 107

Ownership of, 15, 100-1, n.12

Private street. *See* New York City, streets, new.

Public Relations, 62, 67, 71, 78, 83, 88, 99, 103, 122, 127, 157

Restaurants, 80, 91-92, 125

Roof gardens, 39, 61, 88, 91, 94, 101, 129

Tenants, 32, 40, 49-50, 52, 63, 66, 67, 69-71, 73, 76, 78, 88, 90-93, 99, 102-4, 107-8, 111-12, 114, 121, 146

Theaters, 16-17, 53, 57, 62, 64, 69, 76, 78-80, 108, 122-23, 164-95

Trucking ramp, 48, 74, 90, 149, 198

Underground streets, 57, 63, 84, 92, 101, 108, 112, 114, 128-29, 148, 198

Warehouse, bonded, 16, 67

Rockefeller family, 71, 73, 87, 116, 121, n.12, n.13

Abby (Mrs. John D. Jr.), 15, 39, 77, 145, 183, n.206

Abby (Mrs. Jean Mauzé), 14, n.162, n.206

David, 8, 15

John D. Jr., 8, 14, 24, 31, 42, 49, 59, 61, 67, 69, 71, 77, 99-103, 106, 115, 116, 123, 129, 154, 157, 174, 197, 199, n.30, n.79, n.106

  dealings with Metropolitan Opera, 16, 22, 27, 29, 49, n.95

  home and neighborhood, 18, 24, 101

interest and taste in art and architecture, 15, 55, 77, 82, 121, 138-39, 144, 147, 164, 180

real estate, 15, 24-26, 31, 83, 85, 86, 101, 103-4, 108, 132, n.25, n.123

John D. 3rd, 7, 14, 87

Laurance S., 15, 111

Nelson A., 8, 14, 75, 77, 83, 86, 91, 95, 96-97, 103, 117, 146-47, 180, n.58, n.125

Rockettes, 177, 181, 183, 187

Roper, Daniel C., 67

"Roxy" (Samuel Lionel Rothafel), 64-65, 78-80, 164-66, 168, 177, 180-81, 184-87, 190, 192, n.103

Saarinen, Eero, 162

Salzburg, Festival Theater, 166

San Antonio, Milam Building, 73

San Francisco, 73, 128, 137

Sarnoff, David, 55, 77, 112

Schmidt, Mrs. M. B., 80

Schoen, Eugene, 191

Sculptors. *See* Chambellan; Friedlander; Lachaise; Lassaw; Laurent; Lawrie; Lux; Manship; Milles; Noguchi; Zorach.

Sert, José María, 147

Shahn, Ben, 146

Standard Oil Co., 71, 77, 103, 108, 112, 114, 116

Stanislavsky, Konstantin, 65

Steichen, Edward, 192, 195

Steig, William, 92

Stone, Edward Durell, 143, 162, 180, 194, n.150, fig. 55

Streets, multi-level, 10, 20, 28, 36, 40, 42-43, 52, 149, 198, n.68

Thurber, James, 92

Time Inc., 26, 93, 111-12

Todd, Dr. James M., 32, 98, 138

Todd, John R., 32, 35, 42, 44, 46-47, 49-50, 52, 57, 69, 74, 98, 133, 138-39, 144, 147, 150, 156, 165, 174, 192, n.58, n.60, n.95

Todd, Webster B., 33, 50, 65, 75, 79, 98

Todd & Brown, 33, 42, 44, 74, 103, 173, 186

Todd, Robertson & Todd, 30-32, 35, 42, 44-45, 47, 173

Tonnelé, John, 28, 40

Underel Holding Corp., 43, 49, 53, 108, 118, 132, 171
Urban, Joseph, 23, 98, 115, 165, 178, 180, n.198

Van Sweringen family, 43, 83
Versailles, 8, 15

Waid, Daniel Everett, 16, 57
Wars, effects on Rockefeller Center, 101, 103, 107
Washington, D.C., 8, 20, 47, 67
Webb & Knapp, 114
Wenrich, John, 63-64, n.82
White, William A. & Sons, 23, 24, 26, 28, 31, 41, 48, 84, 100

Williamsburg Restoration, 15, 33, 75
Winter, Ezra, 32, 164, 173-74, 187, n.200
Woods, Col. Arthur, 36, 93
World's Fairs and International Expositions, 12
    Chicago, 1933–34, 36, 46-48, 62, 67
    New York, 1939, 126
    Paris, 1925, 183
Wright, Frank Lloyd, 62, 143, 159

York & Sawyer, 36
Young, Owen, 69, 77

Zeckendorf, William, n.6. *See also* Webb & Knapp.
Zoning. *See* New York City, Zoning.
Zorach, William, 176, 183